AMERICA'S ELDERLY:

A SOURCEBOOK

AMERICA'S
ELDERLY:
A SOURCEBOOK

Edited by Edward E. Duensing

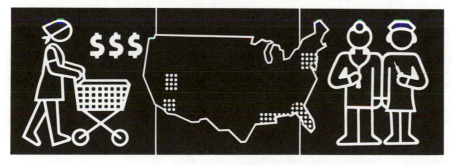

CENTER
FOR URBAN
POLICY RESEARCH

Copyright © 1988 by Rutgers, The State University of New Jersey

Published by the Center for Urban Policy Research
Building 4051—Kilmer Campus
New Brunswick, New Jersey 08903

LIBRARY OF CONGRESS
Library of Congress Cataloging-in-Publication Data

America's elderly: a sourcebook / edited by Edward E. Duensing.
    p.   cm.
  ISBN 0-88285-125-X
  1. Aged—United States—Social conditions—Statistics. 2. Aged—
United States—Economic conditions—Statistics. 3. Aged—Medical
care—United States—Statistics. 4. Aged—Services for—United
States—Statistics.   I. Duensing, Edward.
HQ1064.U5A646 1988
305.2′6′0973—dc19   88-6132
                                                                CIP

CONTENTS

PREFACE

The fact that the population of the United States is rapidly aging has not yet permeated the consciousness of most Americans. After all, who would believe that the United States, a country that prides itself on its youth, has as many senior citizens as teenagers? Or that the fastest-growing segment of its population is comprised of persons 85 years and older? But, believe it or not, these statistics are facts of life—facts that will soon have a dramatic effect on the social, economic, and political framework of the nation.

How America responds to the demographic challenges posed by its aging population will to a large extent be governed by the quality of information available to public officials, policy makers, planners, and others in the fields of business and health care. For good planning requires adequate and timely information. This book represents an attempt to gather together in a single volume the data necessary to create a statistical portrait of America's elderly as they are today and as they will be tomorrow—a portrait highlighting the diversity of senior citizens as well as their commonalities.

The tables and figures included have been selected from among several thousand as those which are current, adequately detailed, and of interest to the widest range of possible users. All statistics chosen have been taken from the most reliable sources available and, where possible, cross-checked to ensure their accuracy.

I would like to express my gratitude to Mary Picarella for creating this book from the myriad styles, fonts, and formats of the original source materials. Her sense of design and attention to detail are deeply appreciated.

I

DEMOGRAPHICS OF THE ELDERLY POPULATION

GENERAL DEMOGRAPHICS

Table 1–1. Resident Population, by Age, Sex, and Race: 1970 to 1985

(In thousands, except as indicated. 1970 and 1980 data based on enumerated population as of April 1; other years based on estimated population as of July 1. Excludes Armed Forces overseas.)

YEAR, SEX, AND RACE	Total, all years	Under 5 years	5–9 years	10–14 years	15–19 years	20–24 years	25–29 years	30–34 years	35–39 years	40–44 years	45–49 years	50–54 years	55–59 years	60–64 years	65–74 years	65 years and over	75 years and over	Median age (yr.)
1970, total[1,2]	**203,235**	**17,163**	**19,969**	**20,804**	**19,084**	**16,383**	**13,486**	**11,437**	**11,113**	**11,988**	**12,124**	**11,111**	**9,979**	**8,623**	**12,443**	**19,972**	**7,530**	**28.0**
Male	98,926	8,750	10,175	10,598	9,641	7,925	6,626	5,599	5,416	5,823	5,855	5,351	4,769	4,030	5,440	8,367	2,927	26.8
Female	104,309	8,413	9,794	10,206	9,443	8,458	6,859	5,838	5,697	6,166	6,269	5,759	5,210	4,593	7,002	11,605	4,603	29.3
White	178,098	14,464	16,941	17,724	16,412	14,327	11,850	10,000	9,749	10,633	10,868	10,019	9,021	7,818	11,300	18,272	6,972	28.9
Black	22,581	2,434	2,749	2,812	2,425	1,816	1,429	1,254	1,196	1,199	1,124	990	874	734	1,043	1,544	501	22.4
1980, total[1]	**226,546**	**16,348**	**16,700**	**18,242**	**21,168**	**21,319**	**19,521**	**17,561**	**13,965**	**11,669**	**11,090**	**11,710**	**11,615**	**10,088**	**15,581**	**25,549**	**9,969**	**30.0**
Male	110,053	8,362	8,539	9,316	10,755	10,663	9,705	8,677	6,862	5,708	5,388	5,621	5,482	4,670	6,757	10,305	3,548	28.8
Female	116,493	7,986	8,161	8,926	10,413	10,655	9,816	8,884	7,104	5,961	5,702	6,089	6,133	5,418	8,824	15,245	6,400	31.3
White[3]	194,713	13,414	13,717	15,095	17,681	18,072	16,658	15,157	12,122	10,110	9,693	10,360	10,394	9,078	14,045	23,162	9,117	30.9
Male[3]	94,924	6,882	7,034	7,730	9,008	9,102	8,363	7,565	6,014	4,991	4,755	5,016	4,928	4,221	6,095	9,316	3,221	29.6
Female[3]	99,788	6,532	6,683	7,365	8,673	8,970	8,295	7,592	6,108	5,119	4,938	5,344	5,466	4,858	7,950	13,846	5,896	32.2
Black[3]	26,683	2,459	2,509	2,691	3,007	2,749	2,342	1,904	1,469	1,260	1,150	1,135	1,041	874	1,344	2,092	748	24.9
Male[3]	12,612	1,240	1,265	1,353	1,500	1,313	1,095	879	667	571	519	507	469	386	567	849	281	23.6
Female[3]	14,071	1,220	1,245	1,338	1,506	1,436	1,247	1,025	801	689	632	628	573	488	777	1,243	467	26.2
1981, total	229,637	16,931	16,093	18,312	20,501	21,614	20,200	18,786	14,381	12,019	10,992	11,616	11,579	10,376	15,914	26,236	10,323	30.3
1982, total	231,996	17,298	16,020	18,172	19,887	21,587	20,753	18,808	15,599	12,450	11,027	11,455	11,510	10,603	16,197	26,827	10,630	30.6
1983, total	234,284	17,650	16,147	17,912	19,274	21,488	21,202	19,211	16,165	13,135	11,226	11,213	11,528	10,705	16,494	27,428	10,934	30.9
1984, total	236,495	17,859	16,464	17,511	18,785	21,327	21,534	19,696	16,932	13,613	11,463	11,030	11,442	10,872	16,733	27,967	11,234	31.2
1985, total[1]	**238,740**	**18,037**	**16,822**	**17,103**	**18,551**	**20,993**	**21,751**	**20,267**	**17,708**	**14,055**	**11,648**	**10,942**	**11,337**	**10,997**	**16,995**	**28,530**	**11,535**	**31.5**
Male	116,161	9,230	8,608	8,762	9,445	10,515	10,886	10,096	8,741	6,889	5,679	5,281	5,380	5,120	7,466	11,529	4,062	30.3
Female	122,579	8,806	8,213	8,340	9,107	10,479	10,865	10,171	8,967	7,166	5,969	5,660	5,957	5,877	9,529	17,002	7,473	32.7
White	202,768	14,636	13,621	13,830	15,194	17,511	18,316	17,158	15,243	12,168	10,046	9,509	9,990	9,804	15,248	25,743	10,495	32.4
Male	99,006	7,509	6,990	7,100	7,746	8,815	9,250	8,636	7,608	6,023	4,946	4,637	4,771	4,585	6,720	10,390	3,670	31.2
Female	103,762	7,127	6,631	6,730	7,448	8,696	9,067	8,522	7,635	6,144	5,099	4,872	5,219	5,219	8,529	15,353	6,824	33.6
Black	28,887	2,706	2,597	2,655	2,770	2,842	2,749	2,408	1,889	1,442	1,255	1,148	1,101	982	1,463	2,343	880	26.6
Male	13,683	1,370	1,314	1,346	1,391	1,369	1,301	1,121	862	653	563	514	500	439	619	940	321	25.2
Female	15,204	1,335	1,283	1,309	1,378	1,473	1,448	1,287	1,027	789	692	634	601	543	844	1,403	559	27.8
Percent:																		
1970	100.0	8.4	9.8	10.2	9.4	8.1	6.6	5.6	5.5	5.9	6.0	5.5	4.9	4.2	6.1	9.8	3.7	(x)
1980	100.0	7.2	7.4	8.1	9.3	9.4	8.6	7.8	6.2	5.2	4.9	5.2	5.1	4.5	6.9	11.3	4.4	(x)
1985, total[1]	**100.0**	**7.6**	**7.0**	**7.2**	**7.8**	**8.8**	**9.1**	**8.5**	**7.4**	**5.9**	**4.9**	**4.6**	**4.7**	**4.6**	**7.1**	**12.0**	**4.8**	**(x)**
Male	100.0	7.9	7.4	7.5	8.1	9.1	9.4	8.7	7.5	5.9	4.9	4.5	4.6	4.4	6.4	9.9	3.5	(x)
Female	100.0	7.2	6.7	6.8	7.4	8.5	8.9	8.3	7.3	5.8	4.9	4.6	4.9	4.8	7.8	13.9	6.1	(x)
White	100.0	7.2	6.7	6.8	7.5	8.6	9.0	8.5	7.5	6.0	5.0	4.7	4.9	4.8	7.5	12.7	5.2	(x)
Black	100.0	9.4	9.0	9.2	9.6	9.8	9.5	9.3	6.5	5.0	4.3	4.0	3.8	3.4	5.1	8.1	3.0	(x)

Notes: X Not applicable.

1. Includes other races, not shown separately.

2. Official count. The revised 1970 resident population count is 203,302,031; the difference of 66,733 is due to errors found after release of the official series.

3. The race data shown for April 1, 1980 have been modified.

Source: U.S. Bureau of the Census, *Current Population Reports*, series P–25, Nos. 870 and 985.

Figure 1–1. Elderly Spanish Origin Population: 1980 and 1985

(Numbers in millions as of April 1980 and March 1985. Persons of Spanish origin may be of any race.)

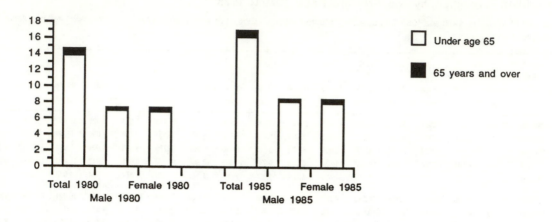

Source: U.S. Bureau of the Census. *1980 Census of Population, Current Population Reports,* series P–20, no. 403; and unpublished data.

Table 1–2. Persons 65 Years Old and Over—Characteristics, by Sex: 1960 to 1985

Characteristic	MALE					FEMALE				
	1960	1970	1975	1980	1985	1960	1970	1975	1980	1985
Total[1,2] **(million)**	**7.5**	**8.3**	**8.7**	**9.9**	**11.0**	**9.0**	**11.5**	**12.4**	**14.2**	**15.8**
Percent of total population	8.6	8.5	8.6	9.2	9.7	9.9	11.1	11.5	12.4	13.1
White[1] (million)	6.9	7.6	7.9	9.0	9.9	8.4	10.6	11.3	12.9	14.3
Black[1] (million)	.5	.7	.8	.8	.9	.6	.9	1.1	1.2	1.3
Age:[3]										
65–69 years (percent)	3.3	3.2	3.5	3.5	3.7	3.7	3.7	4.1	4.2	4.2
70–74 years (percent)	2.5	2.3	2.4	2.6	2.8	2.8	3.0	3.0	3.4	3.6
75–79 years (percent)	1.6	1.6	1.5	1.7	1.9	1.9	2.2	2.2	2.5	2.7
80 years and over (percent)	1.2	1.4	1.5	1.6	1.7	1.6	2.3	2.7	3.0	3.4
Percent below poverty level:[1,4]										
Family householders	29.7	16.6	7.9	8.4	6.0	31.5	23.5	12.3	13.0	13.0
Unrelated individuals	58.5	40.0	25.8	25.3	20.8	69.1	49.9	31.7	30.5	25.2
PERCENT DISTRIBUTION										
Marital status:[1]										
Single	7.3	7.5	4.7	4.9	5.3	8.5	7.7	5.8	5.9	5.1
Married	71.7	73.1	79.3	78.0	77.2	36.8	35.6	39.1	39.5	39.9
Spouse present	69.0	69.9	77.3	76.1	75.0	35.0	33.9	37.6	37.9	38.3
Spouse absent	2.7	3.2	2.0	1.9	2.2	1.8	1.7	1.5	1.7	1.6
Widowed	19.4	17.1	13.6	13.5	13.8	53.1	54.4	52.5	51.2	50.7
Divorced	1.7	2.3	2.5	3.6	3.7	1.5	2.3	2.6	3.4	4.3
Family status:[1]										
In families	82.3	79.2	83.3	[5]83.0	[5]82.4	67.7	58.5	59.3	[5]56.8	[5]56.7
Nonfamily householders	12.8	14.9	15.4	15.7	15.4	26.8	35.2	39.4	42.0	42.1
Secondary individuals	2.4	2.4	1.2	1.3	2.2	3.0	1.9	1.3	1.1	1.1
Residents of institutions[1]	2.5	3.6	(NA)	(NA)	(NA)	2.4	4.4	(NA)	(NA)	(NA)
Living arrangements:[1]										
Living in household	97.4	95.5	99.8	99.9	99.5	97.0	95.0	99.8	99.7	99.6
Living alone	(NA)	14.1	14.8	14.9	14.7	(NA)	33.8	38.0	41.0	41.1
Spouse present	[6]73.2	69.9	77.3	76.1	75.0	[6]36.9	33.9	37.6	37.9	38.3
Living with someone else	(NA)	11.5	7.7	8.9	9.8	(NA)	27.4	24.2	20.8	20.2
Not in household[1,7]	2.6	4.5	.2	.1	.5	3.0	5.0	.2	.3	.4
Years of school completed:										
8 years or less	72.5	61.5	52.6	45.3	37.2	66.4	56.1	48.0	41.6	34.1
1–3 years of high school	10.4	12.6	14.0	15.5	15.7	12.8	13.9	15.5	16.7	17.0
4 years of high school	7.8	12.5	16.8	21.4	26.4	11.6	18.1	21.8	25.8	30.7
1–3 years of college	4.9	5.6	7.2	7.5	9.1	6.1	6.7	8.4	8.6	10.3
4 years or more of college	4.3	7.9	9.4	10.3	11.5	3.2	5.2	6.3	7.4	8.0
Labor force participation:[8]										
Employed	30.9	25.9	20.5	18.4	15.3	9.9	9.4	7.8	7.8	7.0
Unemployed	1.7	.9	1.2	.6	.5	.4	.3	.4	.3	.2
Not in labor force	67.3	73.3	78.4	81.0	84.2	89.7	90.3	91.8	91.9	92.7

Notes: NA Not available.

1. Civilian population as of March. Beginning 1975, excludes institutional population.
2. Includes other races, not shown separately.
3. Estimated total resident population as of July 1.
4. Poverty status based on income in preceding year.
5. Excludes those living in unrelated subfamilies.
6. Includes a small number of "spouse present" in group quarters.
7. In institutions and other group quarters.
8. Annual averages of monthly figures. Source: U.S. Bureau of Labor Statistics, *Employment and Earnings,* monthly.

Source: Except as noted, U.S. Bureau of the Census, *Current Population Reports,* series P-20, No. 410 and earlier reports; series P-23, Nos. 57 and 59; series P-25, Nos. 917 and 985, and series P-60, No. 152 and earlier reports.

Figure 1–2. Number of Men Per 100 Women by Elderly Age Group: 1984

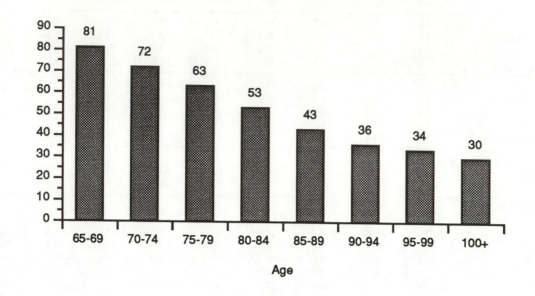

Source: U.S. Bureau of the Census. *Current Population Reports,* Series P–25, no. 952.

Table 1–3. Summary of Characteristics for Persons 85 Years and Over, by Age: 1980

(Range represents a 90–percent confidence interval)

Characteristic	85 years and over Number	85 years and over Range	100 years and over Number	100 years and over Range	100–104 years Number	100–104 years Range	105 years and over Number	105 years and over Range
Race, Sex								
Total	2,240,067	(X)	14,170	(X)	12,838	12,439–13,236	1,332	933–1,731
Male	681,525	678,495–684,555	3,823	3,216–4,430	3,523	2,932–4,114	300	103–497
Female	1,558,542	1,555,512–1,561,572	10,347	9,740–10,954	9,315	8,666–9,964	1,032	677–1,387
White	2,044,961	2,043,104–2,046,818	11,167	10,609–11,725	10,368	9,763–10,973	799	484–1,114
Male	614,407	611,469–617,345	2,629	2,098–3,160	2,464	1,946–2,982	165	18–312
Female	1,430,554	1,427,390–1,433,718	8,538	7,869–9,207	7,904	7,225–8,583	634	351–917
Black	158,920	157,229–160,611	2,450	1,933–2,967	2,001	1,525–2,477	449	210–688
Male	52,966	51,965–53,967	942	602–1,282	807	490–1,124	135	2–268
Female	105,954	104,556–107,352	1,508	1,087–1,929	1,194	814–1,574	314	113–515
Asian or Pacific Islander	13,852	13,336–14,368	135	2–268	135	2–268	–	–
Male	5,197	4,880–5,514	135	2–268	135	2–268	–	–
Female	8,655	8,246–9,064	–	–	–	–	–	–
American Indian, Eskimo, or Aleut	5,871	5,534–6,208	242	65–419	158	15–301	84	0–189
Male	2,311	2,100–2,522	78	0–179	78	0–179	–	–
Female	3,560	3,298–3,822	164	18–310	80	0–182	84	0–189
Other race	16,463	15,900–17,026	176	25–327	176	25–327	–	–
Male	6,644	6,286–7,002	39	0–111	39	0–111	–	–
Female	9,819	9,384–10,254	137	3–271	137	3–271	–	–
Living Arrangements								
Total	2,192,679	2,191,731–2,193,627	14,170	(X)	12,838	12,439–13,237	1,332	933–1,731
In households	1,657,003	1,654,354–1,659,652	7,065	6,382–7,748	6,279	5,600–6,958	786	473–1,099
Male	554,356	551,751–556,961	2,570	2,043–3,097	2,270	1,769–2,771	300	103–497
Female	1,102,647	1,099,629–1,105,665	4,495	3,859–5,131	4,009	3,393–4,625	486	237–735
White	1,493,366	1,490,520–1,496,212	4,758	4,113–5,403	4,378	3,747–5,009	380	159–601
Black	134,587	133,152–136,022	1,873	1,410–2,336	1,551	1,124–1,978	322	118–526
In group quarters	535,676	533,101–538,251	7,105	6,422–7,788	6,559	5,878–7,240	546	283–809
Male	113,622	112,297–114,947	1,253	865–1,641	1,253	865–1,641	–	–
Female	422,054	419,693–424,415	5,852	5,179–6,525	5,306	4,645–5,967	546	283–809
White	510,350	507,818–512,882	6,409	5,729–7,089	5,990	5,315–6,665	419	188–650
Black	20,550	19,974–21,126	577	307–847	450	210–690	127	0–256
Household Relationships								
Total	(NA)	(NA)	14,170	(X)	12,838	12,439–13,237	1,332	933–1,731
Householder	1,089,038	1,086,294–1,091,782	2,728	2,189–3,267	2,500	1,979–3,021	228	56–400
Spouse	102,348	100,858–103,838	81	0–184	81	0–184	–	–
Brother or sister	29,603	28,977–30,229	56	0–142	56	0–142	–	–
Parent	250,376	248,647–252,105	2,487	1,967–3,007	2,345	1,837–2,853	142	6–278
Other relative	156,117	154,720–157,514	1,223	839–1,607	935	596–1,274	288	95–481
Nonrelative	27,408	26,624–28,192	490	240–740	362	146–578	128	0–257
In group quarters	535,676	532,632–538,720	7,105	6,422–7,788	6,559	5,878–7,240	546	283–809
Marital Status								
Total	2,192,679	2,191,731–2,193,627	14,170	(X)	12,838	12,439–13,237	1,332	933–1,731
Married	439,641	437,461–441,821	1,484	1,066–1,902	1,301	906–1,696	183	29–337
Widowed	1,539,377	1,536,832–1,541,922	11,302	10,753–11,851	10,418	9,815–11,021	884	553–1,215
Divorced, separated	56,009	55,152–56,866	322	118–526	104	0–221	218	50–386
Never married	157,652	156,248–159,056	1,062	702–1,422	1,015	663–1,367	47	0–126
Males	667,978	665,467–670,489	3,823	3,216–4,430	3,523	2,932–4,114	300	103–497
Married	317,612	315,697–319,527	1,085	722–1,448	920	583–1,257	165	18–312
Widowed	292,825	290,975–294,675	2,383	1,872–2,894	2,316	1,811–2,821	67	0–161
Divorced, separated	19,876	19,361–20,391	172	22–322	104	0–221	68	0–162
Never married	37,665	36,959–38,371	183	29–337	183	29–337	–	–

Table 1-3. (continued)

Characteristic	85 years and over		100 years and over		100–104 years		105 years and over	
	Number	Range	Number	Range	Number	Range	Number	Range
Females	1,524,701	1,522,142–1,527,260	10,347	9,740–10,954	9,315	8,666–9,964	1,032	677–1,387
Married	122,029	120,783–123,275	399	173–625	381	160–602	18	0–67
Widowed	1,246,552	1,243,825–1,249,279	8,919	8,259–9,579	8,102	7,426–8,778	817	498–1,136
Divorced, separated	36,133	35,442–36,824	150	10–290	–	–	150	10–290
Never married	119,987	118,751–121,223	879	549–1,209	832	511–1,153	47	0–126
In households	1,657,003	1,654,595–1,659,411	7,065	6,382–7,748	6,279	5,600–6,958	786	473–1,099
Married	394,491	392,400–396,582	1,038	682–1,394	873	544–1,202	165	18–312
Widowed	1,125,636	1,122,892–1,128,380	5,401	4,737–6,065	4,998	4,345–5,651	403	176–630
Divorced, separated	43,245	42,490–44,000	322	118–526	104	0–221	218	50–386
Never married	93,631	92,533–94,729	304	106–502	304	106–502	–	–
In group quarters	*508,918	506,626–832,264	7,105	6,422–7,788	6,559	5,878–7,240	546	283–809
Married	42,686	41,936–43,436	446	207–685	428	194–662	18	0–67
Widowed	397,083	394,985–399,177	5,901	5,227–6,575	5,420	4,756–6,084	481	234–728
Divorced, separated	12,101	11,701–12,505	–	–	–	–	–	–
Never married	57,048	56,183–57,913	758	451–1,065	711	413–1,009	47	0–126
Income								
Total	2,192,679	2,191,889–2,193,469	14,048	13,922–14,174	12,800	12,396–13,204	1,248	861–1,635
Less than $5,000	1,760,279	1,758,027–1,762,531	12,123	11,643–12,603	11,065	10,500–11,630	1,058	699–1,417
$5,000–$19,999	424,633	422,482–426,784	1,599	1,167–2,031	1,409	1,000–1,818	190	33–347
$20,000 or more	61,767	60,868–62,666	326	121–531	325	121–531	–	–
Male	667,978	665,467–670,489	3,785	3,180–4,390	3,485	2,897–4,073	300	103–497
Less than $5,000	435,665	433,493–437,837	2,755	2,214–3,296	2,533	2,009–3,057	222	52–392
$5,000–$19,999	199,002	197,440–200,564	793	479–1,107	715	416–1,014	78	0–179
$20,000 or more	33,311	32,647–33,975	237	62–412	237	62–412	–	–
Female	1,524,701	1,522,142–1,527,260	10,263	9,652–10,874	9,315	8,666–9,964	948	607–1,289
Less than $5,000	1,270,614	1,267,895–1,273,333	9,368	8,721–10,015	8,532	7,863–9,201	836	514–1,158
$5,000–$19,999	225,631	223,979–227,283	806	489–1,123	694	399–989	112	0–233
$20,000 or more	28,456	27,841–29,071	89	0–197	89	0–197	–	–
In households	(NA)	(NA)	6,981	6,298–7,664	6,279	5,600–6,958	702	405–999
Less than $5,000	(NA)	(NA)	5,813	5,141–6,485	5,189	4,531–5,847	624	344–904
$5,000–$19,999	(NA)	(NA)	948	607–1,289	870	542–1,198	78	0–179
$20,000 or more	(NA)	(NA)	220	51–389	220	51–389	–	–
In group quarters	(NA)	(NA)	7,067	6,384–7,750	6,521	5,840–7,202	546	283–809
Less than $5,000	(NA)	(NA)	6,310	5,631–6,989	5,876	5,203–6,549	434	199–669
$5,000–$19,999	(NA)	(NA)	651	365–937	539	278–800	112	0–233
$20,000 or more	(NA)	(NA)	106	0–224	106	0–224	–	–
In Poverty								
Total	360,891	356,048–365,734	¹22,410	(X)	(NA)	(NA)	(NA)	(NA)
Male	88,099	85,539–90,659	¹6,871	6,618–7,124	(NA)	(NA)	(NA)	(NA)
Female	272,792	268,484–277,100	¹15,539	15,286–15,792	(NA)	(NA)	(NA)	(NA)
White	298,308	293,833–302,783	¹14,836	14,576–15,096	(NA)	(NA)	(NA)	(NA)
Male	68,360	66,094–70,626	¹4,057	3,846–4,268	(NA)	(NA)	(NA)	(NA)
Female	229,948	225,950–233,946	¹10,779	10,505–11,053	(NA)	(NA)	(NA)	(NA)
Black	54,656	56,624–56,688	¹6,661	6,410–6,912	(NA)	(NA)	(NA)	(NA)
Male	16,756	15,621–17,891	¹2,471	2,299–2,643	(NA)	(NA)	(NA)	(NA)
Female	37,900	36,201–39,599	¹4,190	3,976–4,404	(NA)	(NA)	(NA)	(NA)
Highest Grade Attended								
Total	2,192,679	2,191,731–2,193,627	14,170	(X)	12,838	12,439–13,237	1,332	933–1,731
No school	114,530	113,079–115,981	1,110	743–1,477	931	592–1,270	179	26–332
Grade K to 7	618,550	615,605–621,495	4,162	3,540–4,784	3,526	2,935–4,117	636	353–919
Grade 8	522,813	520,027–525,599	3,614	3,018–4,210	3,411	2,827–3,995	203	41–365
Grade 9 to 11	278,437	276,264–280,610	1,553	1,126–1,980	1,487	1,068–1,906	66	0–159
Grade 12	353,812	351,410–356,214	2,414	1,900–2,928	2,270	1,769–2,771	144	7–281
College, 1 or more	304,537	302,280–306,794	1,317	920–1,714	1,213	831–1,595	104	0–221

Table 1–3. (continued)

Characteristic	85 years and over Number	85 years and over Range	100 years and over Number	100 years and over Range	100–104 years Number	100–104 years Range	105 years and over Number	105 years and over Range
Male	667,978	664,965–670,991	3,823	3,216–4,430	3,523	2,932–4,114	300	103–497
No school	40,861	39,980–41,742	477	231–723	477	231–723	–	–
Grade K to 7	223,602	221,628–225,576	1,604	1,171–2,037	1,304	909–1,699	300	103–497
Grade 8	153,689	152,024–155,354	824	504–1,144	824	504–1,144	–	–
Grade 9 to 11	74,892	73,708–76,076	249	69–429	249	69–429	–	–
Grade 12	83,769	82,519–85,019	320	117–523	320	117–523	–	–
College, 1 or more	91,165	89,864–92,466	349	137–561	349	137–561	–	–
Female	1,524,701	1,521,630–1,527,772	10,347	9,740–10,954	9,315	8,666–9,964	1,032	677–1,387
No school	73,669	72,494–74,844	633	351–915	454	213–695	179	26–332
Grade K to 7	394,948	392,438–397,458	2,558	2,032–3,084	2,222	1,725–2,719	336	128–544
Grade 8	369,124	366,681–371,567	2,790	2,247–3,333	2,587	2,059–3,115	203	41–365
Grade 9 to 11	203,545	201,652–205,438	1,304	909–1,699	1,238	852–1,624	66	0–159
Grade 12	270,043	267,898–272,188	2,094	1,609–2,579	1,950	1,479–2,421	144	7–281
College, 1 or more	213,372	211,439–215,305	968	623–1,313	864	537–1,191	104	0–221
Place of Birth								
Total	2,534,191	(X)	14,170	(X)	12,838	12,439–13,237	1,332	933–1,731
United States	1,785,741	1,779,120–1,792,362	11,468	10,931–12,005	10,471	9,871–11,071	997	648–1,346
Other	748,450	740,683–756,217	2,702	2,165–3,239	2,367	1,857–2,877	335	127–543
U.S. Citizenship								
Total	2,192,679	2,191,731–2,195,048	14,170	(X)	12,838	12,439–13,237	1,332	933–1,731
Born a citizen	1,785,741	1,779,120–1,792,362	11,553	11,023–12,083	10,556	9,960–11,152	997	648–1,346
Naturalized	350,041	344,062–356,020	2,141	1,652–2,630	1,806	1,350–2,262	335	127–543
Not naturalized	56,897	54,306–59,488	476	230–722	476	230–722	–	–
Year of Immigration								
Total	(NA)	(NA)	14,170	(X)	12,838	12,439–13,237	1,332	933–1,731
Born a citizen	(NA)	(NA)	11,553	11,023–12,083	10,556	9,960–11,152	997	648–1,346
1950 to 1980	(NA)	(NA)	338	129–547	338	129–547	–	–
Before 1950	(NA)	(NA)	2,279	1,777–2,781	1,944	1,474–2,414	335	127–543
Language Spoken at Home								
Total	(NA)	(NA)	14,170	(X)	12,838	12,439–13,237	1,332	933–1,731
Only English	(NA)	(NA)	12,035	11,546–12,524	10,929	10,355–11,503	1,106	739–1,473
Other than English	(NA)	(NA)	2,135	1,646–2,624	1,909	1,442–2,376	226	55–397
Ability to Speak English								
Total	(NA)	(NA)	14,170	(X)	12,838	12,439–13,237	1,332	933–1,731
Only speaks English	(NA)	(NA)	12,035	11,546–12,524	10,929	10,355–11,503	1,106	739–1,473
Speaks another language at home	(NA)	(NA)	2,135	1,646–2,624	1,909	1,442–2,376	226	55–397
Speaks English well	(NA)	(NA)	1,278	887–1,669	1,116	748–1,484	162	17–307
Does not speak English well	(NA)	(NA)	857	531–1,183	793	479–1,107	64	0–156
Ancestry								
Total	(NA)	(NA)	13,879	13,685–14,073	12,625	12,199–13,051	1,254	866–1,642
Western European	(NA)	(NA)	6,214	5,536–6,892	5,740	5,069–6,411	474	228–720
Eastern Europe and Russia	(NA)	(NA)	437	201–673	373	154–592	64	0–156
Hispanic Americas, Caribbean	(NA)	(NA)	313	112–514	313	112–514	–	–
Africa	(NA)	(NA)	123	0–250	123	0–250	–	–
Asia and the Pacific	(NA)	(NA)	–	–	–	–	–	–
Canada and Non-Hispanic Caribbean	(NA)	(NA)	3,486	2,897–4,075	2,885	2,335–3,435	601	326–876
Other, not reported	(NA)	(NA)	3,306	2,728–3,884	3,191	2,620–3,762	115	0–238
Male	(NA)	(NA)	3,532	2,941–4,123	3,310	2,732–3,888	222	52–392
Western European	(NA)	(NA)	1,293	899–1,687	1,206	825–1,587	87	0–194
Eastern Europe and Russia	(NA)	(NA)	148	9–287	148	9–287	–	–
Hispanic Americas, Caribbean	(NA)	(NA)	85	0–191	85	0–191	–	–
Africa	(NA)	(NA)	–	–	–	–	–	–

Table 1–3. (continued)

Characteristic	85 years and over		100 years and over		100–104 years		105 years and over	
	Number	Range	Number	Range	Number	Range	Number	Range
Asia and the Pacific	(NA)	(NA)	–	–	–	–	–	–
Canada and Non-Hispanic								
Caribbean	(NA)	(NA)	1,181	803–1,559	1,114	746–1,482	67	0–161
Other, not reported	(NA)	(NA)	825	505–1,145	757	450–1,064	68	0–162
Female	(NA)	(NA)	10,347	9,740–10,954	9,315	8,666–9,964	1,032	677–1,387
Western European	(NA)	(NA)	4,921	4,270–5,572	4,534	3,897–5,171	387	164–610
Eastern Europe and Russia	(NA)	(NA)	289	96–482	225	54–396	64	0–156
Hispanic Americas, Caribbean	(NA)	(NA)	228	56–400	228	56–400	–	–
Africa	(NA)	(NA)	123	0–250	123	0–250	–	–
Asia and the Pacific	(NA)	(NA)	–	–	–	–	–	–
Canada and Non-Hispanic								
Caribbean	(NA)	(NA)	2,305	1,801–2,809	1,771	1,319–2,223	534	274–794
Other, not reported	(NA)	(NA)	2,481	1,962–3,000	2,434	1,919–2,949	47	0–126

Notes: – Represents zero or a range of zero to zero.
      X Not applicable.
      NA Not available.
      * In institutions only for persons 85 and over.
      1. Age 95 and over.

Source: U.S. Bureau of the Census. *Current Population Reports.* Series P-23, No. 153.

Figure 1–3. Population 85 Years and Over, 1950–2050

(Numbers in thousands)

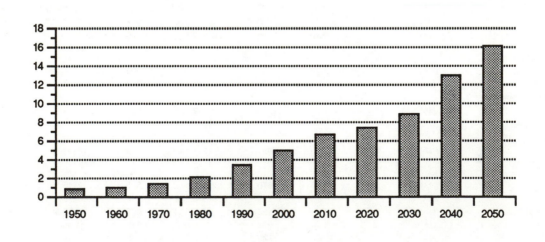

Source: U.S. Bureau of the Census. *Current Population Reports,* series P-23, no. 128.

PROJECTIONS

Table 1–4. Ratio of Males to Females, by Age 65 Years and Over, 1910 to 1985, and by Race, 1985

(Represents number of males per 100 females. Total resident population)

AGE	1910 (Apr. 15)	1920 (Jan. 1)	1930 (Apr. 1)	1940 (Apr. 1)	1950 (Apr. 1)	1960 (Apr. 1)	1970 (Apr. 1)	1980 (Apr. 1)	1985 (Jul. 1)
All ages	**106.0**	**¹104.1**	**¹102.5**	**100.7**	**98.6**	**97.1**	**94.8**	**94.5**	**94.8**
65 years and over	101.1	101.3	100.5	95.5	89.6	82.8	72.1	67.6	67.8

Notes: 1. Includes "age not reported."

Source: U.S. Bureau of the Census, *U.S. Census of Population: 1930*, vol. II; *1940*, vol. II, part 1, and vol. IV, part 1; *1950*, vol. II, part 1; *1960*, vol. I, part 1; *1970*, vol. I, part B; and *Current Population Reports*, series P-25, No. 985.

Table 1–5. Actual and Projected Growth of the Older Population, 1900–2050

(Numbers in thousands)

Year	Total population all ages	55 to 64 Years Number	Percent	65 to 74 Years Number	Percent	75 to 84 Years Number	Percent	85 Years and Over Number	Percent	65 Years and Over Number	Percent
1900	76,303	4,009	5.3	2,189	2.9	772	1.0	123	0.2	3,084	4.0
1910	91,972	5,054	5.5	2,793	3.0	989	1.1	167	0.2	3,950	4.3
1920	105,711	6,532	6.2	3,464	3.3	1,259	1.2	210	0.2	4,933	4.7
1930	122,775	8,397	6.8	4,721	3.8	1,641	1.3	272	0.2	6,634	5.4
1940	131,669	10,572	8.0	6,375	4.8	2,278	1.7	365	0.3	9,019	6.8
1950	150,967	13,295	8.8	8,415	5.6	3,278	2.2	577	0.4	12,270	8.1
1960	179,323	15,572	8.7	10,997	6.1	4,633	2.6	929	0.5	16,560	9.2
1970	203,302	18,608	9.2	12,447	6.1	6,124	3.0	1,409	0.7	19,980	9.8
1980	226,505	21,700	9.6	15,578	6.9	7,727	3.4	2,240	1.0	25,544	11.3
1990	249,657	21,051	8.4	18,035	7.2	10,349	4.1	3,313	1.3	31,697	12.7
2000	267,955	23,767	8.9	17,677	6.6	12,318	4.6	4,926	1.8	34,921	13.0
2010	283,238	34,848	12.3	20,318	7.2	12,326	4.4	6,551	2.3	39,195	13.8
2020	296,597	40,298	13.6	29,855	10.1	14,486	4.9	7,081	2.4	51,422	17.3
2030	304,807	34,025	11.2	34,535	11.3	21,434	7.0	8,612	2.8	64,581	21.2
2040	308,559	34,717	11.3	29,272	9.5	24,882	8.1	12,834	4.2	66,988	21.7
2050	309,488	37,327	12.1	30,114	9.7	21,263	6.9	16,034	5.2	67,411	21.8

Sources: 1900–80: Bureau of the Census. Decennial Censuses of Population, 1990–2050: U.S. Bureau of the Census. *Current Population Reports*, Series P-25, No. 952. May 1984. Projections are middle series.

Table 1–6. Projections of the Total Population by Age, Sex, Race, and Spanish Origin: 1990 to 2000

(In thousands. As of July 1. Includes Armed Forces overseas.)

Age, Sex, Race, and Spanish Origin	Lowest Series (series 19)			Middle Series (series 14)			Highest Series (series 9)		
	1990	1995	2000	1990	1995	2000	1990	1995	2000
Total population[1]	245,753	251,876	256,098	249,657	259,559	267,955	254,122	268,151	281,542
65 years old and over	31,353	33,127	33,621	31,697	33,887	34,921	31,989	34,618	36,246
Male, total	119,620	122,608	124,671	121,518	126,368	130,491	123,698	130,577	137,163
65 years old and over	12,503	13,143	13,255	12,637	13,440	13,762	12,751	13,725	14,277
Female, total	126,133	129,268	131,427	128,139	133,191	137,464	130,424	137,574	144,379
65 years old and over	18,850	19,984	20,366	19,061	20,447	21,158	19,238	20,893	21,969
White, total	207,799	211,481	213,498	210,790	217,412	222,654	213,753	223,236	231,980
65 years old and over	28,313	29,787	30,032	28,596	30,424	31,126	28,810	30,984	32,162
Black, total	30,836	32,506	33,957	31,412	33,651	35,753	31,974	34,780	37,602
65 years old and over	2,538	2,717	2,833	2,579	2,802	2,975	2,597	2,857	3,085
Spanish origin, total[2]	19,148	21,149	23,065	19,887	22,550	25,223	22,053	26,475	31,208
65 years old and over	1,101	1,367	1,627	1,126	1,419	1,719	1,144	1,463	1,804

Notes: 1. Includes other races not shown separately.
2. Persons of Spanish origin may be of any race.

Source: U.S. Bureau of the Census, *Current Population Reports*, series P-25, No. 952.

Table 1–7. Percent Increase in the Older Population, by Age Group, 1950–2020

Period	Percent Change in 10–Year Period			
	65–74 Years	75–84 Years	85 Years and Over	65 Years and Over
Estimates:				
1950–1960	30.1	41.2	59.3	34.5
1960–1970	13.0	31.8	52.3	29.5
1970–1980	25.3	25.9	59.0	28.0
Projections: (Middle Series)				
1980–1990	15.4	32.1	52.2	23.7
1990–2000	-2.0	18.7	48.4	10.2
2000–2010	14.6	-0.3	32.7	12.1
2010–2020	46.8	17.3	7.6	30.9

Source: U.S. Bureau of the Census, *Current Population Reports*, Series P-23, No. 138.

Figure 1–4. Actual and Projected Change in Distribution of Children and Persons 65 Years and Over in the Population: 1900–2050

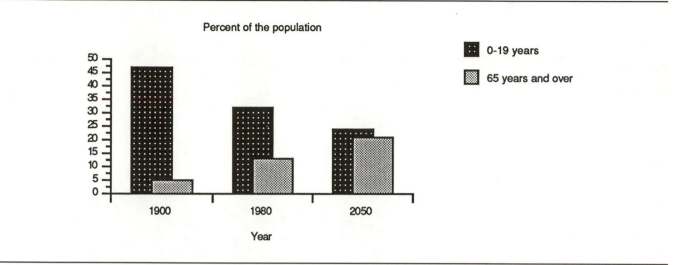

Percent of the population

0-19 years

65 years and over

Year

Source: U.S. Bureau of the Census. *Current Population Reports,* series P–23, no. 952; and *Census of Population,* 1900.

HOUSEHOLD/FAMILY LIVING ARRANGEMENTS

Figure 1–5. Elderly Households in the Population: 1970–1985

(As of March of indicated year)

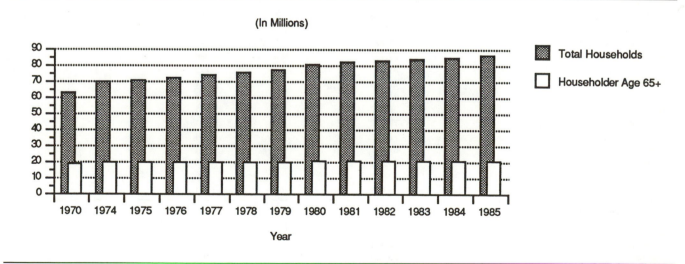

(In Millions)

Total Households

Householder Age 65+

Year

Source: U.S. Bureau of the Census. *Current Population Reports,* series P–20, no. 411 and earlier reports; and unpublished data.

Table 1–8. Elderly Families, by Type, Age, Race, and Spanish Origin of Householder: March 1986

(Numbers in thousands)

Subject	Total (All Ages)	Age of Householder (Years) 65 to 74	Age of Householder (Years) 75 and Over
ALL RACES			
All Families			
Tenure			
Total families	63,558	6,804	3,263
Owner families	45,489	5,955	2,710
Renter families	18,069	849	553
Public housing	1,462	92	71
Private housing	16,607	758	482
Size of Family			
Total families	63,558	6,804	3,263
2 persons	25,472	5,385	2,791
3 persons	15,400	925	295
4 persons	13,355	268	85
5 persons	6,106	138	47
6 persons	2,044	48	30
7 or more persons	1,181	40	14
Age of Members			
Total families	63,558	6,804	3,263
With members:			
Under 18 years	33,562	478	158
18 to 64 years	58,079	3,645	961
65 years and over	11,937	6,804	3,263
Total members	203,963	16,383	7,566
Under 18 years	62,116	783	240
18 to 64 years	123,458	5,104	1,460
65 years and over	18,389	10,496	5,865
Average per family	3.21	2.41	2.32
Under 18 years	0.98	0.12	0.07
18 to 64 years	1.94	0.75	0.45
65 years and over	0.29	1.54	1.80
Age of own children			
Total families	63,558	6,804	3,263
With own children:			
Of any age	41,273	1,543	717
Under 25 years	37,463	390	54
Under 18 years	31,670	113	21
Under 12 years	23,096	27	10
Under 6 years	14,581	5	7
Under 3 years	8,677	1	4
Total own children	79,072	2,291	996
Under 25 years	72,281	554	72
Under 18 years	57,979	151	32
Under 12 years	38,298	36	20
Under 6 years	19,591	6	11
Under 3 years	9,661	1	4
Married-Couple Families			
Tenure			
Total families	50,933	5,784	2,506
Owner families	39,420	5,161	2,117
Renter families	11,513	624	389
Public housing	506	61	47
Private housing	11,007	562	342

Table 1–8. (continued)

Subject	Total (All Ages)	Age of Householder (Years)	
		65 to 74	75 and Over
Size of family			
Total families	50,933	5,784	2,506
2 persons	19,276	4,710	2,221
3 persons	11,714	741	185
4 persons	11,820	195	52
5 persons	5,402	77	22
6 persons	1,755	31	16
7 or more persons	965	31	10
Age of members			
Total families	50,933	5,784	2,506
With members:			
Under 18 years	25,519	250	58
18 to 64 years	45,881	2,831	406
65 years and over	9,573	5,784	2,506
Total members	166,525	13,451	5,558
Under 18 years	47,812	397	98
18 to 64 years	103,220	3,808	611
65 years and over	15,493	9,246	4,848
Average per family	3.27	2.33	2.22
Under 18 years	0.94	0.07	0.04
18 to 64 years	2.03	0.66	0.24
65 years and over	0.30	1.60	1.94
Age of own children			
Total families	50,933	5,784	2,506
With own children:			
Of any age	30,738	890	222
Under 25 years	28,801	324	44
Under 18 years	24,630	94	15
Under 12 years	18,354	24	8
Under 6 years	11,924	4	4
Under 3 years	7,333	1	3
Total own children	60,154	1,345	342
Under 25 years	56,452	469	59
Under 18 years	45,773	130	23
Under 12 years	30,817	33	15
Under 6 years	16,144	5	7
Under 3 years	8,151	1	3
Other Families, Female Householder			
Tenure			
Total families	10,211	807	633
Owner families	4,735	627	484
Renter families	5,476	180	149
Public housing	935	28	24
Private housing	4,542	152	125
Size of family			
Total families	10,211	807	633
2 persons	4,684	525	480
3 persons	3,104	153	93
4 persons	1,355	61	27
5 persons	621	48	21
6 persons	262	16	9
7 or more persons	185	5	3

Table 1-8. (continued)

Subject	Total (All Ages)	Age of Householder (Years) 65 to 74	75 and Over
Age of members			
Total families	10,211	807	633
With members:			
Under 18 years	6,894	185	85
18 to 64 years	9,884	657	466
65 years and over	1,810	807	633
Total members	30,878	2,305	1,683
Under 18 years	12,542	309	118
18 to 64 years	16,120	1,024	714
65 years and over	2,216	972	851
Average per family	3.02	2.86	2.66
Under 18 years	1.23	0.38	0.19
18 to 64 years	1.58	1.27	1.13
65 years and older	0.22	1.20	1.34
Age of own children			
Total families	10,211	807	633
With own children:			
Of any age	9,018	534	413
Under 25 years	7,429	44	8
Under 18 years	6,105	11	6
Under 12 years	4,224	1	2
Under 6 years	2,345	1	2
Under 3 years	1,148	–	1
Total own children	16,597	761	556
Under 25 years	13,952	53	10
Under 18 years	10,840	10	8
Under 12 years	6,724	1	5
Under 6 years	3,038	1	4
Under 3 years	1,286	–	1
WHITE			
All Families			
Tenure			
Total families	54,991	6,129	2,939
Owner families	41,151	5,449	2,471
Renter families	13,840	680	468
Public housing	657	54	48
Private housing	13,184	626	421
Size of family			
Total families	54,991	6,129	2,939
2 persons	22,896	4,995	2,575
3 persons	13,242	800	237
4 persons	11,526	196	61
5 persons	4,981	93	35
6 persons	1,574	26	26
7 or more persons	771	19	5
Age of members			
Total families	54,991	6,129	2,939
With members:			
Under 18 years	27,821	325	97
18 to 64 years	49,867	3,173	786
65 years and over	10,612	6,129	2,939
Total members	173,119	14,265	6,646

Table 1–8. (continued)

Subject	Total (All Ages)	Age of Householder (Years) 65 to 74	75 and Over
Under 18 years	50,629	477	140
18 to 64 years	105,895	4,241	1,145
65 years and over	16,594	9,547	5,361
Average per family	3.15	2.33	2.26
Under 18 years	0.92	0.08	0.05
18 to 64 years	1.93	0.69	0.39
65 years and over	0.30	1.56	1.82
Age of own children			
Total families	54,991	6,129	2,939
With own children:			
Of any age	34,639	1,266	594
Under 25 years	31,476	302	30
Under 18 years	26,575	77	13
Under 12 years	19,286	16	8
Under 6 years	12,264	4	6
Under 3 years	7,393	–	3
Total own children	65,072	1,775	804
Under 25 years	59,805	396	45
Under 18 years	48,114	96	20
Under 12 years	31,898	19	15
Under 6 years	16,462	4	9
Under 3 years	8,178	–	3
Married–Couple Families			
Tenure			
Total families	45,924	5,321	2,322
Owner families	36,283	4,796	1,975
Renter families	9,641	525	346
Public housing	300	38	34
Private housing	9,341	487	313
Size of family			
Total families	45,924	5,321	2,322
2 persons	18,017	4,431	2,094
3 persons	10,532	657	153
4 persons	10,620	148	41
5 persons	4,631	53	17
6 persons	1,441	14	14
7 or more persons	683	17	3
Age of members			
Total families	45,924	5,321	2,322
With members:			
Under 18 years	22,422	174	31
18 to 64 years	41,160	2,538	341
65 years and over	8,727	3,321	2,322
Total members	147,710	12,076	5,068
Under 18 years	41,659	254	53
18 to 64 years	91,823	3,284	503
65 years and over	14,228	8,538	4,512
Average per family	3.22	2.27	2.18
Under 18 years	0.91	0.05	0.02
18 to 64 years	2.00	0.62	0.22
65 years and over	0.31	1.60	1.94
Age of own children			
Total families	45,924	5,321	2,322

Table 1–8. (continued)

Subject	Total (All Ages)	Age of Householder (Years)	
		65 to 74	75 and Over
With own children:			
Of any age	27,156	753	187
Under 25 years	25,432	253	26
Under 18 years	21,756	63	9
Under 12 years	16,178	13	7
Under 6 years	10,561	3	4
Under 3 years	6,560	–	3
Total own children	52,518	1,066	288
Under 25 years	49,432	337	41
Under 18 years	40,222	80	16
Under 12 years	27,191	16	13
Under 6 years	14,338	3	7
Under 3 years	7,275	–	3
Other Families, Female Householder			
Tenure			
Total families	7,111	636	518
Owner families	3,741	515	408
Renter families	3,371	122	110
Public housing	343	15	14
Private housing	3,027	107	96
Size of family			
Total families	7,111	636	518
2 persons	3,625	439	403
3 persons	2,243	118	75
4 persons	765	39	16
5 persons	292	30	15
6 persons	114	10	7
7 or more persons	73	1	2
Age of members			
Total families	7,111	636	518
With members:			
Under 18 years	4,470	121	55
18 to 64 years	6,837	512	374
65 years and over	1,442	636	518
Total members	20,233	1,727	1,317
Under 18 years	7,585	184	67
18 to 64 years	10,844	769	538
65 years and over	1,804	774	712
Average per family	2.85	2.71	2.54
Under 18 years	1.07	0.29	0.13
18 to 64 years	1.52	1.21	1.04
65 years and over	0.25	1.22	1.37
Age of own children			
Total families	7,111	636	518
With own children:			
Of any age	6,224	422	345
Under 25 years	5,008	34	3
Under 18 years	4,040	7	3
Under 12 years	2,697	1	2
Under 6 years	1,463	1	2
Under 3 years	690	–	–
Total own children	10,658	585	445
Under 25 years	8,801	36	4
Under 18 years	6,757	6	4

Table 1–8. (continued)

Subject	Total (All Ages)	Age of Householder (Years) 65 to 74	Age of Householder (Years) 75 and Over
Under 12 years	4,105	1	2
Under 6 years	1,815	1	2
Under 3 years	746	–	–

BLACK

All Families

Tenure
Total families	6,921	573	281
Owner families	3,406	426	205
Renter families	3,515	148	77
Public housing	741	35	21
Private housing	2,774	113	56

Size of family
Total families	6,921	573	281
2 persons	2,178	346	189
3 persons	1,803	94	53
4 persons	1,420	62	21
5 persons	871	39	8
6 persons	338	15	4
7 or more persons	311	18	7

Age of members
Total families	6,921	573	281
With members:			
Under 18 years	4,638	130	53
18 to 64 years	6,615	395	156
65 years and over	1,080	573	281
Total members	24,601	1,789	798
Under 18 years	9,317	272	85
18 to 64 years	13,845	718	282
65 years and over	1,438	799	431
Average per family	3.55	3.12	2.83
Under 18 years	1.35	0.47	0.30
18 to 64 years	2.00	1.25	1.00
65 years and over	0.21	1.39	1.53

Age of own children
Total families	6,921	573	281
With own children:			
Of any age	5,348	224	107
Under 25 years	4,797	67	20
Under 18 years	4,059	29	6
Under 12 years	3,053	8	1
Under 6 years	1,845	1	1
Under 3 years	987	1	1
Total own children	11,339	435	170
Under 25 years	10,015	136	22
Under 18 years	7,849	47	8
Under 12 years	5,082	14	3
Under 6 years	2,471	2	2
Under 3 years	1,154	1	1

Married–Couple Families

Tenure
Total families	3,680	375	150
Owner families	2,323	295	115

Table 1–8. (continued)

Subject	Total (All Ages)	Age of Householder (Years)	
		65 to 74	75 and Over
Renter families	1,357	80	34
Public housing	166	20	11
Private housing	1,191	59	24
Size of family			
Total families	3,680	375	150
2 persons	1,004	242	105
3 persons	908	56	29
4 persons	844	37	7
5 persons	542	20	2
6 persons	195	9	2
7 or more persons	186	11	5
Age of members			
Total families	3,680	375	150
With members:			
Under 18 years	2,185	59	20
18 to 64 years	3,435	228	52
65 years and over	650	375	150
Total members	13,541	1,086	388
Under 18 years	4,320	116	32
18 to 64 years	8,252	398	82
65 years and over	969	572	274
Average per family	3.68	2.90	2.59
Under 18 years	1.17	0.31	0.22
18 to 64 years	2.24	1.06	0.55
65 years and over	0.26	1.53	1.83
Age of own children			
Total families	3,680	375	150
With own children:			
Of any age	2,540	95	25
Under 25 years	2,388	52	13
Under 18 years	1,997	25	4
Under 12 years	1,517	8	–
Under 6 years	937	1	–
Under 3 years	505	1	–
Total own children	5,410	213	37
Under 25 years	4,940	112	14
Under 18 years	3,818	43	4
Under 12 years	2,468	14	–
Under 6 years	1,215	2	–
Under 3 years	578	1	–
Other Families, Female Householder			
Tenure			
Total families	2,874	159	110
Owner families	908	103	71
Renter families	1,966	56	39
Public housing	567	13	10
Private housing	1,399	43	29
Size of family			
Total families	2,874	159	110
2 persons	960	79	72
3 persons	803	32	17
4 persons	552	22	11
5 persons	311	16	7
6 persons	138	6	2
7 or more persons	110	3	1

Table 1–8. (continued)

Subject	Total (All Ages)	Age of Householder (Years)	
		65 to 74	75 and Over
Age of members			
Total families	2,874	159	110
With members:			
Under 18 years	2,270	58	30
18 to 64 years	2,824	134	87
65 years and over	340	159	110
Total members	9,960	542	353
Under 18 years	4,685	118	49
18 to 64 years	4,897	239	172
65 years and over	378	185	133
Average per family	3.47	3.41	3.22
Under 18 years	1.63	0.74	0.45
18 to 64 years	1.70	1.50	1.56
65 years and over	0.13	1.17	1.21
Age of own children			
Total families	2,874	159	110
With own children:			
Of any age	2,601	103	64
Under 25 years	2,256	9	4
Under 18 years	1,934	3	3
Under 12 years	1,441	–	1
Under 6 years	845	–	1
Under 3 years	438	–	1
Total own children	5,583	164	107
Under 25 years	4,842	16	6
Under 18 years	3,843	2	5
Under 12 years	2,476	–	3
Under 6 years	1,169	–	2
Under 3 years	519	–	1

SPANISH ORIGIN

All Families

Tenure			
Total families	4,206	220	106
Owner families	1,892	147	72
Renter families	2,314	74	35
Public housing	191	15	9
Private housing	2,124	58	26
Size of family			
Total families	4,206	220	106
2 persons	1,059	125	67
3 persons	981	44	17
4 persons	1,048	22	7
5 persons	598	14	3
6 persons	286	5	8
7 or more persons	234	9	4
Age of members			
Total families	4,206	220	106
With members:			
Under 18 years	2,981	51	20
18 to 64 years	4,087	156	57
65 years and over	471	220	106
Total members	16,260	714	324
Under 18 years	6,466	102	38
18 to 64 years	9,123	301	105
65 years and over	671	310	181

Table 1–8. (continued)

Subject	Total (All Ages)	Age of Householder (Years) 65 to 74	75 and Over
Average per family	3.87	3.24	3.05
Under 18 years	1.54	0.46	0.36
18 to 64 years	2.17	1.37	0.99
65 years and over	0.16	1.41	1.70
Age of own children			
Total families	4,206	220	106
With own children:			
Of any age	3,297	101	45
Under 25 years	3,067	33	8
Under 18 years	2,755	14	6
Under 12 years	2,237	1	5
Under 6 years	1,505	–	3
Under 3 years	911	–	3
Total own children	7,534	202	77
Under 25 years	6,987	55	14
Under 18 years	5,889	18	12
Under 12 years	4,138	1	11
Under 6 years	2,115	–	6
Under 3 years	1,048	–	3
Married–Couple Families			
Tenure			
Total families	2,962	160	71
Owner families	1,573	113	47
Renter families	1,389	47	24
Public housing	86	10	6
Private housing	1,304	37	18
Size of family			
Total families	2,962	160	71
2 persons	609	91	48
3 persons	614	31	10
4 persons	825	16	3
5 persons	500	11	2
6 persons	229	3	5
7 or more persons	185	8	3
Age of members			
Total families	2,962	160	71
With members:			
Under 18 years	2,075	28	11
18 to 64 years	2,870	111	28
65 years and over	325	160	71
Total members	11,916	512	210
Under 18 years	4,561	62	25
18 to 64 years	6,867	212	49
65 years and over	487	238	135
Average per family	4.02	3.19	(B)
Under 18 years	1.54	0.39	(B)
18 to 64 years	2.32	1.32	(B)
65 years and over	0.16	1.48	(B)
Age of own children			
Total families	2,962	160	71
With own children:			
Of any age	2,293	62	23
Under 25 years	2,176	26	8
Under 18 years	1,987	11	6
Under 12 years	1,631	1	5
Under 6 years	1,145	–	3

Table 1–8. (continued)

Subject	Total (All Ages)	Age of Householder (Years)	
		65 to 74	75 and Over
Under 3 years	709	–	3
Total own children	5,343	127	42
Under 25 years	5,058	46	14
Under 18 years	4,295	16	12
Under 12 years	3,065	1	11
Under 6 years	1,636	–	6
Under 3 years	819	–	3
Other Families, Female Householder			
Tenure			
Total families	980	43	27
Owner families	232	24	19
Renter families	749	20	8
Public housing	104	5	3
Private housing	644	15	5
Size of family			
Total families	980	43	27
2 persons	310	24	17
3 persons	305	10	4
4 persons	195	5	4
5 persons	83	3	–
6 persons	47	1	1
7 or more persons	40	–	1
Age of members			
Total families	980	43	27
With members:			
Under 18 years	771	18	6
18 to 64 years	961	33	21
65 years and over	111	43	27
Total members	3,516	140	85
Under 18 years	1,691	29	8
18 to 64 years	1,684	59	40
65 years and over	140	51	37
Average per family	3.59	(B)	(B)
Under 18 years	1.73	(B)	(B)
18 to 64 years	1.72	(B)	(B)
65 years and over	0.14	(B)	(B)
Age of own children			
Total families	980	43	27
With own children:			
Of any age	879	30	16
Under 25 years	788	2	–
Under 18 years	684	–	–
Under 12 years	553	–	–
Under 6 years	328	–	–
Under 3 years	181	–	–
Total own children	1,971	51	29
Under 25 years	1,757	2	–
Under 18 years	1,458	–	–
Under 12 years	979	–	–
Under 6 years	432	–	–
Under 3 years	205	–	–

Notes: Persons of Spanish origin may be of any race.

– Represents zero.

B Base less than 75,000.

Source: U.S. Bureau of the Census. *Current Population Reports* Series P-20, No. 419

Table 1–9. Living Arrangements of Persons 65 and Over: 1980 to 2000

(in millions and percent)

	Actual		Projected			
	1980		1990		2000	
	Mil.	%	Mil.	%	Mil.	%
Total Elderly	25.5	100.0	29.8	100.0	34.2	100.0
Not in Households[1]	1.8	7.1	1.6	5.4	1.4	4.0
In Households	23.7	92.9	28.2	94.6	32.8	96.0
Family	(16.1)	(63.0)	(17.8)	(59.8)	(19.6)	(57.3)
Nonfamily[2]	(7.6)	(29.9)	(10.4)	(34.8)	(13.2)	(38.7)

Notes: 1. Mostly in institutions.

2. Consists of a person maintaining a household while living alone or with nonrelatives.

Source: Benjamin Handler, *Housing Needs of the Elderly: A Quantitative Analysis.* Ann Arbor, Michigan: National Policy Center on Housing and Living Arrangements for Older Americans, University of Michigan, 1982, p. 7. Handler's source for 1980 was the U.S. Bureau of the Census. Current Population Reports, *Population Characteristics*, Series P-20, Nos. 365 and 366.

Table 1-10. Elderly Households, by Type, Age of Members, and Age, Race, and Spanish Origin of Householder: March 1986

(Numbers in thousands)

Subject	Total (All Ages)	Age of Householder (Years)	
		65 to 74	75 and Over
ALL RACES			
Households by Type			
All Households	88,458	11,157	7,439
Family households	63,558	6,804	3,263
Married–couple family	50,933	5,784	2,506
Other family, male householder	2,414	213	124
Other family, female householder	10,211	807	633
Nonfamily households	24,900	4,352	4,177
Male householder	10,648	1,005	756
Female householder	14,252	3,347	3,421
Age of Household Members			
All Members	236,229	21,022	11,891
Under 18 years	62,952	802	244
18 to 64 years	146,070	5,287	1,555
65 years and over	27,206	14,933	10,091
Households with Members:			
Under 18 years	33,975	493	162
18 to 64 years	74,593	3,744	1,018
65 years and over	20,596	11,157	7,439
Average per Household	2.67	1.88	1.60
Under 18 years	0.71	0.07	0.03
18 to 64 years	1.65	0.47	0.21
65 years and over	0.31	1.34	1.36
Members of Married–Couple Households	167,218	13,486	5,587
Under 18 years	47,961	398	100
18 to 64 years	103,661	3,824	626
65 years and over	15,596	9,264	4,861
Households with Members:			
Under 18 years	25,552	251	59
18 to 64 years	45,892	2,836	412
65 years and over	9,638	5,784	2,506
Average per Household	3.28	2.33	2.23
Under 18 years	0.94	0.07	0.04
18 to 64 years	2.04	0.66	0.25
65 years and over	0.31	1.60	1.94
Members of Other Households with Female Householder	47,805	5,826	5,187
Under 18 years	12,684	325	119
18 to 64 years	25,996	1,135	766
65 years and over	9,124	4,365	4,302
Households with Members:			
Under 18 years	6,955	196	86
18 to 64 years	17,449	708	502
65 years and over	8,627	4,155	4,054
Average per Household	1.95	1.40	1.28
Under 18 years	0.52	0.08	0.03
18 to 64 years	1.06	0.27	0.19
65 years and over	0.37	1.03	1.06
WHITE			
Households by Type			
All Households	76,576	9,953	6,790

Table 1–10. (continued)

Subject	Total (All Ages)	Age of Householder (Years) 65 to 74	75 and Over
Family households	54,991	6,129	2,939
Married–couple family	45,924	5,321	2,322
Other family, male householder	1,956	171	99
Other family, female householder	7,111	636	518
Nonfamily households	21,585	3,824	3,851
Male householder	9,013	845	668
Female householder	12,572	2,979	3,183
Age of Household Members			
All Members	200,952	18,291	10,610
Under 18 years	51,297	489	143
18 to 64 years	125,146	4,364	1,213
65 years and over	24,510	13,437	9,254
Households with Members:			
Under 18 years	28,146	335	100
18 to 64 years	63,889	3,250	829
65 years and over	18,395	9,953	6,790
Average per Household	2.62	1.84	1.56
Under 18 years	0.67	0.05	0.02
18 to 64 years	1.63	0.44	0.18
65 years and over	0.32	1.35	1.36
Members of Married–Couple Households	148,308	12,103	5,084
Under 18 years	41,790	255	54
18 to 64 years	92,198	3,291	508
65 years and over	14,320	8,556	4,522
Households with Members:			
Under 18 years	22,447	174	32
18 to 64 years	41,167	2,541	345
65 years and over	8,784	5,321	2,322
Average per Household	3.23	2.27	2.19
Under 18 years	0.91	0.05	0.02
18 to 64 years	2.01	0.62	0.22
65 years and over	0.31	1.61	1.95
Members of Other Households with Female Householder	35,092	4,814	4,574
Under 18 years	7,694	193	69
18 to 64 years	19,324	838	584
65 years and over	8,074	3,783	3,921
Households with Members:			
Under 18 years	4,516	128	56
18 to 64 years	13,312	551	405
65 years and over	7,642	3,616	3,701
Average per Household	1.78	1.33	1.24
Under 18 years	0.39	0.05	0.02
18 to 64 years	0.98	0.23	0.16
65 years and over	0.41	1.05	1.06
BLACK			
Households by Type			
All Households	9,797	1,058	586
Family households	6,921	573	281
Married–couple family	3,680	375	150
Other family, male householder	368	40	22
Other family, female householder	2,874	159	110

Table 1–10. (continued)

Subject	Total (All Ages)	Age of Householder (Years)	
		65 to 74	75 and Over
Nonfamily households	2,876	484	305
Male householder	1,412	148	79
Female householder	1,464	336	226
Age of Household Members			
All Members	28,373	2,354	1,138
Under 18 years	9,454	279	86
18 to 64 years	16,644	773	309
65 years and over	2,275	1,302	743
Households with Members:			
Under 18 years	4,713	135	54
18 to 64 years	8,731	415	170
65 years and over	1,889	1,058	586
Average per Household	2.90	2.23	1.94
Under 18 years	0.96	0.26	0.15
18 to 64 years	1.70	0.73	0.53
65 years and over	0.23	1.23	1.27
Members of Married–Couple Households	13,607	1,095	401
Under 18 years	4,332	116	32
18 to 64 years	8,295	407	91
65 years and over	981	572	277
Households with Members:			
Under 18 years	2,193	59	20
18 to 64 years	3,439	231	53
65 years and over	658	375	150
Average per Household	3.70	2.92	2.68
Under 18 years	1.18	0.31	0.22
18 to 64 years	2.25	1.09	0.61
65 years and over	0.27	1.35	1.85
Members of Other Households with			
Female Householder	11,759	942	589
Under 18 years	4,713	125	49
18 to 64 years	6,075	279	178
65 years and over	972	538	362
Households with Members:			
Under 18 years	2,282	63	30
18 to 64 years	3,741	146	92
65 years and over	912	495	335
Average per Household	2.71	1.90	1.75
Under 18 years	1.09	0.25	0.15
18 to 64 years	1.40	0.56	0.53
65 years and over	0.22	1.09	1.08
SPANISH ORIGIN			
Households by Type			
All Households	5,213	352	196
Family households	4,206	220	106
Married–couple family	2,962	160	71
Other family, male householder	264	16	8
Other family, female householder	980	43	27
Nonfamily households	1,006	131	90
Male householder	541	35	20
Female householder	465	96	70

Table 1–10. (Continued)

Subject	Total (All Ages)	Age of Householder (Years)	
		65 to 74	75 and Over
Age of Household Members			
All Members	17,890	855	416
Under 18 years	6,566	102	38
18 to 64 years	10,419	308	106
65 years and over	906	445	272
Households with Members:			
Under 18 years	3,019	51	20
18 to 64 years	4,875	158	59
65 years and over	701	352	196
Average per Household	3.43	2.43	2.12
Under 18 years	1.26	0.29	0.19
18 to 64 years	2.00	0.87	0.54
65 years and over	0.17	1.27	1.39
Members of Married–Couple Households	12,014	515	210
Under 18 years	4,586	62	25
18 to 64 years	6,931	212	49
65 years and over	496	240	135
Households with Members:			
Under 18 years	2,077	28	11
18 to 64 years	2,870	111	28
65 years and over	331	160	71
Average per Household	4.06	3.21	(B)
Under 18 years	1.55	0.39	(B)
18 to 64 years	2.34	1.32	(B)
65 years and over	0.17	1.50	(B)
Members of Other Households with Female Householder	4,157	239	158
Under 18 years	1,707	29	8
18 to 64 years	2,141	63	42
65 years and over	309	148	108
Households with Members:			
Under 18 years	775	18	6
18 to 64 years	1,263	35	22
65 years and over	279	140	97
Average per Household	2.88	1.71	1.62
Under 18 years	1.18	0.20	0.09
18 to 64 years	1.48	0.45	0.43
65 years and over	0.21	1.06	1.11

Notes: Persons of Spanish origin may be of any race.

B Base is less than 75,000.

Source: U.S. Bureau of the Census. *Current Population Reports*, P-20, No. 419.

Table 1–11. Elderly Households, by Age of Householder, Race of Members, Region, and Residence: March 1986

(Number in thousands)

Subject	United States			North-east	Midwest[1]	South			West
	Total	White	Black			Total	White	Black	
UNITED STATES									
Age of Householder									
Total	88,458	76,576	9,797	18,562	21,847	30,311	24,798	5,159	17,738
65 to 74 years	11,157	9,953	1,058	2,525	2,701	4,065	3,416	635	1,866
75 years and over	7,439	6,790	586	1,768	1,916	2,503	2,153	344	1,252
Age of Household Members									
All members	236,229	200,952	28,373	49,341	58,582	80,551	64,068	15,355	47,755
65 years and over	27,206	24,510	2,275	6,385	6,646	9,554	8,175	1,335	4,621
Households with Members:									
65 years and over	20,596	18,395	1,889	4,816	5,016	7,251	6,097	1,122	3,512
Average per Household	2.67	2.62	2.90	2.66	2.68	2.66	2.58	2.98	2.69
65 years and over	0.31	0.32	0.23	0.34	0.30	0.32	0.33	0.26	0.26
Members of Married–Couple Households	167,218	148,308	13,607	34,557	42,262	57,045	48,397	7,752	33,354
65 years and over	15,596	14,320	981	3,539	3,830	5,487	4,872	583	2,741
Households with Members:									
65 years and over	9,638	8,784	658	2,174	2,345	3,422	3,001	399	1,697
Average per Household	3.28	3.23	3.70	3.32	3.30	3.22	3.14	3.74	3.34
65 years and over	0.31	0.31	0.27	0.34	0.30	0.31	0.32	0.28	0.27
Members of Other Households with Female Householder	47,805	35,092	11,759	10,513	11,499	16,798	10,647	6,013	8,994
65 years and over	9,124	8,074	972	2,220	2,219	3,257	2,691	557	1,428
Households with Members:									
65 years and over	8,627	7,642	912	2,062	2,124	3,058	2,523	527	1,383
Average per Household	1.95	1.78	2.71	1.92	1.92	2.00	1.74	2.76	1.95
65 years and over	0.37	0.41	0.22	0.41	0.37	0.39	0.44	0.26	0.31
METROPOLITAN									
Age of Householder									
Total	68,363	58,326	8,265	16,352	15,398	21,670	17,653	3,736	14,944
65 to 74 years	8,069	7,108	839	2,193	1,718	2,658	2,223	426	1,500
75 years and over	5,386	4,919	422	1,548	1,203	1,624	1,434	188	1,011
Age of Household Members									
All members	182,811	153,277	23,686	43,582	41,477	57,612	45,749	10,997	40,139
65 years and over	19,928	17,821	1,755	5,563	4,228	6,354	5,490	837	3,783
Households with Members:									
65 years and over	15,108	13,383	1,464	4,218	3,230	4,801	4,065	715	2,859
Average per Household	2.67	2.63	2.87	2.67	2.69	2.66	2.59	2.94	2.69
65 years and over	0.29	0.31	0.21	0.34	0.27	0.29	0.31	0.22	0.25
Members of Married–Couple Households	127,342	111,628	11,157	30,299	28,920	40,481	34,274	5,513	27,641
65 years and over	11,429	10,437	741	3,063	2,385	3,736	3,364	350	2,245
Households with Members:									
65 years and over	7,097	6,425	503	1,891	1,486	2,334	2,071	248	1,385
Average per Household	3.30	3.25	3.66	3.33	3.32	3.23	3.16	3.68	3.34
65 years and over	0.30	0.30	0.24	0.34	0.27	0.30	0.31	0.23	0.27
Members of Other Households with Female Householder	38,392	27,630	10,032	9,540	8,948	12,157	7,694	4,363	7,747
65 years and over	6,706	5,873	777	1,956	1,474	2,108	1,733	371	1,167
Households with Members:									
65 years and over	6,329	5,554	724	1,820	1,410	1,978	1,627	348	1,122
Average per Household	1.98	1.81	2.69	1.93	2.02	2.02	1.76	2.73	1.95
65 years and over	0.35	0.38	0.21	0.40	0.33	0.35	0.40	0.23	0.29

Table 1–11. (continued)

| Subject | United States | | | North-east | Midwest[1] | South | | | West |
	Total	White	Black			Total	White	Black	
NONMETROPOLITAN									
Age of Householder									
Total	20,094	18,250	1,532	2,210	6,450	8,641	7,145	1,423	2,794
65 to 74 years	3,088	2,845	218	332	983	1,407	1,193	209	366
75 years and over	2,053	1,872	164	221	713	879	719	156	241
Age of Household Members									
All members	53,419	47,675	4,686	5,759	17,104	22,939	18,319	4,358	7,616
65 years and over	7,278	6,689	520	822	2,418	3,201	2,686	498	839
Households with Members:									
65 years and over	5,488	5,012	425	598	1,786	2,451	2,032	407	653
Average per Household	2.66	2.61	3.06	2.61	2.65	2.65	2.56	3.06	2.73
65 years and over	0.36	0.37	0.34	0.37	0.37	0.37	0.38	0.35	0.30
Members of Married–Couple Households	39,876	36,681	2,450	4,258	13,342	16,563	14,123	2,239	5,713
65 years and over	4,167	3,883	240	476	1,445	1,750	1,507	232	496
Households with Members:									
65 years and over	2,541	2,359	156	282	859	1,088	931	151	312
Average per Household	3.23	3.18	3.87	3.19	3.26	3.19	3.09	3.89	3.32
65 years and over	0.34	0.34	0.38	0.36	0.35	0.34	0.33	0.40	0.29
Members of Other Households with Female Householder	9,413	7,462	1,728	973	2,551	4,642	2,953	1,650	1,247
65 years and over	2,419	2,202	195	263	745	1,149	958	186	261
Households with Members:									
65 years and over	2,297	2,088	188	242	715	1,080	896	179	261
Average per Household	1.84	1.69	2.82	1.79	1.64	1.97	1.68	2.83	1.90
65 years and over	0.47	0.50	0.32	0.49	0.48	0.49	0.54	0.32	0.40

Notes: 1. Formerly North Central.
Source: U.S. Bureau of the Census. *Current Population Reports*, P-20, No. 419.

MARITAL STATUS

Table 1–12. Marital Status of the Population, by Sex and Age: 1985

(As of March)

| Sex and Age | Number of Persons (1,000) | | | | | Percent Distribution | | | | |
	Total	Single	Mar-ried	Wid-owed	Di-vorced	Total	Sin-gle	Mar-ried	Wid-owed	Di-vorced
Male	**81,452**	**20,543**	**53,536**	**2,109**	**5,264**	**100.0**	**25.2**	**65.7**	**2.6**	**6.5**
65–74 years	7,259	380	5,899	672	307	100.0	5.2	81.3	9.3	4.2
75 years and over	3,755	200	2,604	851	100	100.0	5.3	69.3	22.7	2.7
Female	**89,917**	**16,377**	**54,354**	**11,372**	**7,814**	**100.0**	**18.2**	**60.4**	**12.6**	**8.7**
65–74 years	9,317	412	4,764	3,622	519	100.0	4.4	51.1	38.9	5.6
75 years and over	6,487	400	1,543	4,390	154	100.0	6.2	23.8	67.7	2.4

Source: U.S. Bureau of the Census, *Current Population Reports*, series P-20, No. 410.

Table 1-13. Married Couples, by Age of Husband and Wife, Race, and Spanish Origin of Householder or Subfamily Reference Person: March 1986

(Numbers in thousands)

Subject	Total	Age of Wife (Years)										Median
		Under 25	25 to 34	35 to 44	45 to 54	55 to 59	60 and 61	62 to 64	65 to 69	70 to 74	75 and Over	
ALL RACES												
Total	51,704	4,024	13,435	11,783	8,388	4,179	1,531	2,211	2,832	1,811	1,510	42.1
Age of Husband:												
Under 25 years	2,224	1,902	298	19	–	–	3	–	1	–	2	20.8
25 to 34 years	11,907	1,982	9,226	674	21	3	–	–	–	–	2	29.3
35 to 44 years	11,929	124	3,524	7,854	394	14	6	3	2	6	1	37.9
45 to 54 years	8,801	10	317	2,894	5,209	287	31	34	15	2	3	47.3
55 to 59 years	4,414	1	31	235	1,955	1,816	184	106	68	16	2	54.9
60 and 61 years	1,672	–	10	33	323	766	319	159	47	12	2	58.1
62 to 64 years	2,264	1	11	45	248	667	456	577	208	47	3	60.7
65 to 69 years	3,373	–	11	17	163	443	415	951	1,115	211	47	64.0
70 to 74 years	2,518	2	4	9	55	136	85	262	1,027	782	157	68.4
75 years and over	2,602	–	3	3	21	47	33	119	350	735	1,293	74.9
Median	44.8	25.6	32.0	41.6	52.3	59.9	63.5	66.2	69.8	73.9	75+	(X)
WHITE												
Total	46,546	3,646	11,894	10,479	7,571	3,781	1,419	2,036	2,617	1,694	1,409	42.4
Age of Husband:												
Under 25 years	2,059	1,775	263	17	–	–	2	–	1	–	2	20.8
25 to 34 years	10,610	1,752	8,223	609	21	3	–	–	–	–	2	29.3
35 to 44 years	10,614	110	3,083	7,047	341	14	6	3	2	6	1	38.0
45 to 54 years	7,835	7	269	2,516	4,715	257	22	34	11	2	3	47.4
55 to 59 years	4,017	1	28	201	1,778	1,661	174	95	61	16	2	55.0
60 and 61 years	1,538	–	8	28	291	713	296	143	43	12	2	58.1
62 to 64 years	2,081	1	9	40	224	596	446	544	179	38	3	60.8
65 to 69 years	3,073	–	4	10	138	383	377	872	1,060	196	33	64.1
70 to 74 years	2,317	–	4	6	42	122	71	244	958	729	142	68.5
75 years and over	2,404	–	3	3	21	34	24	100	303	695	1,221	75+
Median	45.0	25.3	31.9	41.5	52.3	59.9	63.4	66.1	69.8	74.0	75+	(X)
BLACK												
Total	3,736	290	1,094	898	568	296	96	141	174	91	88	40.4
Age of Husband:												
Under 25 years	130	107	23	–	–	–	–	–	–	–	–	21.1
25 to 34 years	946	170	732	45	–	–	–	–	–	–	–	29.1
35 to 44 years	892	7	293	559	33	–	–	–	–	–	–	37.6
45 to 54 years	688	4	37	259	354	23	8	–	3	–	–	46.3
55 to 59 years	286	–	3	22	114	118	10	11	7	–	–	55.1
60 and 61 years	101	–	2	3	18	43	21	11	4	–	–	58.2
62 to 64 years	148	–	2	3	18	57	6	27	26	9	–	59.5
65 to 69 years	225	–	3	7	18	34	30	61	44	14	14	63.0
70 to 74 years	164	2	–	–	13	13	12	12	58	42	12	67.6
75 years and over	155	–	–	–	–	7	9	18	32	27	62	72.2
Median	43.9	27.2	32.2	42.2	52.1	60.3	65.4	66.7	70.2	72.7	75+	(X)
SPANISH ORIGIN												
Total	3,085	465	1,012	698	458	184	51	62	74	43	39	35.9
Age of Husband:												
Under 25 years	270	232	37	1	–	–	–	–	–	–	–	20.8
25 to 34 years	967	213	683	68	3	–	–	–	–	–	–	29.0
35 to 44 years	724	14	248	435	27	–	1	–	–	–	–	37.3
45 to 54 years	529	3	34	168	297	21	2	3	1	–	–	47.0
55 to 59 years	176	1	3	15	66	72	10	4	6	–	–	55.2

Table 1–13. (continued)

Subject	Total	Under 25	25 to 34	35 to 44	45 to 54	55 to 59	60 and 61	62 to 64	65 to 69	70 to 74	75 and Over	Median
						Age of Wife (Years)						
60 and 61 years	83	–	1	5	23	30	12	8	3	1	–	57.0
62 to 64 years	89	1	3	4	17	30	10	14	5	2	1	58.1
65 to 69 years	108	–	–	–	20	19	15	22	24	6	3	62.1
70 to 74 years	59	–	–	1	3	10	–	7	21	14	3	67.1
75 years and over	80	–	3	1	2	2	1	4	14	21	32	73.0
Median	39.2	25.0	31.9	41.4	51.7	60.0	62.3	65.4	69.7	74.7	75 +	(X)

Notes: Persons of Spanish origin may be of any race.

– Represents zero or rounds to zero.

X Not applicable.

Source: U.S. Bureau of the Census, *Current Population Reports*, Series P-20, No. 419

LIFE EXPECTANCY AND MORTALITY

Figure 1–6. Life Expectancy at Age 65: 1900–2050

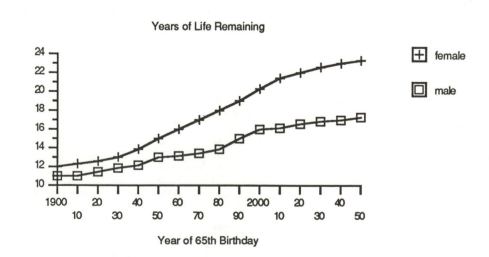

Years of Life Remaining

Year of 65th Birthday

Source: U.S. Bureau of the Census. *Current Population Reports*, series P-23, no. 128.

Table 1–14. Life Expectancy at Birth and Age 65 by Sex and Calendar Year, 1900–2050

	Male		Female	
	At birth	At age 65	At birth	At age 65
1900	46.4	11.3	49.0	12.0
1910	50.1	11.4	53.6	12.1
1920	54.5	11.8	56.3	12.3
1930	58.0	11.8	61.3	12.9
1940	61.4	11.9	65.7	13.4
1950	65.6	12.8	71.1	15.1
1960	66.7	12.9	73.2	15.9
1970	67.1	13.1	74.9	17.1
1980	69.9	14.0	77.5	18.4
1990	71.4	14.5	78.9	19.2
2000	72.1	14.8	79.5	19.5
2010	72.4	15.0	79.8	19.8
2020	72.7	15.2	80.1	20.1
2030	73.0	15.4	80.4	20.3
2040	73.3	15.6	80.7	20.6
2050	73.6	15.8	81.0	20.8

Source: U.S. Social Security Administration; *Social Security Area Population Projections, 1984*; Actuarial Study No. 92, Alternative 1.

Table 1–15. Death Rates, by Age, Sex, and Race: 1960 to 1984

(Number of deaths per 100,000 population in specified group)

Sex, Year, and Race	All Ages[1]	65–74 yr. Old	75–84 yr. Old	85 yr. Old and Over
Male				
1960[2]	1,105	4,914	10,178	21,186
1970	1,090	4,874	10,010	17,822
1975	1,002	4,409	9,154	18,135
1980	977	4,105	8,817	18,801
1982	938	3,929	8,391	17,782
1983	943	3,885	8,539	17,977
1984[2,3]	946	3,859	8,473	18,034
White: 1970	1,087	4,810	10,099	18,552
1980	983	4,036	8,830	19,097
1983	957	3,816	8,557	18,443
1984[2,3]	962	3,783	8,511	18,512
Black: 1970	1,187	5,803	9,455	12,222
1980	1,034	5,131	9,232	16,099
1983	963	4,949	9,100	14,156
1984[2,3]	963	4,992	8,869	14,708
Female				
1960[2]	809	2,872	7,633	19,008
1970	808	2,580	6,678	15,518
1975	761	2,237	5,743	14,455
1980	785	2,145	5,440	14,747
1982	771	2,085	5,121	13,895
1983	787	2,092	5,200	14,011
1984[2,3]	792	2,092	5,197	13,614
White: 1970	813	2,471	6,699	15,980
1980	806	2,067	5,402	14,980
1983	815	2,025	5,162	14,278
1984[2,3]	822	2,031	5,162	13,910
Black: 1970	829	3,861	6,692	10,707
1980	733	3,057	6,212	12,367
1983	711	2,931	6,065	11,330
1984[2,3]	711	2,882	6,095	10,730

Notes: 1. Includes unknown age.
2. Includes deaths of nonresidents.
3. Based on a 10–percent sample of deaths—preliminary data.

Source: U.S. National Center for Health Statistics, *Vital Statistics, Vital Statistics of the United States*, annual; and unpublished data.

Figure 1–7. Death Rates Among Persons 65 Years of Age and Over, by Age: 1940–

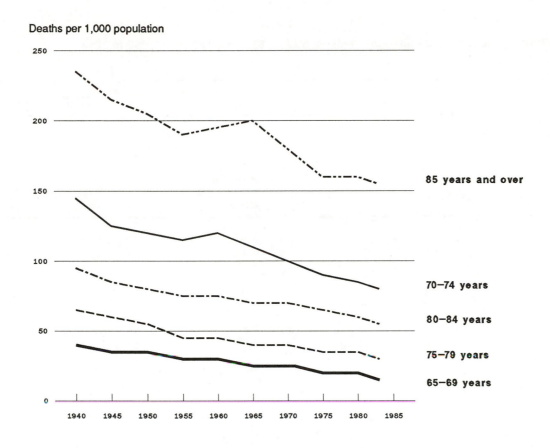

Deaths per 1,000 population

85 years and over

70–74 years

80–84 years

75–79 years

65–69 years

Source: U.S. National Center for Health Statistics, *Vital and Health Statistics,* Series 3, No. 22a; *Monthly Vital Statistics Report,* Vol. 33, No. 3, *Supplement;* Vol. 33, No. 9, *Supplement;* and Vol. 34, No. 6, *Supplement* (2).

GEOGRAPHIC

Table 1–16. Projections of the Population of Regions, by Age 65 Years and Over: 1980 to 2000

(In thousands)

	Total	65 Years & Over
Total Resident Population		
April 1, 1980 (r)		
U.S. total	226,546	25,549
Northeast	49,135	6,072
Midwest*	58,866	6,692
South	75,372	8,488
West	43,172	4,298
July 1, 1990		
U.S. total	249,203	31,799
Northeast	48,423	6,912
Midwest*	60,265	7,656
South	87,594	11,403
West	52,920	5,829
July 1, 2000		
U.S. total	267,462	35,036
Northeast	46,401	6,828
Midwest*	59,714	7,763
South	98,828	13,582
West	62,519	6,864
Percent of U.S. Total		
1980 (r)		
U.S. Total	100.00	100.00
Northeast	21.69	23.77
Midwest*	25.98	26.20
South	33.27	33.21
West	19.06	16.82
1990		
U.S. Total	100.00	100.00
Northeast	19.43	21.74
Midwest*	24.18	24.07
South	35.15	35.86
West	21.24	18.33
2000		
U.S. Total	100.00	100.00
Northeast	17.35	19.49
Midwest*	22.33	22.16
South	36.95	38.77
West	23.38	19.59

Notes: * Formerly the North Central Region
       (r) revised

Source: U.S. Bureau of the Census, *Current Population Reports*, Series P-25, No. 937; P-25, No. 970.

Table 1–17. Resident Population, by Age and State: 1985

(In thousands, except percent. As of July 1. Includes Armed Forces stationed in area.)

Region Division, and State	Total	65 years and over	Percent, 65 years and over
U.S.	238,740	28,530	12.0
Region:			
Northeast	49,859	6,573	13.2
Midwest	59,197	7,297	12.3
South	81,858	9,632	11.8
West	47,826	5,028	10.5
New England	**12,660**	**1,668**	**13.2**
Maine	1,164	153	13.2
New Hampshire	998	116	11.6
Vermont	535	63	11.8
Massachusetts	5,822	783	13.4
Rhode Island	968	139	14.4
Connecticut	3,174	413	13.0
Middle Atlantic	**37,199**	**4,905**	**13.2**
New York	17,783	2,254	12.7
New Jersey	7,562	954	12.6
Pennsylvania	11,853	1,698	14.3
East North Central	**41,642**	**4,948**	**11.9**
Ohio	10,744	1,296	12.1
Indiana	5,499	645	11.7
Illinois	11,535	1,368	11.9
Michigan	9,088	1,022	11.2
Wisconsin	4,775	617	12.9
West North Central	**17,555**	**2,349**	**13.4**
Minnesota	4,193	522	12.5
Iowa	2,884	413	14.3
Missouri	5,029	687	13.7
North Dakota	685	87	12.7
South Dakota	708	97	13.7
Nebraska	1,606	217	13.5
Kansas	2,450	326	13.3
South Atlantic	**40,227**	**5,094**	**12.7**
Delaware	622	70	11.2
Maryland	4,392	458	10.4
District of Columbia	626	76	12.1
Virginia	5,706	587	10.3
West Virginia	1,936	257	13.3
North Carolina	6,255	708	11.3
South Carolina	3,347	342	10.2
Georgia	5,976	594	9.9
Florida	11,366	2,001	17.6
East South Central	**15,122**	**1,816**	**12.0**
Kentucky	3,726	444	11.9
Tennessee	4,762	576	12.1
Alabama	4,021	487	12.1
Mississippi	2,613	310	11.9

Table 1–17. (continued)

Region Division, and State	Total	65 years and over	Percent, 65 years and over
West South Central	**26,510**	**2,722**	**10.3**
Arkansas	2,359	338	14.3
Louisiana	4,481	441	9.8
Oklahoma	3,301	405	12.3
Texas	16,370	1,538	9.4
Mountain	**12,789**	**1,288**	**10.1**
Montana	826	98	11.8
Idaho	1,005	109	10.9
Wyoming	509	42	8.3
Colorado	3,231	285	8.8
New Mexico	1,450	139	9.6
Arizona	3,187	392	12.3
Utah	1,645	130	7.9
Nevada	936	93	9.9
Pacific	**35,037**	**3,740**	**10.7**
Washington	4,409	505	11.4
Oregon	2,687	354	13.2
California	26,365	2,766	10.5
Alaska	521	17	3.2
Hawaii	1,054	99	9.4

Source: U.S. Bureau of the Census, *Current Population Reports* series P-25, No. 985.

Figure 1–8. Ten States With Highest Proportion of Persons Age 65 Years and Over: July 1, 1985

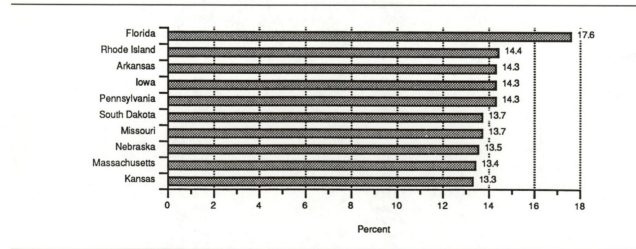

Source: U.S. Bureau of the Census. *Current Population Reports,* series P–25, no. 970.

Table 1–18. Growth of Each State's Elderly Population 1970–80 and 1980–84

(Numbers in thousands)

State	1980 all ages Number	Rank	1980 65 plus Number	Rank	Percent	Rank	Percent increase, 1970–80	1984 65 plus Number	Percent	Percent increase, 1970–80
Alabama	3,894	22	440	19	11.3	24	35.0	476	11.9	8.3
Alaska	402	51	12	51	2.9	51	67.7	15	3.1	32.6
Arizona	2,718	29	307	28	11.3	25	90.4	375	12.3	21.9
Arkansas	2,286	33	312	27	13.7	2	31.4	336	14.3	7.4
California	23,668	1	2,414	1	10.2	34	34.1	2,693	10.5	11.5
Colorado	2,890	28	247	33	8.6	46	31.6	280	8.8	13.4
Connecticut	3,108	25	365	26	11.7	18	26.3	407	12.9	11.6
Delaware	594	48	59	48	10.0	36	35.0	67	11.0	13.8
D.C.	638	47	74	46	11.6	20	4.9	75	12.1	1.5
Florida	9,746	7	1,688	3	17.3	1	70.6	1,931	17.6	14.4
Georgia	5,463	13	517	16	9.5	41	40.6	577	9.9	11.7
Hawaii	965	39	76	45	7.9	49	72.4	94	9.0	22.9
Idaho	944	41	94	41	9.9	37	38.2	108	10.8	14.9
Illinois	11,427	5	1,262	6	11.0	29	15.4	1,356	11.8	7.5
Indiana	5,490	12	585	13	10.7	31	18.5	638	11.6	8.9
Iowa	2,913	27	388	24	13.3	4	10.7	410	14.1	5.9
Kansas	2,364	32	306	29	13.0	8	15.1	323	13.3	5.6
Kentucky	3,661	23	410	21	11.2	27	21.5	438	11.8	6.8
Louisiana	4,206	19	404	22	9.6	39	31.8	435	9.7	7.5
Maine	1,125	38	141	36	12.5	11	23.0	152	13.1	7.6
Maryland	4,217	18	396	23	9.4	42	32.0	447	10.3	13.0
Massachusetts	5,737	11	727	10	12.7	10	14.2	777	13.4	6.9
Michigan	9,262	8	912	8	9.9	38	21.2	1,007	11.1	10.3
Minnesota	4,076	21	480	18	11.8	17	17.3	517	12.4	7.7
Mississippi	2,521	31	289	31	11.5	21	30.1	306	11.8	5.9
Missouri	4,917	15	648	11	13.2	5	15.6	682	13.6	5.3
Montana	787	44	85	43	10.8	32	23.0	96	11.6	13.2
Nebraska	1,570	35	206	35	13.1	7	12.1	216	13.4	4.8
Nevada	800	43	66	47	8.2	47	112.3	87	9.5	32.2
New Hampshire	921	42	103	40	11.2	28	31.3	114	11.7	10.6
New Jersey	7,365	9	860	9	11.7	19	23.4	942	12.5	9.6
New Mexico	1,303	37	116	38	8.9	45	64.2	135	9.5	16.6
New York	17,558	2	2,161	2	12.3	13	10.2	2,247	12.7	4.0
North Carolina	5,882	10	603	12	10.2	35	45.7	688	11.2	14.1
North Dakota	653	46	80	44	12.3	14	21.2	87	12.6	7.6
Ohio	10,798	6	1,169	7	10.8	30	17.2	1,280	11.9	9.5
Oklahoma	3,025	26	376	25	12.4	12	25.5	401	12.1	6.5
Oregon	2,633	30	303	30	11.5	22	33.8	344	12.9	13.4
Pennsylvania	11,864	4	1,531	4	12.9	9	20.3	1,676	14.1	9.5
Rhode Island	947	40	127	37	13.4	3	22.1	138	14.3	8.7
South Carolina	3,122	24	287	32	9.2	44	50.5	331	10.0	15.1
South Dakota	691	45	91	42	13.2	6	13.1	96	13.6	5.8
Tennessee	4,591	17	518	15	11.3	26	34.8	566	12.0	9.4
Texas	14,229	3	1,371	5	9.6	40	38.2	1,514	9.5	10.4
Utah	1,461	36	109	39	7.5	50	40.8	128	7.7	16.9
Vermont	511	49	58	49	11.4	23	22.5	63	11.8	7.8
Virginia	5,346	14	505	17	9.5	43	38.1	572	10.2	13.2
Washington	4,132	20	432	20	10.4	33	34.0	492	11.3	14.0
West Virginia	1,950	34	238	34	12.2	15	22.3	255	13.0	7.1
Wisconsin	4,705	16	564	14	12.0	16	19.3	611	12.8	8.4
Wyoming	470	50	37	50	7.9	48	23.1	42	8.2	12.3

Source: U.S. Bureau of the Census, Decennial Census of the Population, Current Population Reports, Series P-25, No. 95, and Current Population Reports, Series P-25, No. 970.

Table 1–19. Resident Population of States, People Age 85 and Older: 1980

	Number*	Percent Women	Percent Naturalized Citizens
Alabama	34,019	68.6%	1.4%
Alaska	619	64.3	17.9
Arizona	19,878	66.4	13.3
Arkansas	26,354	65.7	1.4
California	218,017	69.9	19.5
Colorado	24,363	68.3	10.4
Connecticut	35,729	73.2	33.7
Delaware	5,269	75.6	10.9
District of Columbia	6,385	71.6	6.8
Florida	117,342	63.7	21.1
Georgia	39,434	72.2	1.3
Hawaii	5,561	60.8	26.2
Idaho	8,476	66.3	8.4
Illinois	114,682	70.7	20.1
Indiana	54,410	69.8	5.9
Iowa	44,940	71.2	6.7
Kansas	33,455	68.2	3.4
Kentucky	35,036	66.5	1.2
Louisiana	30,535	68.7	2.3
Maine	14,099	74.7	15.3
Maryland	32,665	72.4	10.7
Massachusetts	73,908	72.5	36.7
Michigan	81,653	68.9	21.2
Minnesota	52,789	66.4	15.4
Mississippi	23,509	69.5	1.0
Missouri	61,072	69.7	5.0
Montana	8,837	63.1	15.2
Nebraska	23,744	66.4	6.9
Nevada	3,640	64.7	22.5
New Hampshire	9,650	69.5	21.9
New Jersey	72,231	70.0	32.9
New Mexico	8,783	67.3	5.1
New York	192,983	69.4	35.9
North Carolina	45,203	68.1	1.7
North Dakota	8,140	65.0	24.4
Ohio	108,426	69.1	13.4
Oklahoma	33,981	68.7	2.0
Oregon	28,431	68.1	11.3
Pennsylvania	129,960	69.5	18.0
Rhode Island	11,978	74.0	33.1
South Carolina	20,004	73.6	1.8
South Dakota	10,427	67.0	9.2
Tennessee	41,443	69.4	1.8
Texas	112,022	69.6	6.2
Utah	8,852	67.2	13.7
Vermont	6,007	71.6	14.7
Virginia	41,131	73.1	3.7
Washington	41,476	70.2	15.6
West Virginia	19,409	67.0	3.8
Wisconsin	55,637	67.4	13.7
Wyoming	3,473	61.6	16.6
U.S.	2,240,067	69.2	16.0

Notes: * Totals are slightly different from the 100 percent count from the 1980 census because of sampling.

Source: U.S. Bureau of the Census. Decennial Census of the Population, 1980

Figure 1–9. Ten States With Largest Percent Increase of Population Age 65 Years and Over: 1980–1984

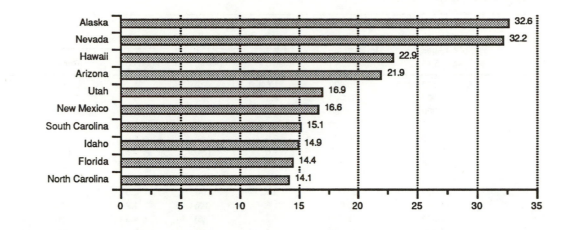

Source: U.S. Bureau of the Census. *Current Population Reports,* series P–23, no. 128.

Figure 1–10. Migration Streams: 1975–1980

From 1975 to 1980, the 20 largest Frostbelt to Sunbelt migration streams of older migrants went to Florida, California, Texas, and North Carolina

(major interstate streams of older migrants from the frostbelt to the sunbelt states: 1975–80)

Source: © *American Demographics,* Vol. 6, No. 12, December 1984, p. 24. Reprinted with permission.

Table 1–20. Migration to the Sunbelt: 1975–1980

(Fifty–six percent of older interstate migrants moved from Frostbelt to Sunbelt between 1975 and 1980, compared to less than half of all interstate migrants. Florida received 26 percent of all older migrants.)

Sunbelt state	In–Migrants of All Ages (Aged 5 +)	Older In–Migrants (Aged 60 +)	Share of National Interstate Migration				Older Migrants as a Percent of All Migrants
			Aged 5 +	(Rank)	Aged 60 +	(Rank)	
Alabama	320,000	20,000	1.6%	(25)	1.2%	(27)	6.3%
Arizona	598,000	94,000	2.9	(8)	5.7	(3)	15.7
California	1,877,000	145,000	9.2	(1)	8.8	(2)	7.7
Florida	1,801,000	429,000	8.9	(2)	25.9	(1)	23.8
Georgia	582,000	26,000	2.9	(9)	1.6	(14)	4.5
Louisiana	325,000	13,000	1.6	(24)	0.8	(35)	4.0
Mississippi	213,000	15,000	1.0	(33)	0.9	(31)	6.9
New Mexico	207,000	17,000	1.0	(34)	1.0	(30)	8.3
North Carolina	538,000	38,000	2.6	(14)	2.3	(7)	7.0
South Carolina	332,000	20,000	1.6	(23)	1.2	(25)	6.1
Texas	1,436,000	75,000	7.1	(3)	4.5	(4)	5.2
Virginia	695,000	34,000	3.4	(4)	2.1	(11)	4.9
Total Sunbelt in–migrants	8,924,000	926,000	43.8		56.0		10.4
Total other interstate migrants	11,434,000	728,000	56.2		44.0		6.4
Total interstate migrants	20,358,000	1,654,000	100.0		100.0		8.1

Source: ©American Demographics, Vol. 6, No. 12, December 1984, p. 24. Reprinted with permission.

Table 1–21. Metropolitan Statistical Areas—Elderly Population, 1980

Metropolitan Area	Total (1,000)	65 years old and over (%)
	1980	
Albany–Schenectady–Troy, NY MSA	836	13.1
Albuquerque, NM MSA	420	8.1
Allentown–Bethlehem, PA–NJ MSA	635	12.9
Appleton–Oshkosh–Neenah, WI MSA	291	10.7
Atlanta, GA MSA	2,138	7.8
Atlantic City, NJ MSA	276	17.2
Augusta, GA–SC MSA	346	8.4
Austin, TX MSA	537	7.8
Bakersfield, CA MSA	403	9.7
Baltimore, MD MSA	2,200	10.1
Baton Rouge, LA MSA	494	7.0
Beaumont–Port Arthur, TX MSA	375	10.3
Binghamton, NY MSA	263	12.2
Birmingham, AL MSA	884	11.7
Boston–Lawrence–Salem, MA–NH CMSA	3,972	11.8
Boston, MA PMSA	2,806	12.2
Brockton, MA PMSA	183	10.6
Lawrence–Haverhill, MA–NH PMSA	339	12.0
Lowell, MA–NH PMSA	243	9.2
Nashua, NH PMSA	143	7.5
Salem–Gloucester, MA PMSA	258	13.0
Buffalo–Niagara Falls, NY CMSA	1,243	12.3
Buffalo, NY PMSA	1,015	12.4
Niagara Falls, NY PMSA	227	11.9
Canton, OH MSA	404	11.1
Charleston, SC MSA	430	6.9
Charleston, WV MSA	270	11.5
Charlotte–Gastonia–Rock Hill, NC–SC MSA	971	9.6
Chattanooga, TN–GA MSA	427	10.9
Chicago–Gary–Lake County (IL), IL–IN–WI CMSA	7,937	9.9
Aurora–Eligin, IL PMSA	316	8.9
Chicago, IL PMSA	6,060	10.4
Gary–Hammond, IN PMSA	643	8.4
Joliet, IL PMSA	355	7.7
Kenosha, WI PMSA	123	10.8
Lake County, IL PMSA	440	7.2
Cincinnati–Hamilton, OH–KY–IN CMSA	1,660	10.6
Cincinnati, OH–KY–IN PMSA	1,401	10.9
Hamilton–Middletown, OH PMSA	259	8.9
Cleveland–Akron–Lorain, OH CMSA	2,834	11.1
Akron, OH PMSA	660	10.4
Cleveland, OH PMSA	1,899	11.7
Lorain–Elyria, OH PMSA	275	8.5
Colorado Springs, CO MSA	309	6.8
Columbia, SC MSA	410	7.3
Columbus, OH MSA	1,244	9.0
Corpus Christi, TX MSA	326	8.4
Dallas–Fort Worth, TX CMSA	2,931	8.2
Dallas, TX PMSA	1,957	7.9
Fort Worth–Arlington, TX PMSA	973	8.9

Table 1–21. (continued)

Metropolitan Area	Total (1,000)	1980 — 65 years old and over (%)
Davenport–Rock Island–Moline, IA–IL MSA	384	10.7
Dayton–Springfield, OH MSA	942	9.8
Daytona Beach, FL MSA	259	22.3
Denver–Boulder, CO CMSA	1,618	7.8
Boulder–Longmont, CO PMSA	190	6.8
Denver, CO PMSA	1,429	7.9
Des Moines, IA MSA	368	10.5
Detroit–Ann Arbor, MI CMSA	4,753	9.3
Ann Arbor, MI PMSA	265	6.4
Detroit, MI PMSA	4,488	9.5
El Paso, TX MSA	480	6.6
Erie, PA MSA	280	10.9
Eugene–Springfield, OR MSA	275	9.6
Evansville, IN–KY MSA	276	12.3
Fayetteville, NC MSA	247	4.5
Fort Myers–Cape Coral, FL MSA	205	22.3
Flint, MI MSA	450	8.0
Fort Wayne, IN MSA	354	9.8
Fresno, CA MSA	515	10.1
Grand Rapids, MI MSA	602	9.8
Greensboro–Winston-Salem–High Point, NC MSA	852	10.2
Greenville–Spartanburg, SC MSA	569	9.8
Harrisburg–Lebanon–Carlisle, PA MSA	555	11.8
Hartford–New Britain–Middletown, CT CMSA	1,014	11.4
Bristol, CT PMSA	74	10.3
Hartford, CT PMSA	716	11.4
Middletown, CT PMSA	82	10.7
New Britain, CT PMSA	142	12.4
Honolulu, HI MSA	763	7.3
Houston–Galveston–Brazoria, TX CMSA	3,101	6.4
Brazoria, TX PMSA	170	6.1
Galveston–Texas City, TX PMSA	196	9.1
Houston, TX PMSA	2,736	6.2
Huntington–Ashland, WV–KY–OH MSA	336	11.7
Indianapolis, IN MSA	1,167	9.8
Jackson, MS MSA	362	9.4
Jacksonville, FL MSA	722	9.7
Johnson City–Kingsport–Bristol, TN–VA MSA	434	11.4
Johnstown, PA MSA	265	13.6
Kansas City, MO–KS MSA	1,433	10.5
Knoxville, TN MSA	566	11.2
Lakeland–Winter Haven, FL MSA	322	14.3
Lancaster, PA MSA	362	11.7
Lansing–East Lansing, MI MSA	420	7.6
Las Vegas, NV MSA	463	7.6
Lexington–Fayette, KY MSA	318	9.2
Little Rock–North Little Rock, AR MSA	474	9.9
Los Angeles–Anaheim–Riverside, CA CMSA	11,498	9.9

Table 1–21. (continued)

Metropolitan Area	Total (1,000)	1980 65 years old and over (%)
Anaheim–Santa Ana, CA PMSA	1,933	8.3
Los Angeles–Long Beach, CA PMSA	7,478	9.9
Oxnard–Ventura, CA PMSA	529	8.3
Riverside–San Bernardino, CA PMSA	1,558	12.1
Louisville, KY–IN MSA	957	10.4
Macon–Warner Robins, GA MSA	264	8.9
Madison, WI MSA	324	8.4
McAllen–Edinburg–Mission, TX MSA	283	9.2
Melbourne–Titusville–Palm Bay, FL MSA	273	12.7
Memphis, TN–AR–MS MSA	913	9.3
Miami–Fort Lauderdale, FL CMSA	2,644	18.1
Fort Lauderdale–Hollywood–Pompano Beach, FL PMSA	1,018	22.0
Miami–Hialeah, FL PMSA	1,626	15.7
Milwaukee–Racine, WI CMSA	1,570	11.0
Milwaukee, WI PMSA	1,397	11.1
Racine, WI PMSA	173	10.2
Minneapolis–St. Paul, MN–WI MSA	2,137	9.6
Mobile, AL MSA	444	10.2
Modesto, CA MSA	266	11.0
Montgomery, AL MSA	273	10.1
Nashville–Davidson, TN MSA	851	10.4
New Haven–Meriden, CT MSA	500	12.3
New London–Norwich, CT–RI MSA	251	10.5
New Orleans, LA MSA	1,256	9.1
New York–Northern New Jersey–Long Island, NY–NJ–CT CMSA	17,539	12.2
Bergen–Passaic, NJ PMSA	1,293	12.3
Bridgeport–Milford, CT PMSA	439	12.1
Danbury, CT PMSA	170	9.1
Jersey City, NJ PMSA	557	12.6
Middlesex–Somerset–Hunterdon, NJ PMSA	886	8.9
Monmouth–Ocean, NJ PMSA	849	15.5
Nassau–Suffolk, NY PMSA	2,606	9.8
New York, NY PMSA	8,275	13.2
Newark, NJ PMSA	1,879	11.1
Norwalk, CT PMSA	127	9.9
Orange County, NY PMSA	260	10.9
Stamford, CT PMSA	199	12.4
Norfolk–Virginia Beach–Newport News, VA MSA	1,160	7.7
Oklahoma City, OK MSA	861	10.0
Omaha, NE–IA MSA	585	9.6
Orlando, FL MSA	700	10.9
Pensacola, FL MSA	290	8.6
Peoria, IL MSA	366	10.9
Philadelphia–Wilmington–Trenton, PA–NJ–DE–MD CMSA	5,681	11.5
Philadelphia, PA–NJ PMSA	4,717	11.7
Trenton, NJ PMSA	308	11.4
Vineland–Millville–Bridgeton, NJ PMSA	133	11.7
Wilmington, DE–NJ–MD PMSA	523	9.7
Phoenix, AZ MSA	1,509	11.6

Table 1–21. (continued)

Metropolitan Area	Total (1,000)	1980 65 years old and over (%)
Pittsburgh–Beaver Valley, PA CMSA	2,423	13.4
Beaver County, PA PMSA	204	11.9
Pittsburgh, PA PMSA	2,219	13.5
Portland–Vancouver, OR–WA CMSA	1,298	11.0
Portland, OR PMSA	1,106	11.3
Vancouver, WA PMSA	192	9.0
Poughkeepsie, NY MSA	245	11.1
Providence–Pawtucket–Fall River, RI–MA—CMSA	1,083	13.4
Fall River, MA–RI PMSA	157	14.7
Pawtucket–Woonsocket–Attleboro, RI–MA—PMSA	307	13.3
Providence, RI PMSA	619	13.3
Raleigh–Durham, NC MSA	561	8.5
Reading, PA MSA	313	14.1
Richmond–Petersburg, VA MSA	761	9.9
Rochester, NY MSA	971	11.0
Rockford, IL MSA	280	10.2
Sacramento, CA MSA	1,100	9.6
Saginaw–Bay City–Midland, MI MSA	422	9.1
St. Louis, MO–IL MSA	2,377	11.7
Salem, OR MSA	250	12.6
Salinas–Seaside–Monterey, CA MSA	290	9.2
Salt Lake City–Ogden, UT MSA	910	7.3
San Antonio, TX MSA	1,072	9.0
San Diego, CA MSA	1,862	10.3
San Francisco–Oakland–San Jose, CA CMSA	5,368	10.4
Oakland, CA PMSA	1,762	9.9
San Francisco, CA PMSA	1,489	12.6
San Jose, CA PMSA	1,295	7.5
Santa Cruz, CA PMSA	188	13.2
Santa Rosa–Petaluma, CA PMSA	300	13.5
Vallejo–Fairfield–Napa, CA PMSA	334	9.9
Santa Barbara–Santa Maria–Lompoc, CA MSA	299	11.3
Scranton–Wilkes-Barre, PA MSA	729	15.6
Seattle–Tacoma, WA CMSA	2,093	9.8
Seattle, WA PMSA	1,607	9.9
Tacoma, WA PMSA	486	9.4
Shreveport, LA MSA	333	10.4
Spokane, WA MSA	342	11.5
Springfield, MA MSA	515	12.8
Stockton, CA MSA	347	11.3
Syracuse, NY MSA	643	10.7
Tampa–St. Petersburg–Clearwater, FL MSA	1,614	21.5
Toledo, OH MSA	617	11.0
Tucson, AZ MSA	531	11.7
Tulsa, OK MSA	657	10.1
Utica–Rome, NY MSA	320	13.5
Visalia–Tulare–Porterville, CA MSA	246	10.7

Table 1–21. (continued)

Metropolitan Area	1980	
	Total (1,000)	65 years old and over (%)
Washington, DC–MD–VA MSA	3,251	7.6
West Palm Beach–Boca Raton–Delray Beach, FL MSA	577	23.3
Wichita, KS MSA	412	9.9
Worcester, MA MSA	403	13.3
York, PA MSA	381	11.5
Youngstown–Warren, OH MSA	531	11.4

Source: U.S. Bureau of the Census, *1980 Census of Population, Supplementary Report, Metropolitan Statistical Areas* (PC80–S1–18) and *General Population Characteristics* (PC80–1–B)

Table 1–22. Elderly Population by Age, Sex and Farm–Nonfarm Residence

(Current Population Survey Annual Averages. Numbers in thousands.)

Age	Farm			Nonfarm		
	Both sexes	Male	Female	Both sexes	Male	Female
All ages	5,226	2,733	2,493	231,107	111,584	119,523
65 to 69 years	278	144	134	9,245	4,169	5,075
70 to 74 years	219	119	100	7,230	3,058	4,172
75 years and over	226	109	117	10,300	3,748	6,552
Percent Distribution of Total U.S. Population						
All ages	100.0	100.0	100.0	100.0	100.0	100.0
65 to 69 years	5.3	5.3	5.4	4.0	3.7	4.2
70 to 74 years	4.2	4.4	4.0	3.1	2.7	3.5
75 years and over	4.3	4.0	4.7	4.5	3.4	5.5

Source: Current Population Reports, Series P-27, No. 60

Table 1–23. Cities With Largest Numbers and Highest Percentage of Persons 65 Years of Age and Older, 1980

City	Elderly		City	Elderly	
	Population	%		Population	%
New York, NY	954,671	13.5	Sun City, AZ	29,973	74.1
Chicago, IL	342,578	11.4	Miami Beach, FL	49,882	51.8
Los Angeles, CA	314,486	10.6	Hallandale, FL	18,185	49.8
Philadelphia, PA	238,037	14.1	Hemet, CA	10,854	48.3
Detroit, MI	140,790	11.7	Tamarac City, FL	13,131	44.7
San Francisco, CA	104,253	15.4	Deerfield Beach, FL	16,186	41.3
Baltimore, MD	100,707	12.8	Boynton Beach, FL	12,860	36.1
St. Louis, MO	79,742	17.6	Dunedin, FL	10,842	35.9
Milwaukee, WI	79,526	12.5	Seal Beach, CA	9,117	35.1
Seattle, WA	76,052	15.4	Delray Beach, FL	10,263	29.9
Cleveland, OH	74,596	13.0	Pompano Beach, FL	15,680	29.8
Washington, DC	74,046	11.6	Largo, FL	17,339	29.4
Indianapolis, IN	72,184	10.3	North Miami Beach, FL	9,576	26.2
Boston, MA	71,500	12.5	Clearwater, FL	22,322	26.1
Pittsburgh, PA	67,830	16.0	Sarasota, FL	12,754	26.1
Memphis, TN	67,221	10.4	Sunrise, FL	10,277	25.9
New Orleans, LA	65,229	11.7	St. Petersburg, FL	61,760	25.8
Denver, CO	62,037	12.6	Hollywood, FL	30,452	25.1
St. Petersburg, FL	61,670	25.8	Boca Raton, FL	11,732	23.7
Miami, FL	58,967	17.0	Atlantic City, NJ	9,446	23.5

Source: U.S. Bureau of Census, 1980 Census of Population and Housing, Summary Characteristics for Government Units and Standard Metropolitan Statistical Areas. PHC 80-3; and United States Conference of Mayors, Assessing Elderly Housing: A Planning Guide for Mayors and Local Officials (Washington, D.C.: United States Conference of Mayors, 1985), p. 3.

Table 1–24. Percentage of Population Age 65 and Over in Cities With 100,000 Inhabitants or More: 1980

City	total population (1,000)	Percent— 65 years old and over	City	total population (1,000)	Percent— 65 years old and over
	1980			1980	
Abilene, TX	98	10.3	Garland, TX	139	4.1
Akron, OH	237	13.5	Gary, IN	152	8.2
Albuquerque, NM	332	8.4	Glendale, AZ	97	7.0
Alexandria, VA	103	9.2	Glendale, CA	139	16.3
Allentown, PA	104	16.1	Grand Rapids, MI	182	13.4
Amarillo, TX	149	10.1	Greensboro, NC	156	9.8
Anaheim, CA	219	7.7	Hampton, VA	123	7.0
Anchorage, AK	174	2.0	Hartford, CT	136	11.4
Ann Arbor, MI	108	5.9	Hialeah, FL	145	11.4
Arlington, TX	160	4.5	Hollywood, FL	121	25.1
Atlanta, GA	425	11.5	Honolulu, HI	365	10.4
Aurora, CO	159	4.3	Houston, TX	1,595	6.9
Austin, TX	345	7.5	Huntington Beach, CA	171	5.9
Bakersfield, CA	106	9.2	Huntsville, AL	143	7.0
			Independence, MO	112	10.9
Baltimore, MD	787	12.8			
Baton Rouge, LA	219	8.7	Indianapolis, IN	701	10.3
Beaumont, TX	118	11.4	Irving, TX	110	4.7
Berkeley, CA	103	10.8	Jackson, MS	203	9.7
Birmingham, AL	284	13.9	Jacksonville, FL	541	9.6
Boise City, ID	102	10.2	Jersey City, NJ	224	11.8
Boston, MA	563	12.7	Kansas City, KS	161	11.7
Bridgeport, CT	143	13.4	Kansas City, MO	448	12.3
Buffalo, NY	358	15.0	Knoxville, TN	175	13.8
Cedar Rapids, IA	110	11.0	Lakewood, CO	113	7.2
Charlotte, NC	314	8.6			
Chattanooga, TN	170	12.7	Lansing, MI	130	8.7
Chesapeake, VA	114	7.1	Laredo, TX	91	8.6
Chicago, IL	3,005	11.4	Las Vegas, NV	165	8.3
			Lexington–Fayette, KY	204	8.6
Cincinnati, OH	385	14.5	Lincoln, NE	172	10.3
Cleveland, OH	574	13.0	Little Rock, AR	158	11.0
Colorado Springs, CO	215	8.3	Livonia, MI	105	7.8
Columbus, GA	169	8.9	Long Beach, CA	361	14.0
Columbus, OH	565	8.9	Los Angeles, CA	2,967	10.6
Concord, CA	103	7.3			
Corpus Christi, TX	232	8.2	Louisville, KY	298	15.3
Dallas, TX	904	9.5	Lubbock, TX	174	7.8
Davenport, IA	103	10.5	Macon, GA	117	11.9
Dayton, OH	203	11.8	Madison, WI	171	8.7
Denver, CO	492	12.6	Memphis, TN	646	10.4
Des Moines, IA	191	12.5	Mesa, AZ	152	11.2
Detroit, MI	1,203	11.7	Miami, FL	347	17.0
Durham, NC	101	12.1	Milwaukee, WI	636	12.5
Elizabeth, NJ	106	13.2	Minneapolis, MN	371	15.4
El Paso, TX	425	6.9	Mobile, AL	200	11.1
Erie, PA	119	13.4	Modesto, CA	107	9.7
Eugene, OR	106	9.5	Montgomery, AL	178	10.1
Evansville, IN	130	15.2	Nashville–Davidson, TN	456	11.0
Flint, MI	160	10.0	New Haven, CT	126	13.1
Fort Lauderdale, FL	153	19.1	New Orleans, LA	558	11.7
Fort Wayne, IN	172	11.9			
Fort Worth, TX	385	11.8	New York, NY	7,072	13.5
Fremont, CA	132	5.2	Bronx Borough	1,169	12.9
Fresno, CA	218	10.9	Brooklyn Borough	2,231	12.5
Fullerton, CA	102	8.0	Manhattan Borough	1,428	14.3
Garden Grove, CA	123	7.4	Queens Borough	1,891	14.9
			Staten Island Borough	352	10.0

Table 1–24. (continued)

City	1980 total population (1,000)	Percent— 65 years old and over
Newark, NJ	329	8.8
Newport News, VA	145	7.8
Norfolk, VA	267	9.2
Oakland, CA	339	13.2
Odessa, TX	90	7.4
Oklahoma City, OK	403	11.3
Omaha, NE	314	12.2
Ontario, CA	89	7.3
Orlando, FL	128	12.7
Oxnard, CA	108	6.6
Pasadena, CA	119	14.9
Pasadena, TX	113	4.8
Paterson, NJ	138	10.3
Peoria, IL	124	12.3
Philadelphia, PA	1,688	14.1
Phoenix, AZ	790	9.3
Pittsburgh, PA	424	16.0
Pomona, CA	93	8.9
Portland, OR	366	15.3
Portsmouth, VA	105	10.7
Providence, RI	157	15.3
Raleigh, NC	150	8.3
Reno, NV	101	10.5
Richmond, VA	219	14.1
Riverside, CA	171	8.8
Roanoke, VA	100	15.6
Rochester, NY	242	14.0
Rockford, IL	140	12.6
Sacramento, CA	276	13.6
St. Louis, MO	453	17.6
St. Paul, MN	270	15.0
St. Petersburg, FL	239	25.8
Salt Lake City, UT	163	14.7
San Antonio, TX	786	9.5
San Bernardino, CA	117	11.9
San Diego, CA	876	9.7

City	1980 total population (1,000)	Percent— 65 years old and over
San Francisco, CA	679	15.4
San Jose, CA	629	6.2
Santa Ana, CA	204	7.4
Savannah, GA	141	11.4
Seattle, WA	494	15.4
Shreveport, LA	206	11.7
South Bend, IN	110	14.8
Spokane, WA	171	15.3
Springfield, IL	100	14.3
Springfield, MA	152	13.8
Springfield, MO	133	13.2
Stamford, CT	102	12.0
Sterling Heights, MI	109	4.5
Stockton, CA	150	11.0
Sunnyvale, CA	107	8.2
Syracuse, NY	170	14.6
Tacoma, WA	159	13.5
Tallahassee, FL	82	7.4
Tampa, FL	272	14.8
Tempe, AZ	107	4.7
Toledo, OH	355	12.5
Topeka, KS	119	13.9
Torrance, CA	130	8.5
Tucson, AZ	331	11.7
Tulsa, OK	361	10.8
Virginia Beach, VA	262	4.5
Waco, TX	101	14.3
Warren, MI	161	8.0
Washington, DC	638	11.6
Waterbury, CT	103	15.5
Wichita, KS	279	10.6
Winston–Salem, NC	132	12.1
Worcester, MA	162	16.3
Yonkers, NY	195	14.8
Youngstown, OH	115	14.6

Source: U.S. Bureau of the Census, *Census of Population: 1970,* vol. 1, chapters A and B; *1980 Census of Population,* vol. 1, chapters A and B; press release (CB85–140) and unpublished data.

RACE/NATIONAL ORIGIN

Table 1–25. Selected Characteristics of the Population Age 65 and Over by Selected Country of Birth: 1980

(In percent, except as indicated. As of April 1.)

Nativity and Selected Country of Birth	Total persons (1,000)	65 yrs. and over
Total[1]	**226,546**	**11.3**
Native	212,466	10.6
Foreign born	14,080	21.2
Asia: Phillipines	501	10.4
Korea	290	2.6
China	286	14.8
Vietnam	231	1.7
Japan	222	9.8
India	206	2.0
Iran	122	3.3
Hong Kong	80	1.4
Taiwan	75	1.5
Israel	67	5.7
Latin America: Mexico	2,199	7.6
Cuba	608	13.8
Jamaica	197	7.3
Dominican Republic	169	4.2
Columbia	144	3.6
El Salvador	94	2.9
Haiti	92	4.1
Ecuador	86	3.9
Argentina	69	6.7
Trinidad and Tobago	66	4.4
Guatemala	63	2.8
North America: Canada	843	29.3
Europe: Germany	849	27.9
Italy	832	44.5
England	442	26.8
Poland	418	51.1
Portugal[2]	212	14.8
Greece	211	21.7
Ireland	198	47.1
Yugoslavia	153	28.0
Austria	146	62.7
Hungary	144	48.0
Scotland	142	42.2
France	120	20.4
Czechoslovakia	113	48.4
Netherlands	103	27.2
Sweden	77	63.4
Spain	74	29.3
Romania	67	38.1
Norway	63	56.3
Soviet Union	406	57.8

Notes: 1. Includes other countries not shown separately.

2. Includes persons born in Azores.

Source: U.S. Bureau of the Census, unpublished data.

Figure 1–11. Age of Foreign-Born Residents of the United States: 1980

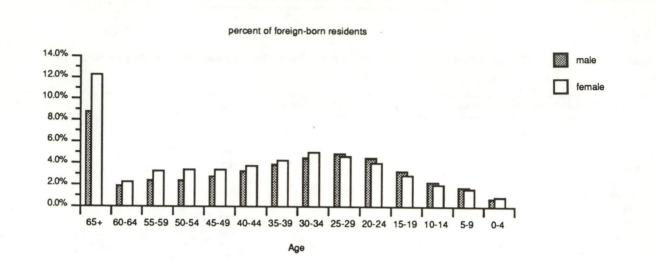

percent of foreign-born residents

Note: Illegals counted by the 1980 Census are included in the foreign-born total.
Source: U.S. Bureau of the Census. *1980 Census of the Population.*

DEPENDENCY RATIOS

Table 1–26. Population 65 Years Old and Over, and Societal Support Ratios: 1960 to 1985

(In millions, except as indicated. As of July. Includes Armed Forces overseas. The support ratio is the number of elderly persons of a specified age per 100 persons defined by age or work status.)

Age Group	1960	1970	1980	1985	Support Ratio	1960	1970	1980	1985
Persons 65 years and over	**16.7**	**20.1**	**25.7**	**28.5**	Persons, 65 years old and over, per				
Percent of all ages	9.2	9.8	11.3	11.9	100 persons, 18–64 years old	17	17	19	19
65–69 years	6.3	7.0	8.8	9.4	Persons, 60 years old and over, per				
70–74 years	4.8	5.5	6.8	7.6	100 persons, 20–59 years old	27	29	30	31
75–79 years	3.1	3.9	4.8	5.5	Nonworkers, 65 years old and over,				
80–84 years	1.6	2.3	3.0	3.3	per 100 workers, 18–64 years old[1]	21	22	23	22
85 years and over	.9	1.4	2.3	2.7	Nonworkers, 60 years old and over,				
					per 100 workers, 20–59 years old[1]	28	30	31	30

Notes: 1. Nonworkers are persons not in labor force and workers are persons in civilian labor force. Labor force data are monthly averages based on the Current Population Survey. Data from U.S. Bureau of Labor Statistics.

Source: U.S. Bureau of the Census, *Current Population Reports*, series P-25, No. 985 and earlier reports; and unpublished data.

Figure 1–12. Ratio of U.S. Elderly and Dependent U.S. Elderly to Offspring, 1980–2050

**Number of elderly
per 1000 offspring**

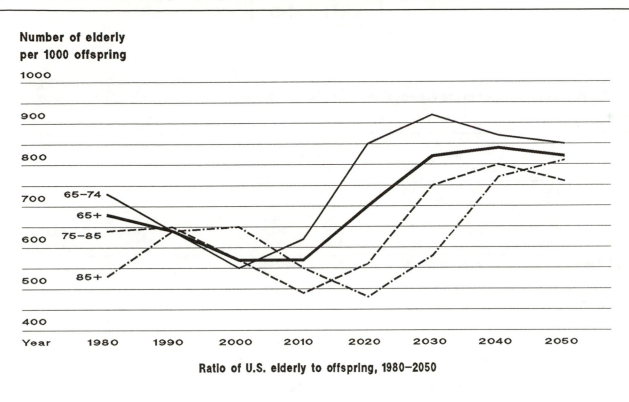

Ratio of U.S. elderly to offspring, 1980–2050

**Number of elderly
per 1000 offspring**

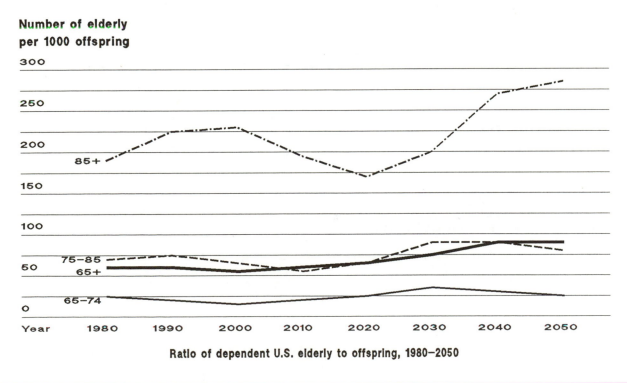

Ratio of dependent U.S. elderly to offspring, 1980–2050

Note: Illegals counted by the 1980 Census not included.
Source: Population Reference Bureau, Inc., *Population Trends and Public Policy,* No. 9, September 1985.

VETERANS

Table 1–27. Projected Changes in the Veteran Population: 1980–2020

(in millions)

Year	Total Veteran Population	65 to 74 Years Number	%	75 to 84 Years Number	%	85 Years and over Number	%	65 Years and over Number	%
1980	28.6	2.18	7.6	.64	2.2	.22	0.8	3.04	10.6
1990	27.1	5.62	20.7	1.33	4.9	.21	0.8	7.16	26.4
2000	24.3	5.01	20.6	3.45	14.2	.52	2.1	8.97	36.9
2010	20.7	3.72	18.0	3.02	14.6	1.38	6.7	8.13	39.3
2020	17.5	4.05	23.1	2.35	13.4	1.37	7.8	7.77	44.4

Source: Veterans Administration. *Caring for the Older Veteran.* Washington, D.C., July 1984.

Table 1–28. Estimated Number of Living Veterans By Age and Period of Service, March 31, 1984

(in thousands)

Age	Total Veterans [a]	Vietnam Era [b]	Korean Conflict [c]	World War II	World War I	Peace-Time
All ages	28,135	7,603	4,233	10,840	272	5,186
Under 25	492	–	–	–	–	492
25–34	3,636	2,500	–	–	–	1,137
35–44	6,020	4,737	–	–	–	1,283
45–54	5,958	344	3,524	162	–	1,927
55–64	7,656	22	676	6,826	–	132
65–74	3,396	1	25	3,265	–	104
75–84	709	–	7	555	53	94
85 +	267	–	1	31	219	17
Median Age	52.0	36.8	52.5	62.8	87.8	44.0

Notes: a Detail may not add to total due to rounding.

b Not including those who served also during the Korean Conflict.

c Not including those who served also during World War II.

Source: Veterans Administration, Office of Information Management and Statistics. *Veteran Population, Mar. 31, 1984.*

II

INCOME AND EXPENDITURES

PERSONAL INCOME

Table 2–1. Median Income of Persons Age 65 and Older by Age, Race, and Sex: 1984

Race	Both sexes 65 to 69	Both sexes 70 and over	Male 65 to 69	Male 70 and over	Female 65 to 69	Female 70 and over
All races	$8,512	$7,045	$12,292	$9,407	$6,229	$5,950
White	8,971	7,457	12,749	9,853	6,527	6,225
Black	5,321	4,646	7,545	5,679	4,446	4,304
Hispanic	5,593	5,117	8,778	5,705	4,342	4,825

Source: U.S. Bureau of the Census unpublished data from the March 1985 Current Population Survey.

Table 2–2. Money Income of Persons Age 65 and Over—Percent Distribution by Sex, Income Level, Median, and Mean Income: 1984

SEX, YEAR AND AGE	All persons (mil.)	Total (mil.)	1 to 1,999 or less[1]	2,000-3,999	4,000-5,999	6,000-7,999	8,000-9,999	10,000-14,999	15,000-24,999	25,000 and over	Median Income (dol.)	Mean Income (dol.)
MALE												
Total	87.0	82.2	8.1	6.5	6.8	6.7	5.6	14.6	22.4	29.2	15,600	19,438
15–19 years old	9.2	6.2	52.8	22.0	11.2	8.9	3.2	1.5	.4		1,893	2,967
20–24 years old	10.1	9.4	13.0	13.6	11.6	20.7	21.2	15.8	4.0		8,046	9,464
25–34 years old	20.2	19.8	3.6	4.0	4.9	10.2	16.5	31.7	29.1		18,093	19,534
35–44 years old	15.3	15.1	3.3	2.8	2.8	6.4	10.1	25.6	49.1		24,566	26,894
45–54 years old	10.8	10.6	4.1	3.0	3.4	6.8	11.1	22.3	49.2		24,589	27,513
55–64 years old	10.4	10.2	3.6	3.7	6.0	11.3	14.0	23.4	38.0		19,527	24,350
65 yrs. old and over	11.0	10.9	1.4	7.4	13.3	25.6	22.2	18.1	12.1		10,450	14,440
FEMALE												
Total	95.3	85.6	19.2	13.6	12.6	9.8	7.4	15.0	15.6	6.6	6,868	9,584
15-19 years old	9.1	5.9	58.2	20.8	10.3	7.3	2.5	.9	.2		1,719	2,521
20–24 years old	10.4	9.3	20.3	16.7	13.6	21.1	18.0	9.1	1.2		5,911	7,125
25–34 years old	20.7	19.0	18.9	9.3	8.5	15.3	18.6	22.7	6.7		9,392	10,686
35–44 years old	16.0	14.6	19.2	9.2	8.4	14.7	16.0	21.0	11.5		9,561	11,828
45–54 years old	11.6	10.4	19.2	9.7	8.6	16.1	16.9	19.6	9.8		8,903	11,397
55–64 years old	11.8	10.7	19.1	14.4	12.5	17.2	14.3	14.8	7.6		6,837	9,954
65 yrs. old and over	15.8	15.6	4.3	20.7	24.8	24.2	12.0	9.4	4.6		6,020	8,800

Note: 1. Includes persons with income deficit.
Source: U.S. Bureau of the Census, Current Population Reports, series P-60, No. 151.

Figure 2–1. Median Money Income of Year-Round Full-Time Workers With Income, by Sex and Age 65 + : 1970–1984

(Age as of March of following year)

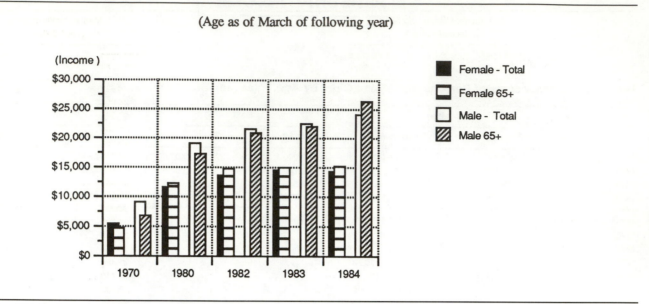

Note: "Total" refers to workers age 14 and over.

Source: U.S. Bureau of the Census, *Current Population Reports,* Series P–60, No. 151, and earlier issues.

HOUSEHOLD AND FAMILY INCOME

Figure 2–2. Median Money Income of Persons Age 65 and Older by Marital Status: 1984

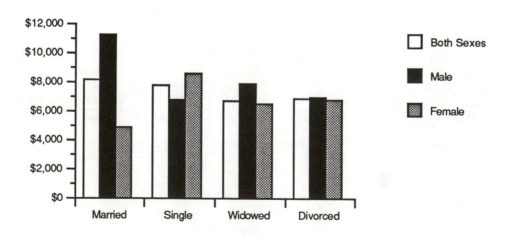

Source: U.S. Bureau of the Census. Unpublished data from the March 1985 *Current Population Survey.*

Table 2–3. Median Family Income, 1965-84, Elderly and Non-Elderly Families

Year	Median family income (actual dollars) Head aged 25 to 64	Head aged 65 +	CPI	Median family income (1984 dollars) Head aged 25 to 64	Head aged 65 +
1965	$ 7,537	$ 3,460	94.5	$24,822	$11,396
1966	8,146	3,645	97.2	26,083	11,671
1967	8,753	3,928	100.0	27,242	12,225
1968	9,511	4,592	104.2	28,408	13,715
1969	10,438	4,803	109.8	29,587	13,614
1970	10,879	5,053	116.3	29,113	13,522
1971	11,406	5,453	121.3	29,266	13,991
1972	12,717	5,968	125.3	31,587	14,824
1973	13,496	6,426	133.1	31,558	15,027
1974	14,380	7,505	147.7	30,301	15,814
1975	15,331	8,057	161.2	29,599	15,555
1976	16,624	8,721	170.5	30,345	15,919
1977	17,960	9,110	181.5	30,798	15,622
1978	19,764	10,141	195.4	31,480	16,153
1979	22,175	11,318	217.4	31,746	16,203
1980	23,392	12,881	246.8	29,499	16,244
1981	25,138	14,335	272.4	28,721	16,378
1982	26,003	16,118	289.1	27,993	17,351
1983	27,243	16,862	298.4	28,414	17,587
1984	29,292	18,236	311.1	29,292	18,236

Note: CPI (Consumer Price Index) figures establish a baseline (100) of the cost of goods and services in 1967, against which price increases and decreases can be measured. Consumer prices in 1979, for example, were more than double the prices in 1967 for the same goods and services (217.4 compared to 100). The Census Bureau revised its method for imputing interest income when calculating 1984 income levels in order to correct an historical bias which underestimated missing interest income data. Data for 1965-83 were computed under the earlier methodology, while 1984 median family income levels were calculated using the revised method.

Source: U.S. Bureau of the Census, *Current Population Reports*, series P-60, 1965-83 and unpublished data from the 1985 Current Population Survey.

Table 2–4. Money Income of Households by Age of Householder, Race, Spanish Origin, and Aggregate and Mean Income: 1984

(As of March 1985)

Characteristic	ALL RACES[1] Aggregate money income (bil. dol.)	Mean income (dol.)	WHITE Aggregate money income (bil. dol.)	Mean income (dol.)	BLACK Aggregate money income (bil. dol.)	Mean income (dol.)	SPANISH ORIGIN[2] Aggregate money income (bil. dol.)	Mean income (dol.)
Total	2,383.5	27,464	2,154.2	28,597	170.3	17,966	103.2	21,129
Age of householder:								
15–24 years old	90.5	16,644	80.8	17,472	6.9	10,387	6.9	14,115
25–34 years old	523.9	26,178	467.6	27,490	41.9	16,956	28.2	20,709
35–44 years old	583.7	33,389	522.6	34,784	43.7	22,459	28.1	23,735
45–54 years old	454.6	36,003	407.8	37,792	34.6	23,215	19.8	26,699
55–64 years old	398.9	30,516	367.0	31,996	24.5	18,135	13.1	21,627
65 years old and over	331.9	18,279	308.3	18,790	18.7	12,042	7.0	14,045

Notes: 1. Includes other races not shown separately.
2. Persons of Spanish origin may be of any race.

Source: U.S. Bureau of the Census, *Current Population Reports*, series P-60, No. 151.

Table 2–5. Households with Householders Age 65 Years Old and Over and Persons in Households, by Household Money Income and Poverty Status of the Primary Family or Individual: 1984

(Numbers in thousands. Households as of March 1985.)

Characteristic	Total	Under $2,500	$2,500 to $4,999	$5,000 to $7,499	$7,500 to $9,999	$10,000 to $12,499	$12,500 to $14,999	$15,000 to $19,999	$20,000 and over	Median income (dollars) Value	Median income Stand-ard error	Mean income (dollars) Value	Mean income Stand-ard error	Below current poverty level Number	Below current poverty level Poverty rate
ALL HOUSEHOLDS															
Total	86,789	2,168	4,716	6,185	5,287	5,578	4,979	9,871	48,004	22,415	102	27,464	101	11,887	13.7
HOUSEHOLDER 65 YEARS OLD AND OVER															
Total	18,155	250	1,980	2,881	2,029	1,755	1,532	2,352	5,376	12,799	144	18,279	182	2,683	14.8
Region															
Northeast	4,165	49	428	658	463	411	346	521	1,289	13,027	304	18,899	388	530	12.7
Midwest	4,595	65	389	777	570	422	421	623	1,328	12,943	266	17,425	296	556	12.1
South	6,304	91	982	959	680	645	487	755	1,707	11,710	200	17,719	337	1,332	21.1
West	3,091	46	182	487	315	276	278	454	1,052	14,651	301	19,856	406	265	8.6
Race and Spanish Origin of Householder[1]															
White	16,406	189	1,592	2,510	1,831	1,605	1,418	2,207	5,053	13,339	148	18,790	195	2,088	12.7
Black	1,556	60	369	337	186	136	99	120	249	7,672	320	12,042	415	566	36.4
Spanish origin	497	7	93	110	56	43	39	44	105	9,229	823	14,045	1,043	137	27.5
Type of Household															
Family households	9,806	61	223	641	901	1,013	970	1,605	4,391	18,296	216	24,311	282	713	7.3
Married-couple families	8,057	42	133	471	702	860	813	1,356	3,679	18,616	233	24,876	319	476	5.9
Male householder, no wife present	295	4	11	19	29	23	25	37	147	19,886	1,277	23,770	1,438	27	9.2
Female householder, no husband present	1,454	15	80	151	169	131	131	211	565	16,134	569	21,293	623	209	14.4
Nonfamily households	8,350	189	1,757	2,240	1,128	741	563	747	985	7,488	94	11,195	169	1,970	23.6
Male householder	1,693	34	285	409	216	162	151	180	256	8,867	312	12,836	409	319	18.9
Female householder	6,656	155	1,472	1,830	911	580	411	568	729	7,323	73	10,777	184	1,651	24.8
Size of Household															
One person (living alone)	8,111	184	1,756	2,213	1,086	712	544	709	907	7,390	67	10,910	166	1,913	23.6
Two persons	8,124	55	189	572	842	919	856	1,405	3,286	17,064	194	22,664	295	540	6.7
Three persons	1,239	10	24	52	75	78	97	174	729	24,710	771	29,332	830	110	8.9
Four persons	377	—	6	19	17	28	16	36	256	29,480	1,618	32,907	1,490	46	12.3
Five persons	150	—	—	13	3	7	11	13	103	29,485	3,066	34,338	2,703	26	17.6
Six persons	82	1	—	6	3	10	2	10	50	28,162	3,089	35,758	5,411	21	26.0
Seven persons or more	73	—	5	7	3	1	5	5	46	(B)	(B)	(B)	(B)	26	(B)
Mean size of household	1.73	1.32	1.15	1.30	1.54	1.71	1.78	1.85	2.20	(X)	(X)	(X)	(X)	1.48	(X)
Presence of Children Under 18 Years Old															
Households with children under 18 years old	650	2	38	84	51	58	65	76	275	17,009	1,189	23,101	1,126	182	28.0
Households with children under 6 years old	216	—	5	35	12	16	16	21	110	21,156	2,757	27,647	2,507	69	31.8
Households with no children under 18 years old	17,506	248	1,943	2,797	1,977	1,696	1,467	2,276	5,101	12,657	148	18,100	184	2,501	14.3

Table 2–5. (continued)

Characteristic	Total	Under $2,500	$2,500 to $4,999	$5,000 to $7,499	$7,500 to $9,999	$10,000 to $12,499	$12,500 to $14,999	$15,000 to $19,999	$20,000 and over	Median income (dollars) Value	Median income Standard error	Mean income (dollars) Value	Mean income Standard error	Below current poverty level Number	Poverty rate
Work Experience in 1984 of Householder															
Total civilian hhldrs	18,155	250	1,980	2,881	2,029	1,755	1,532	2,352	5,376	12,799	144	18,279	182	2,683	14.8
Worked	3,206	22	71	219	245	273	271	455	1,650	20,753	597	28,978	637	128	4.0
Worked at full-time jobs	1,412	16	17	46	43	102	99	174	915	28,035	1,114	37,181	1,116	52	3.6
40 weeks or more	1,021	10	10	23	24	58	60	117	719	31,785	1,339	41,320	1,420	30	3.0
27 to 39 weeks	99	1	1	8	6	12	3	14	53	23,619	3,917	26,623	2,884	5	4.6
26 weeks or less	292	4	7	15	12	32	36	43	143	19,728	1,876	26,296	1,505	17	5.7
Worked at part-time jobs	1,793	6	53	173	202	170	172	281	735	16,953	453	22,517	658	77	4.3
40 weeks or more	1,015	1	26	93	105	84	98	172	436	17,472	624	23,651	862	37	3.7
27 to 39 weeks	162	—	5	15	15	16	15	20	75	17,963	2,335	20,899	1,401	5	3.3
26 weeks or less	617	5	22	65	82	70	59	89	224	15,318	926	21,077	1,226	34	5.5
Did not work	14,950	228	1,910	2,662	1,784	1,482	1,261	1,897	3,727	11,504	135	15,985	164	2,555	17.1
Weeks of Unemployment in 1984 of Householder															
Total	266	1	18	21	36	17	32	39	102	15,800	1,041	23,106	2,020	25	9.6
1 to 4 weeks	106	—	4	4	14	7	15	13	50	17,311	2,936	29,487	4,391	5	4.4
5 to 14 weeks	62	—	5	6	9	5	12	10	16	(B)	(B)	(B)	(B)	8	(B)
15 to 26 weeks	53	1	2	4	10	3	2	11	21	(B)	(B)	(B)	(B)	3	(B)
27 weeks or more	46	—	8	8	4	2	3	6	16	(B)	(B)	(B)	(B)	10	(B)
Total Money Earnings in 1984[2]															
With earnings	3,199	22	71	219	243	274	271	455	1,643	20,705	596	28,886	636	128	4.0
Without earnings	14,956	228	1,910	2,662	1,786	1,481	1,261	1,897	3,733	11,508	135	16,010	165	2,555	17.1
Tenure															
Owner occupied	13,665	158	1,058	1,772	1,471	1,338	1,244	1,943	4,682	14,582	154	20,161	222	1,550	11.3
Renter occupied, including no cash rent	4,490	93	922	1,109	557	417	288	409	695	8,044	197	12,552	265	1,133	25.2

Notes: 1. Persons of Spanish origin may be of any race.
2. Excludes relatively small number of households reporting, "no income."
(B) = Base less than 75,000
(—) = Represents zero or rounds to zero
(X) = Not applicable

Source: U.S. Bureau of the Census. "Characteristics of Households and Persons Receiving Selected Noncash Benefits: 1984." *Current Population Reports: Consumer Income* Series P-60, No. 150.

Table 2–6. Comparison of Mean Earnings of Husbands and Wives in 1983 and 1981, by Selected Characteristics

Characteristic	Husband				Wife			
		Mean Earnings		Per-cent change in real money income		Mean earnings		Per-cent change in real money income
			1981				1981	
	1983	Constant dollars	Current dollars		1983	Constant dollars	Current dollars	
Total, 15 years and over	$22,980	$22,858	$20,866	0.5	$10,164	$9,419	$8,598	7.9
Age								
15 to 24 years	12,217	13,559	12,378	− 9.9	7,258	7,047	6,433	3.0
25 to 34 years	20,000	20,497	18,711	− 2.4	10,352	9,654	8,813	7.2
35 to 44 years	26,336	26,477	24,170	− 0.5	10,998	9,842	8,984	11.7
45 to 54 years	27,008	26,223	23,938	3.0	10,956	10,089	9,210	8.6
55 to 64 years	24,048	23,962	21,874	0.4	9,777	9,664	8,822	1.2
65 years and over	11,932	11,681	10,663	2.1	4,948	6,025	5,500	− 17.9

Source: U.S. Bureau of the Census, "Earnings in 1983 of Married-Couple Families, by Characteristics of Husbands and Wives." *Current Population Reports: Consumer Income,* series P-60, No. 153.

AFTER-TAX AND DISCRETIONARY INCOME

Figure 2–3. Money Income of Elderly Households—Mean After-Tax Household Income in Constant (1984) Dollars: 1970–1984

(Households as of March of following year. Estimates of after-tax income were derived from tax simulation procedures based on a "statistical" combination of data from the Internal Revenue Service, summaries of State individual income tax regulations, data on the characteristics of persons paying FICA payroll taxes from the Social Security Administration, property tax information from the Annual Housing Survey, and the March Current Population Survey microdata file.)

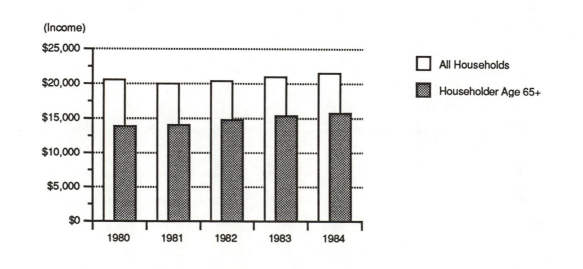

Source: U.S. Bureau of the Census. *Current Population Reports,* Series P–23, No. 147, and unpublished data.

Table 2–7. Household Income Before and After Taxes: 1984

(Households as of March 1985)

Before-tax money income level	All households Number (thous.)	All households Percent distribution	Before taxes Aggregate income Amount (bil. of dol.)	Before taxes Aggregate income Percent distribution	Before taxes Mean income Value (dol.)	Before taxes Mean income Standard error (dol.)	Before taxes Income per household member (dol.)	After taxes Aggregate income Amount (bil. of dol.)	After taxes Aggregate income Percent distribution	After taxes Mean income Value (dol.)	After taxes Mean income Standard error (dol.)	After taxes Income per household member (dol.)	Total number of persons in households (thous.)
All Households													
Total	86,789	100.0	2,383.5	100.0	27,464	101	10,207	1,871.5	100.0	21,564	70	8,015	233,516
Under $2,500	2,168	2.5	1.2	.1	566	68	263	.7	-	327	71	152	4,666
$2,500 to $4,999	4,716	5.4	18.5	.8	3,923	13	2,115	17.7	.9	3,755	14	2,024	8,749
$5,000 to $7,499	6,185	7.1	38.3	1.6	6,200	12	3,155	36.3	1.9	5,875	14	2,989	12,155
$7,500 to $9,999	5,287	6.1	46.0	1.9	8,700	13	3,930	42.6	2.3	8,056	17	3,638	11,706
$10,000 to $12,499	5,578	6.4	62.4	2.6	11,196	13	4,836	56.2	3.0	10,079	19	4,353	12,914
$12,500 to $14,999	4,979	5.7	68.2	2.9	13,707	13	5,805	60.3	3.2	12,104	23	5,126	11,757
$15,000 to $17,499	5,269	6.1	85.2	3.6	16,170	14	6,744	73.4	3.9	13,928	30	5,809	12,632
$17,500 to $19,999	4,603	5.3	85.9	3.6	18,668	14	7,320	73.3	3.9	15,934	29	6,248	11,738
$20,000 to $22,499	4,772	5.5	100.9	4.2	21,136	15	7,893	84.2	4.5	17,636	31	6,586	12,777
$22,500 to $24,999	4,240	4.9	100.5	4.2	23,699	14	8,501	82.8	4.4	19,522	33	7,003	11,821
$25,000 to $27,499	4,422	5.1	115.6	4.8	26,140	15	9,137	94.0	5.0	21,246	34	7,427	12,651
$27,500 to $29,999	3,599	4.1	103.2	4.3	28,661	15	9,803	83.5	4.5	23,202	40	7,936	10,523
$30,000 to $32,499	3,702	4.3	115.3	4.8	31,137	17	10,355	91.9	4.9	24,815	41	8,252	11,132
$32,500 to $34,999	2,941	3.4	99.1	4.2	33,687	17	11,017	78.7	4.2	26,772	46	8,755	8,994
$35,000 to $37,499	2,998	3.5	108.4	4.5	36,159	18	11,565	85.1	4.5	28,381	47	9,077	9,373
$37,500 to $39,999	2,432	2.8	94.0	3.9	38,661	19	12,228	73.3	3.9	30,155	54	9,538	7,688
$40,000 to $44,999	4,472	5.2	188.8	7.9	42,205	29	13,281	145.9	7.8	32,621	49	10,265	14,212
$45,000 to $49,999	3,346	3.9	158.0	6.6	47,228	33	14,563	120.8	6.5	36,102	61	11,133	10,850
$50,000 to $59,999	4,495	5.2	244.1	10.2	54,302	56	16,007	100.4	9.0	40,795	65	12,318	14,888
$60,000 to $74,999	3,328	3.8	220.4	9.2	66,237	98	19,448	161.6	8.6	48,568	103	14,260	11,335
$75,000 and over	3,256	3.8	329.5	13.8	101,172	707	30,077	225.9	12.1	69,359	397	20,619	10,954
Householder 65 Years Old And Over													
Total	18,155	100.0	331.9	100.0	18,279	182	10,316	285.9	100.0	15,745	130	8,886	32,169
Under $2,500	250	1.4	.3	.1	1,120	106	817	.2	.1	885	113	646	343
$2,500 to $4,999	1,980	10.9	8.1	2.4	4,070	17	3,501	7.7	2.7	3,909	20	3,362	2,302
$5,000 to $7,499	2,881	15.9	17.8	5.4	6,196	17	4,681	17.1	6.0	5,930	20	4,480	3,813
$7,500 to $9,999	2,029	11.2	17.7	5.3	8,731	21	5,512	16.8	5.9	8,304	27	5,242	3,213
$10,000 to $12,499	1,755	9.7	19.7	5.9	11,229	23	6,473	18.7	6.6	10,673	32	6,152	3,014
$12,500 to $14,999	1,532	8.4	21.1	6.3	13,749	23	7,524	19.8	6.9	12,898	39	7,058	2,800
$15,000 to $17,499	1,299	7.2	21.0	6.3	16,200	26	8,745	19.4	6.8	14,911	86	8,049	2,407
$17,500 to $19,999	1,053	5.8	19.7	5.9	18,685	29	9,633	18.2	6.4	17,253	55	8,895	2,043
$20,000 to $22,499	774	4.3	16.4	4.9	21,190	34	10,981	14.8	5.2	19,183	65	9,941	1,493
$22,500 to $24,999	677	3.7	16.0	4.8	23,643	36	11,306	14.3	5.0	21,130	78	10,105	1,415
$25,000 to $27,499	592	3.3	15.5	4.7	26,153	40	12,055	13.7	4.8	23,124	96	10,659	1,283
$27,500 to $29,999	497	2.7	14.2	4.3	28,676	40	13,300	12.5	4.4	25,162	101	11,670	1,071
$30,000 to $32,499	390	2.1	12.2	3.7	31,260	49	13,217	10.5	3.7	26,979	124	11,407	923
$32,500 to $34,999	356	2.0	12.0	3.6	33,782	47	14,265	10.3	3.6	28,943	139	12,222	842
$35,000 to $37,499	265	1.5	9.6	2.9	36,285	59	14,817	8.1	2.8	30,604	177	12,497	650
$37,500 to $39,999	232	1.3	9.0	2.7	38,676	69	15,964	7.5	2.6	32,255	196	13,314	562
$40,000 to $44,999	375	2.1	15.9	4.8	42,429	102	18,124	13.1	4.6	34,939	177	14,925	878
$45,000 to $49,999	278	1.5	13.1	4.0	47,229	106	18,503	10.7	3.7	38,426	223	15,054	710
$50,000 to $59,999	317	1.7	17.2	5.2	54,307	207	20,632	13.6	4.8	43,037	252	16,350	834
$60,000 to $74,999	293	1.6	19.2	5.8	65,657	304	26,555	14.5	5.1	49,521	349	20,029	72.1
$75,000 and over	332	1.8	36.1	10.9	108,744	2,685	44,015	24.3	8.5	73,164	1,421	29,614	820

Source: U.S. Bureau of the Census, "After-Tax Money Income Estimates of Households: 1984." *Current Population Reports: Special Studies P-23, No. 147.*

Figure 2–4. Disposable and Discretionary Household Income

(Dollars in billions)

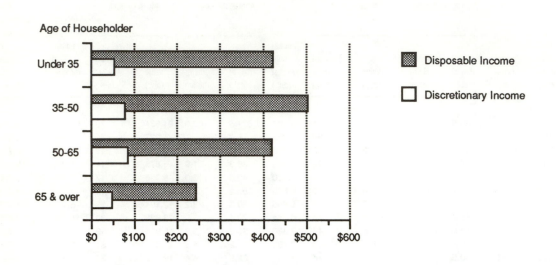

Notes: 1. Disposable income is the amount of money remaining after taxes. The term discretionary income is generally used to define the money available to households after all basic everyday expenditures have been paid.

2. Household figures are for 1983; income figures are for the preceding year.

Source: Midlife and Beyond: The $800 Billion Over-Fifty Market. New York: The Conference Board, 1985.

Figure 2–5. The Dimensions of Discretionary Income by Age of Household Head

(Based on households in the discretionary income bracket, 1983. Income figures refer to previous year.)

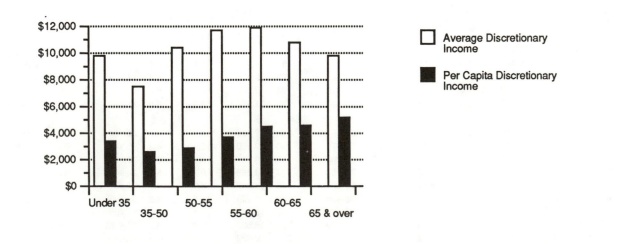

Note: The term discretionary income is generally used to define the money available to households after all basic everyday expenditures have been paid.

Source: Midlife and Beyond: The $800 Billion Over-Fifty Market. New York: The Conference Board, 1985.

SOURCE OF INCOME

Table 2-8. Source of Income as a Percentage of Income: 1968-1983

Year	Social Security/ Railroad Retirement	Asset Income	SSI/Public Assistance	Pensions	Earnings
Families with head 65 and older					
1968	22.9	14.6	1.3	12.3	48.2
1970	25.0	14.5	1.4	12.5	46.6
1972	28.1	14.0	1.1	12.5	44.2
1974	31.1	15.4	1.3	13.5	38.8
1976	32.3	15.6	1.4	14.5	36.1
1978	32.2	15.7	1.2	13.8	37.1
1980	32.4	19.4	1.1	15.6	31.4
1981	33.0	21.7	1.0	14.9	29.5
1982	33.1	21.4	0.8	14.8	29.9
1983	34.3	20.9	0.8	16.0	28.0
Unrelated individuals 65 and older					
1968	34.2	26.5	4.1	14.4	20.8
1970	37.3	24.1	4.1	15.4	19.1
1972	41.7	24.2	3.2	14.3	16.6
1974	44.9	21.7	3.7	16.2	13.6
1976	46.9	20.9	3.0	15.7	13.4
1978	45.9	22.7	2.7	16.9	11.8
1980	47.4	24.4	2.5	14.6	11.2
1981	45.9	26.6	1.9	14.1	11.5
1982	45.3	28.7	1.8	14.1	10.1
1983	44.0	28.7	1.9	15.5	9.8

Source: U.S. Bureau of the Census, *Current Population Reports* Series P-60, 1969-83.

Table 2–9. Income Sources by Age, Sex, Race, and Spanish Origin: Percent of Aged Persons with Money Income from Specified Sources, 1984[1]

Source of income	White			Black			Spanish origin[2]		
	55–61	62–64	65 and older	55–61	62–64	65 and older	55–61	62–64	65 and older
				Men					
Number (in thousands)	6,921	2,691	9,969	696	258	896	394	108	356
Percent of units with									
Earnings	82	60	22	65	47	19	74	60	22
Retirement benefits	22	57	94	27	58	90	17	50	82
Social Security [3,4]	8	47	90	14	53	86	11	42	77
Benefits other than Social Security	17	36	46	14	26	33	9	20	27
Other public pensions	9	14	16	9	8	14	5	9	9
Railroad retirement	0	1	2	1	1	4	0	0	3
Government employee pensions	9	13	14	8	7	10	5	9	6
Private pensions or annuities	8	24	31	5	18	20	4	11	19
Income from assets	72	74	75	30	25	33	39	50	37
Veterans' benefits	5	7	5	4	7	7	2	2	4
Public assistance	4	7	10	11	8	18	8	5	25
				Women					
Number (in thousands)	7,345	3,044	14,263	837	305	1,347	417	152	466
Percent of units with									
Earnings	52	34	10	55	38	13	45	26	9
Retirement benefits	13	61	94	19	58	87	10	50	76
Social Security [3,4]	8	57	92	13	50	85	7	48	74
Benefits other than Social Security	9	16	23	8	16	12	4	9	10
Other public pensions	3	8	11	6	9	7	1	4	5
Railroad retirement	0	1	2	0	0	1	0	0	1
Government employee pensions	2	4	7	3	6	4	1	3	3
Private pensions or annuities	5	9	12	3	8	5	3	5	5
Income from assets	69	71	70	30	30	27	34	35	35
Veterans' benefits	1	2	2	2	5	4	1	1	1
Public assistance	5	7	13	20	30	32	14	13	30

Notes: 1. Receipt of sources is ascertained by response to a yes/no question which is imputed by CPS. A married couple receives a source if one or both persons are recipients of that source.

2. Persons of Spanish origin may be of any race.

3. Recipients of Social Security may be receiving retired-worker benefits, dependents' or survivors' benefits, disability benefits, transitionally insured, or special age-72 benefits.

4. Comparison of record data and survey data from the 1972 Survey of the Aged indicates sizable under-reporting of receipt of Social Security benefits by married women, many of whom are attributing the income to their husbands.

Source: U.S. Department of Health and Human Services. Social Security Administration. Office of Policy. *Income of the Population 55 and Over, 1984.* Washington, D.C.: U.S. Department of Health and Human Services. 1985.

Table 2–10. Income Sources: Percent of Aged Units[1] 55 and Older with Money Income From Specified Sources,[2] by Age, Sex, and Marital Status, 1984

Source of income	Age 55-61	Age 62-64	Age 65 and older				
			Total	65–69	70–74	75–79	80 and older
			All units				
Number (in thousands)	10,388	4,271	20,790	6,498	5,529	4,211	4,553
Percent of units with							
Earnings	80	59	21	36	22	13	5
Wages and salaries	74	54	18	32	19	10	4
Self-employment	11	8	3	6	3	3	1
Retirement benefits	26	63	94	91	96	96	94
Social Security[3]	12	55	91	87	94	93	91
Benefits other than Social Security	18	33	38	44	41	36	28
Other public pensions	9	14	16	17	17	16	12
Railroad retirement	0	1	2	2	2	2	3
Government employee pensions	9	13	14	16	16	14	10
Military	3	4	2	3	2	1	1
Federal	3	4	5	5	5	4	3
State/local	3	6	8	8	9	9	6
Private pensions or annuities	9	22	24	29	26	22	16
Income from assets	66	68	68	69	70	68	63
Interest	63	65	66	67	68	67	61
Other income from assets	28	28	23	25	24	22	21
Dividends	19	19	16	18	16	14	14
Rent or royalties	13	12	10	11	11	9	9
Estates or trusts	2	2	2	2	1	2	2
Veterans' benefits	5	6	5	6	5	4	4
Unemployment compensation	7	4	1	1	1	0	0
Workers'compensation	2	2	1	1	1	1	1
Public assistance	8	11	16	15	17	17	17
Supplemental security income	7	10	16	14	17	17	17
Other public assistance	2	1	1	1	0	1	1
Personal contributions	2	1	1	1	1	1	1
			Married couples				
Number (in thousands)	6,352	2,469	8,289	3,326	2,430	1,452	1,080
Percent of units with							
Earnings	90	71	34	48	32	25	12
Wages and salaries	84	64	29	42	26	21	9
Self-employment	14	12	6	8	6	5	3
Retirement benefits	26	62	96	92	98	99	97
Social Security[3]	11	52	93	88	96	97	96
Benefits other than Social Security	19	39	52	54	53	49	43
Other public pensions	10	15	20	21	21	19	16
Railroad retirement	0	1	2	2	2	2	4
Government employee pensions	10	14	18	19	19	17	13
Military	5	5	3	4	3	2	1
Federal	3	4	6	6	6	5	5
State/local	3	7	10	10	12	11	8
Private pensions or annuities	10	27	35	37	37	34	29
Income from assets	76	76	79	79	80	79	73
Interest	73	73	77	78	78	78	71
Other income from assets	34	33	30	32	30	27	29
Dividends	24	24	22	24	21	19	21
Rent or royalties	17	14	13	14	14	11	11
Estates or trusts	2	2	2	2	2	2	1
Veterans' benefits	5	7	5	6	5	2	2
Unemployment compensation	8	6	1	2	1	1	0
Workers'compensation	3	3	1	1	1	0	0
Public assistance	5	9	13	12	15	13	14
Supplemental security income	4	8	13	12	14	13	14
Other public assistance	1	1	0	0	1	0	0
Personal contributions	0	0	0	0	1	0	1

Table 2–10. (continued)

Source of income	Age 55-61	Age 62-64	Age 65 and older				
			Total	65–69	70–74	75–79	80 and older
			Non-married persons				
Number (in thousands)	4,037	1,802	12,501	3,171	3,099	2,759	3,473
Percent of units with							
Earnings	64	43	12	24	15	6	3
Wages and salaries	60	40	10	21	13	5	2
Self-employment	5	3	2	3	2	1	1
Retirement benefits	26	65	93	90	95	95	93
Social Security[3]	15	58	90	87	92	91	89
Benefits other than Social Security	15	25	29	33	31	29	23
Other public pensions	7	11	13	14	15	14	11
Railroad retirement	0	1	2	1	2	2	2
Government employee pensions	6	10	11	12	13	12	9
Military	2	2	1	2	2	1	1
Federal	3	4	4	4	4	3	3
State/local	2	4	7	7	7	8	5
Private pensions or annuities	8	15	17	21	18	16	12
Income from assets	50	57	61	59	61	63	60
Interest	48	54	59	56	59	61	58
Other income from assets	17	20	19	18	19	19	19
Dividends	11	13	12	11	12	12	12
Rent or royalties	7	9	8	7	8	8	8
Estates or trusts	1	1	2	1	1	2	2
Veterans' benefits	5	6	5	5	5	5	4
Unemployment compensation	5	2	0	1	1	0	0
Workers'compensation	1	2	1	1	1	1	1
Public assistance	14	14	18	18	19	20	18
Supplemental security income	10	13	18	17	19	19	17
Other public assistance	4	2	1	1	0	1	1
Personal contributions	3	2	1	1	1	1	1
			Non-married men				
Number (in thousands)	1,425	531	2,755	840	690	566	658
Percent of units with							
Earnings	66	47	16	26	18	10	5
Wages and salaries	57	42	12	21	15	7	3
Self-employment	9	4	3	4	4	2	1
Retirement benefits	25	60	92	89	94	95	92
Social Security[3]	12	52	88	84	90	91	87
Benefits other than Social Security	15	32	37	38	38	40	33
Other public pensions	9	15	14	16	14	14	12
Railroad retirement	1	1	2	2	3	2	2
Government employee pensions	8	14	12	14	11	12	10
Military	2	3	3	4	3	3	1
Federal	3	5	4	5	4	3	3
State/local	3	7	5	6	4	6	5
Private pensions or annuities	7	17	24	24	25	26	21
Income from assets	48	54	57	55	55	59	61
Interest	45	51	55	53	53	57	59
Other income from assets	16	18	18	17	18	16	19
Dividends	12	12	11	11	11	10	11
Rent or royalties	6	8	8	7	8	7	9
Estates or trusts	1	0	1	0	0	0	2
Veterans' benefits	6	8	8	11	11	5	4
Unemployment compensation	5	2	0	1	1	0	0
Workers'compensation	1	1	1	1	1	2	1
Public assistance	12	15	15	15	13	16	18
Supplemental security income	9	14	15	14	13	16	18
Other public assistance	3	2	1	1	0	1	0
Personal contributions	1	1	0	1	0	1	1

Table 2–10. (continued)

Source of income	Age 55-61	Age 62-64	Age 65 and older				
			Total	65–69	70–74	75–79	80 and older
			Non-married women				
Number (in thousands)	2,612	1,272	9,747	2,331	2,408	2,193	2,814
Percent of units with							
Earnings	63	42	11	23	14	5	2
Wages and salaries	61	40	10	21	12	4	2
Self-employment	3	3	1	2	1	1	0
Retirement benefits	27	67	93	91	95	95	93
Social Security[3]	16	61	90	88	92	91	90
Benefits other than Social Security	15	23	27	31	29	26	21
Other public pensions	6	10	13	13	15	14	11
Railroad retirement	0	1	2	1	2	2	3
Government employee							
pensions	6	9	11	12	13	12	9
Military	2	1	1	1	1	0	1
Federal	2	4	4	4	5	3	3
State/local	2	3	7	7	8	8	5
Private pensions or annuities	9	14	15	20	16	13	10
Income from assets	52	58	62	60	63	63	60
Interest	49	55	59	58	61	61	58
Other income from assets	17	21	19	18	20	20	19
Dividends	11	13	12	11	12	12	12
Rent or royalties	7	10	8	8	8	8	8
Estates or trusts	2	1	2	1	1	2	2
Veterans' benefits	4	5	4	3	3	4	5
Unemployment compensation	5	2	0	1	1	0	0
Workers'compensation	1	3	1	1	2	1	1
Public assistance	14	14	19	19	21	21	18
Supplemental security income	11	13	19	18	21	20	17
Other public assistance	5	2	1	1	0	1	1
Personal contributions	5	3	1	2	1	1	1

Notes: 1. An aged unit is a married couple living together or a non-married person. The concept of the aged unit allows one to measure incomes of the entire aged population either separately from or in combination with the income of other members of the families in which they live.

2. Receipt of sources is ascertained by response to a yes/no question which is imputed by CPS. A married couple receives a source if one or both persons are recipients of that source.

3. Recipients of Social Security may be receiving retired-worker benefits, dependents' or survivors' benefits, disability benefits, transitionally insured, or special age-72 benefits.

Source: U.S. Department of Health and Human Services. Social Security Administration. Office of Policy. *Income of the Population 55 and Over, 1984.* Washington, D.C.: U.S. Department of Health and Human Services. 1985.

Table 2–11. Income Sources by Levels of Total Money Income and Marital Status: Percent of Aged Units[1] 65 and Older with Money Income From Specified Sources, 1984[2]

Source of income	Total	Under $5,000	$5,000–$9,999	$10,000–$19,999	$20,000 or more
			All units		
Number (in thousands)	20,790	4,044	6,220	5,910	4,617
Percent of units with					
Earnings	21	4	11	25	43
Retirement benefits	94	84	98	98	93
Social Security[3]	91	83	95	94	88
Benefits other than Social Security	38	5	26	56	59
Other public pensions	16	2	10	21	29
Railroad retirement	2	1	3	3	2
Government employee pensions	14	2	7	19	28
Private pensions or annuities	24	3	17	38	35
Income from assets	68	27	59	84	95
Veterans' benefits	5	5	6	5	3
Public assistance	16	29	13	12	15
			Married couples		
Number (in thousands)	8,289	242	1,382	3,258	3,407
Percent of units with					
Earnings	34	20	16	28	50
Retirement benefits	96	78	97	99	93
Social Security[3]	93	72	96	96	90
Benefits other than Social Security	52	14	20	57	62
Other public pensions	20	2	7	18	29
Railroad retirement	2	1	1	3	2
Government employee pensions	18	1	5	15	27
Private pensions or annuities	35	13	13	42	40
Income from assets	79	39	45	80	94
Veterans' benefits	5	3	7	5	4
Public assistance	13	13	17	11	15
			Non-married persons		
Number (in thousands)	12,501	3,802	4,838	2,652	1,209
Percent of units with					
Earnings	12	3	9	22	25
Retirement benefits	93	84	98	97	93
Social Security[3]	90	83	95	92	85
Benefits other than Social Security	29	5	28	54	52
Other public pensions	13	2	11	25	32
Railroad retirement	2	1	3	2	3
Government employee pensions	11	2	8	23	30
Private pensions or annuities	17	2	18	32	23
Income from assets	61	26	63	88	96
Veterans' benefits	5	5	6	4	2
Public assistance	18	30	12	14	16

Notes: 1. An aged unit is a married couple living together or a non-married person. The concept of the aged unit allows one to measure incomes of the entire aged population either separately from or in combination with the income of other members of the families in which they live.

2. Receipt of sources is ascertained by response to a yes/no question which is imputed by CPS. A married couple receives a source if one or both persons are recipients of that source.

3. Recipients of Social Security may be receiving retired-worker benefits, dependents' or survivors' benefits, transitionally insured, or special age-72 benefits.

Source: U.S. Department of Health and Human Services. Social Security Administration. Office of Policy. *Income of the Population 55 and Over, 1984.* Washington, D.C.: U.S. Department of Health and Human Services. 1985.

Table 2–12. Income from Earnings by Race, Spanish Origin, and Marital Status: Percentage Distribution of Aged Units 65 and Older, 1984

Income (recipients only)	White			Black			Spanish origin[1]		
	All units	Married couples	Non-married persons	All units	Married couples	Non-married persons	All units	Married couples	Non-married persons
Number (in thousands)	3,844	2,572	1,272	383	203	179	130	88	42
Total percent	100.0	100.0	100.0	100.0	100.0	100.0	100.0	100.0	100.0
Less than $1,000	15.9	13.2	21.3	12.9	11.5	14.4	10.8	6.8	[2]
$1,000–$1,999	8.3	7.5	9.8	9.4	4.9	14.5	7.3	8.4	[2]
$2,000–$2,999	9.1	8.3	10.7	18.2	10.4	27.0	8.0	7.0	[2]
$3,000–$3,999	6.6	5.6	8.7	6.9	6.3	7.6	7.3	4.0	[2]
$4,000–$4,999	5.3	4.7	6.5	5.5	4.2	7.0	5.6	7.9	[2]
$5,000–$5,999	6.1	5.2	8.0	4.7	4.1	5.5	8.2	4.0	[2]
$6,000–$6,999	6.6	5.6	8.5	6.1	4.8	7.6	7.4	4.6	[2]
$7,000–$7,999	3.6	3.3	4.2	3.6	4.5	2.5	5.5	6.1	[2]
$8,000–$8,999	3.2	3.6	2.5	3.2	5.2	1.0	4.1	5.0	[2]
$9,000–$9,999	1.9	2.4	.9	2.3	3.1	1.4	3.5	3.2	[2]
$10,000–$10,999	2.4	2.9	1.3	1.9	.9	3.1	2.2	.8	[2]
$11,000–$11,999	1.4	1.6	1.1	1.7	2.5	.8	2.3	2.3	[2]
$12,000–$12,999	2.9	3.4	1.8	1.7	3.0	.2	6.9	10.2	[2]
$13,000–$13,999	1.5	1.6	1.3	2.3	1.5	3.3	0	0	[2]
$14,000–$14,999	1.2	1.0	1.7	2.2	4.1	0	1.5	2.2	[2]
$15,000–$19,999	6.8	8.0	4.3	4.5	7.7	.9	9.7	13.3	[2]
$20,000–$24,999	4.8	5.9	2.5	4.4	6.6	1.9	2.7	4.0	[2]
$25,000–$29,999	3.6	4.0	2.7	2.7	5.0	0	4.3	6.4	[2]
$30,000–$34,999	2.7	3.3	1.4	1.5	2.1	.8	.8	1.2	[2]
$35,000–$39,999	1.5	2.2	.2	0	0	0	0	0	[2]
$40,000–$44,999	1.1	1.5	.3	.3	.6	0	1.1	1.6	[2]
$45,000–$49,999	.9	1.2	.2	1.5	1.8	1.1	.2	.3	[2]
$50,000 or more	4.4	5.7	1.8	2.7	5.0	0	1.4	2.1	[2]
Median dollar income[3]	5,700	7,000	3,950	4,590	7,350	2,730	6,270	7,970	[2]

Notes: 1. Persons of Spanish origin may be of any race.
2. Fewer than 75,000 weighted cases.
3. Rounded to the nearest $10.

Source: U.S. Department of Health and Human Services. Social Security Administration. Office of Policy. *Income of Population 55 and Over, 1984*. Washington, D.C.: U.S. Department of Health and Human Services, 1985.

Table 2–13. Wage and Salary Projections by Age and Sex: 1970–2055

Average Hourly Wage by Age and Sex (1972 Dollars)

	Male			Female		
	55–64	65 +	Total	55–64	65 +	Total
1970	$3.29	$4.84	$2.24	$2.79	$1.84	$2.78
1975	5.57	3.96	5.22	2.97	1.91	3.00
1980	7.09	4.66	6.44	3.62	2.41	3.66
1985	7.41	4.87	6.72	3.78	2.52	3.81
1990	8.54	5.61	7.38	4.35	2.90	4.14
1995	9.92	6.53	8.28	5.06	3.37	4.59
2000	10.77	7.08	9.06	5.50	3.66	4.99
2005	11.12	7.31	9.85	5.67	3.78	5.44
2010	11.35	7.47	10.57	5.79	3.86	5.88
2015	11.51	7.57	11.18	5.87	3.91	6.27
2020	12.04	7.92	11.81	6.14	4.09	6.64
2025	13.39	8.81	12.53	6.83	4.55	7.02
2030	15.29	10.06	13.40	7.80	5.20	7.49
2035	17.17	11.29	14.58	8.76	5.84	8.15
2040	18.21	11.98	15.93	9.29	6.19	8.93
2045	19.54	12.85	17.51	9.97	6.64	9.83
2050	21.56	14.18	19.20	11.00	7.33	10.77
2055	24.38	16.04	21.10	12.44	8.29	11.81

Average Annual Compensation by Age and Sex (1972 Dollars)

	Male			Female			All		
	55–64	65 +	Total	55–64	65 +	Total	55–64	65 +	Total
1970	$9,390	$4,772	$8,513	$4,061	$2,212	$3,609	$7,557	$3,951	$6,782
1975	10,101	5,409	8,876	4,254	2,196	3,834	8,068	4,361	6,951
1980	12,697	6,146	10,767	5,132	2,689	4,634	9,861	4,897	8,312
1985	13,255	6,389	11,278	5,357	2,797	4,829	10,289	5,068	8,684
1990	15,159	7,207	12,398	6,137	3,169	5,274	11,616	5,596	9,434
1995	17,453	8,147	13,823	7,083	3,606	5,849	13,152	6,289	10,358
2000	18,717	8,545	14,867	7,620	3,814	6,325	13,936	6,774	10,998
2005	19,078	8,510	15,791	7,793	3,832	6,856	14,165	6,990	11,628
2010	19,280	8,431	16,657	7,898	3,824	7,390	14,294	7,064	12,287
2015	19,376	8,338	17,359	7,955	3,805	7,861	14,385	7,058	12,842
2020	20,126	8,550	18,117	8,279	3,921	8,290	14,880	7,263	13,398
2025	22,247	9,340	18,983	9,166	4,302	8,713	16,249	7,944	14,019
2030	25,241	10,468	20,066	10,419	4,844	9,240	18,289	8,920	14,806
2035	28,105	11,480	21,582	11,628	5,344	10,004	20,336	9,815	15,920
2040	29,517	11,841	23,271	12,246	5,551	10,919	21,326	10,168	17,185
2045	31,319	12,315	25,183	13,035	5,818	11,939	22,629	10,599	18,640
2050	34,186	13,172	27,115	14,273	6,272	12,965	24,654	11,339	20,123
2055	38,227	14,429	29,250	16,012	6,927	14,093	27,591	12,458	21,763

Source: U.S. Department of Health and Human Services. National Institute on Aging. *The National Institute on Aging Macroeconomic–Demographic Model.* Washington, D.C.: National Institutes of Health, 1984.

Table 2-14. Income and Source of Income of Persons Age 85 and Older (1980)

State	Number[1]	Percent receiving wage or salary	Percent self-employed	Percent with Social Security	Percent with interest, dividends, rental Income	Percent with pension or other Income	Percent receiving Supplemental Security Income or welfare	Average per capita Income in 1985[2]	Average household income in 1985[2]	Percent below poverty level
Alabama	34,019	3.7%	2.1%	20.9%	72.4%	26.5%	19.3%	$6,613	$16,559	27.2%
Alaska	619	3.6	0.0	17.9	60.7	25.0	42.9	8,675	31,553	10.7
Arizona	19,878	2.3	1.4	35.7	78.5	10.4	21.4	8,996	21,864	17.6
Arkansas	26,354	3.0	1.7	22.0	76.2	18.7	17.3	5,823	13,099	26.3
California	218,017	3.3	1.3	36.6	71.0	19.0	21.6	9,685	22,752	9.6
Colorado	24,363	2.8	2.2	33.9	74.6	12.4	22.3	7,999	18,356	16.4
Connecticut	35,729	3.2	0.5	39.7	71.3	6.3	21.6	9,291	25,168	10.1
Delaware	5,269	4.5	1.5	38.0	75.6	6.0	17.3	7,537	22,822	16.9
District of Columbia	6,385	9.3	0.9	33.3	60.2	8.6	32.1	13,053	28,798	16.7
Florida	117,342	3.8	1.3	39.2	77.4	10.6	21.0	9,639	20,907	16.7
Georgia	39,434	4.1	2.2	23.6	71.4	20.6	15.7	6,545	17,654	23.8
Hawaii	5,561	3.8	1.2	29.6	76.9	10.8	22.3	7,047	37,754	12.3
Idaho	8,476	3.9	2.4	32.4	79.7	7.4	16.8	7,454	15,474	21.1
Illinois	114,682	5.0	3.4	41.4	74.9	8.2	19.0	8,802	22,893	14.0
Indiana	54,410	4.8	4.1	38.7	77.3	7.6	20.6	7,812	17,980	15.8
Iowa	44,940	6.5	6.4	45.1	78.1	7.7	13.6	8,541	15,435	15.9
Kansas	33,455	6.5	5.4	40.3	76.7	6.8	15.4	8,434	16,227	17.6
Kentucky	35,036	5.4	5.4	29.7	75.2	15.6	19.1	7,054	16,761	23.8
Louisiana	30,535	4.8	1.9	19.4	66.5	25.5	16.6	6,555	18,334	26.2
Maine	14,099	1.7	1.4	33.1	79.0	11.4	22.7	7,242	17,574	19.1
Maryland	32,665	4.3	1.3	36.6	73.0	10.0	21.0	8,817	27,323	12.7
Massachusetts	73,908	2.3	0.7	30.7	71.6	13.5	20.5	7,669	20,731	11.2
Michigan	81,653	2.5	1.5	36.4	75.2	10.8	21.2	7,277	20,121	15.2
Minnesota	52,789	2.8	2.3	39.3	74.9	7.3	21.8	7,995	16,900	15.7
Mississippi	23,509	3.8	2.3	15.6	71.2	32.1	15.2	5,660	15,070	30.8
Missouri	61,072	3.3	3.1	37.0	74.0	14.1	19.7	8,026	17,251	44.1
Montana	8,837	3.2	1.8	31.4	76.7	5.9	21.7	7,287	16,067	12.9
Nebraska	23,744	8.4	5.7	38.8	76.8	5.8	14.9	7,979	15,949	18.1
Nevada	3,640	2.7	0.5	27.3	78.6	14.4	21.9	7,825	21,691	14.4
New Hampshire	9,650	2.5	0.8	38.8	76.1	6.4	21.0	7,744	18,909	15.3
New Jersey	72,231	2.9	0.9	34.1	75.9	7.3	21.2	8,423	25,736	11.7
New Mexico	8,783	4.4	2.5	27.7	77.0	14.6	17.7	7,494	18,375	23.7
New York	192,983	2.9	1.1	33.1	74.0	11.4	21.6	8,241	22,422	12.0
North Carolina	45,203	5.5	4.5	27.6	76.9	15.3	17.6	6,940	17,840	23.6
North Dakota	8,140	8.1	5.0	35.0	81.1	7.8	8.8	7,574	17,339	15.1
Ohio	108,426	3.3	2.0	37.1	76.1	7.3	21.9	7,889	19,895	14.9
Oklahoma	33,981	3.9	3.6	27.5	74.1	22.6	19.0	7,442	14,936	23.1
Oregon	28,431	2.7	1.9	41.7	78.1	7.8	21.4	8,273	17,320	16.4
Pennsylvania	129,960	2.4	0.9	37.0	77.6	8.7	23.1	7,843	21,523	13.8
Rhode Island	11,978	2.8	0.6	31.7	77.0	9.4	17.3	8,215	21,889	12.7
South Carolina	20,004	5.2	2.4	23.6	71.7	21.5	14.4	6,555	18,629	25.4
South Dakota	10,427	5.6	3.7	36.1	75.8	9.0	18.2	6,430	12,836	24.6
Tennessee	41,443	3.5	3.4	26.7	75.2	16.9	18.6	6,669	17,492	24.2
Texas	112,022	4.5	3.0	26.8	72.3	16.4	16.9	7,843	19,241	21.6
Utah	8,852	3.4	3.2	36.3	77.2	9.1	21.6	7,997	17,275	39.7
Vermont	6,007	2.5	3.2	43.8	78.4	14.4	20.0	8,937	19,419	16.9
Virginia	41,131	5.2	2.5	32.8	75.6	13.0	22.7	7,884	23,012	17.0
Washington	41,476	3.8	1.8	36.2	75.1	10.6	21.9	8,184	17,624	15.4
West Virginia	19,409	2.8	1.8	29.4	81.2	12.0	25.1	7,170	17,544	33.8
Wisconsin	55,637	2.5	1.2	42.4	77.6	8.9	20.8	7,403	17,842	44.0
Wyoming	3,473	4.0	1.3	33.1	75.5	6.0	21.9	7,672	15,591	45.7
United States	2,240,067	3.7	2.2	34.4	74.7	12.5	20.2	8,089	20,161	16.2

Notes: 1. Totals are slightly different from the 100 percent count from the 1980 Census because of sampling.
2. 1979 income in 1985 dollars, inflated using the Consumer Price Index.

Source: U.S. Bureau of the Census. *1980 Census of Population.*

PENSIONS

Table 2–15. Former Industry of Retirement Pension Recipients—Mean Monthly Pension Income, Total Household Income, and Social Security Income: 1984

Industry	Number (thous.)	Pension income		Total household income		Social Security income			Pension and Social Security income	
		Mean	Standard error	Mean	Standard error	Number (thous.)	Mean	Standard error	Mean[1]	Standard error
Total	11,547	$568	$25	$2,251	$79	8,688	$487	$8	$934	$23
Agriculture, forestry, and fisheries	50	(B)	(B)	(B)	(B)	41	(B)	(B)	(B)	(B)
Mining	87	(B)	(B)	(B)	(B)	71	(B)	(B)	(B)	(B)
Construction	486	468	92	1,960	326	436	536	36	949	87
Manufacturing, total	3,602	395	37	1,962	139	3,123	532	11	856	36
Durable goods	1,255	318	45	1,882	177	1,161	518	18	798	49
Nondurable goods	2,348	436	50	2,005	191	1,962	540	15	887	49
Transportation, communication, and other public utilities	1,196	689	77	2,276	241	823	474	28	1,015	74
Wholesale trade	249	396	114	2,515	584	200	543	40	834	107
Retail trade	519	279	72	1,750	300	434	471	32	674	73
Finance, insurance, and real estate	382	365	129	1,782	257	345	517	36	832	138
Business and repair services	107	(B)	(B)	(B)	(B)	89	(B)	(B)	(B)	(B)
Personal services	68	(B)	(B)	(B)	(B)	58	(B)	(B)	(B)	(B)
Entertainment and recreation services	33	(B)	(B)	(B)	(B)	28	(B)	(B)	(B)	(B)
Professional and related services	2,208	493	43	2,194	171	1,816	450	18	863	44
Public administration, total	1,636	896	75	2,537	215	990	377	26	1,125	71
Federal government	790	1,113	116	2,543	257	438	279	30	1,268	111
State government	384	646	107	2,494	542	254	455	52	947	113
Local government	462	733	126	2,564	425	299	455	45	1,026	126
Armed Forces	924	1,067	103	3,549	311	232	471	43	1,186	109

Notes: (B) Base less than 200,000.

1. Based on all retirement pension recipients, including those not receiving Social Security income.

Source: Bureau of the Census. *Current Population Reports*, Series P-70, No. 12.

Table 2–16. Projected Beneficiaries and Benefit Payments in Private Pension Plans by Type of Plan, 1980-2055

Year	Defined Benefit Plans			Defined Contribution Plans		
	Beneficiaries (Millions)	Average Benefits (1972 $)	Total Payment (Billions of 1972 $)	Beneficiaries (Millions)	Average Benefits (1972 $)	Total Payments (Billions of 1972 $)
1980	5.90	$1,981	$ 11.69	3.01	$1,263	$ 3.79
1990	9.31	2,263	21.06	4.73	1,483	7.02
2000	11.35	3,091	35.08	5.77	2,101	12.11
2010	15.73	3,820	60.10	7.99	2,524	20.17
2020	22.38	4,272	95.59	11.37	2,728	31.02
2030	25.15	4,788	120.39	12.78	2,946	37.65
2040	23.03	5,533	127.43	11.70	3,263	38.18
2050	24.04	6,380	153.40	12.22	3,638	44.45
2055	25.37	6,826	173.19	12.89	3,830	49.38
Rate of Growth						
1980–2010	3.32%	2.21%	5.60%	3.31%	2.33%	5.73%
2010–2055	1.07	1.30	2.38	1.07	0.93	2.01
1980–2055	1.96	1.66	3.66	1.96	1.49	3.48

Source: National Institute on Aging Macroeconomic—Demographic Model. Washington, D.C.: U.S. Department of Health and Human Services, 1984.

Table 2–17. Retirees in the Private Pension System by Age and Sex

(Millions)

	Male						Female					
	55–57	58–61	62–64	65–67	68–71	72 +	55–57	58–61	62–64	65–67	68–71	72 +
1970	0.058	0.300	0.469	0.632	0.700	0.847	0.040	0.243	0.315	0.377	0.353	0.403
1975	0.027	0.369	0.741	0.835	0.791	0.830	0.030	0.402	0.814	0.925	0.641	0.485
1980	0.033	0.445	0.829	1.129	1.110	0.940	0.036	0.496	0.958	1.352	1.370	0.866
1985	0.036	0.505	1.041	1.370	1.375	1.312	0.038	0.561	1.196	1.679	1.784	1.770
1990	0.037	0.539	1.130	1.586	1.724	1.696	0.039	0.585	1.280	1.943	2.241	2.457
1995	0.043	0.556	1.174	1.716	1.914	2.120	0.046	0.604	1.311	2.048	2.471	3.057
2000	0.059	0.666	1.304	1.758	2.037	2.415	0.063	0.726	1.469	2.090	2.567	3.449
2005	0.077	0.877	1.728	2.066	2.166	2.591	0.082	0.950	1.927	2.468	2.735	3.626
2010	0.086	1.096	2.214	2.725	2.670	2.804	0.091	1.185	2.447	3.228	3.355	3.886
2015	0.093	1.231	2.473	3.348	3.478	3.489	0.098	1.321	2.734	3.942	4.319	4.780
2020	0.089	1.296	2.749	3.748	4.119	4,537	0.095	1.391	3.029	4.377	5.099	6.148
2025	0.078	1.212	2.778	4.029	4.652	5.431	0.083	1.302	3.061	4.698	5.710	7.339
2030	0.071	1.119	2.406	3.883	4.865	6.170	0.076	1.201	2.657	4.524	5.957	8.290
2035	0.076	1.005	2.336	3.483	4.446	6.533	0.081	1.075	2.568	4.049	5.440	8.749
2040	0.089	1.123	2.236	3.176	4.245	6.126	0.093	1.198	2.449	3.673	5.160	8.188
2045	0.090	1.261	2.628	3.454	3.892	5.713	0.095	1.341	2.865	3.976	4.697	7.552
2050	0.087	1.267	2.761	3.975	4.461	5.437	0.092	1.346	3.001	4.550	5.351	7.085
2055	0.084	1.217	2.713	4.048	4.913	6.051	0.088	1.291	2.944	4.616	5.863	7.765

Source: National Institute on Aging Macroeconomic—Demographic Model. Washington, D.C.: U.S. Department of Health and Human Services, 1984.

Table 2–18. Projected Beneficiaries and Total Benefit Payments in Public Pension Plans by Type of Plan, 1980–2055

Year	Total Beneficiaries (Millions)			Total Benefit Payments (Billions of 1972 Dollars)		
	Civil Service	Military	State & Local	Civil Service	Military	State & Local
1980	1.41	1.19	3.09	$6.72	$6.27	$9.34
1990	1.96	1.35	3.83	10.78	8.27	13.54
2000	2.31	1.45	3.80	13.54	10.20	15.47
2010	2.35	1.43	4.16	16.43	11.73	20.07
2020	2.44	1.43	4.27	18.29	13.28	22.96
2030	2.52	1.43	5.25	20.94	15.00	28.53
2040	2.61	1.43	5.45	25.81	17.12	35.45
2050	2.70	1.43	5.12	30.90	19.62	36.32
2055	2.75	1.43	5.07	33.79	21.10	36.42
Rate of Growth						
1980–2010	1.72%	0.61%	1.00%	3.02%	2.11%	2.58%
2010–2055	0.34	0.0	0.44	1.62	1.31	1.33
1980–2055	0.89	0.46	0.66	2.18	1.63	1.83

Projected Average Benefits Paid by Public Employee Pension Plans By Type of Plan, 1980-2055

(1972 Dollars)

Year	Civil Service	Military	State and Local	Total
1980	$ 4,902	$5,259	$3,022	$3,949
1990	5,608	6,127	3,539	4,592
2000	5,967	7,038	4,073	5,217
2010	7,116	8,187	4,823	6,103
2020	7,645	9,272	5,381	6,739
2030	8,452	10,475	5,435	7,040
2040	10,059	11,954	6,510	8,300
2050	11,649	13,701	7,100	9,439
2055	12,536	14,735	7,190	9,933
Rate of Growth				
1980–2010	1.25%	1.49%	1.57%	1.46%
2010–2055	1.27	1.31	0.89	1.09
1980–2055	1.26	1.38	1.16	1.24

Source: *National Institute on Aging Macroeconomic—Demographic Model.* Washington, D.C.: U.S. Department of Health and Human Services, 1984.

Table 2–19. Retirees in the Public Pension System by Age and Sex

(Millions)

	Male							Female					
	55–57	58–61	62–64	65–67	68–71	72+		55–57	58–61	62–64	65–67	68–71	72+
1970	0.14	0.28	0.27	0.29	0.35	0.54		0.03	0.08	0.10	0.17	0.16	0.19
1975	0.16	0.40	0.44	0.39	0.50	1.02		0.03	0.09	0.13	0.15	0.28	0.46
1980	0.19	0.44	0.49	0.52	0.66	1.53		0.03	0.09	0.13	0.17	0.29	0.79
1985	0.19	0.45	0.52	0.56	0.76	2.06		0.03	0.10	0.13	0.17	0.29	1.04
1990	0.19	0.43	0.47	0.54	0.77	2.51		0.03	0.08	0.12	0.16	0.27	1.17
1995	0.18	0.42	0.47	0.50	0.72	2.82		0.03	0.08	0.11	0.15	0.26	1.23
2000	0.20	0.46	0.48	0.50	0.69	2.92		0.03	0.09	0.11	0.14	0.26	1.25
2005	0.20	0.52	0.55	0.55	0.71	2.80		0.03	0.09	0.12	0.15	0.28	1.26
2010	0.20	0.52	0.60	0.63	0.80	2.75		0.04	0.10	0.13	0.16	0.29	1.30
2015	0.20	0.48	0.54	0.62	0.85	2.84		0.04	0.09	0.13	0.16	0.28	1.30
2020	0.20	0.48	0.54	0.59	0.83	3.01		0.04	0.10	0.14	0.17	0.30	1.31
2025	0.20	0.47	0.54	0.60	0.83	3.11		0.04	0.10	0.14	0.19	0.33	1.38
2030	0.21	0.53	0.60	0.65	0.93	3.26		0.04	0.12	0.18	0.24	0.46	1.57
2035	0.20	0.48	0.59	0.67	0.95	3.47		0.04	0.11	0.16	0.23	0.47	1.87
2040	0.20	0.45	0.51	0.59	0.90	3.55		0.04	0.10	0.14	0.19	0.41	2.02
2045	0.20	0.46	0.51	0.56	0.79	3.52		0.04	0.10	0.14	0.17	0.38	2.04
2050	0.20	0.46	0.52	0.58	0.80	3.38		0.04	0.11	0.15	0.19	0.38	2.02
2055	0.20	0.45	0.52	0.58	0.84	3.31		0.04	0.11	0.15	0.20	0.41	2.01

Source: *National Institute on Aging Macroeconomic—Demographic Model*. Washington, D.C.: U.S. Department of Health and Human Services, 1984.

NET WORTH AND ASSETS

Figure 2–6. Net Worth of Families With Householder Age 55 and Over: 1983

(Net worth is the difference between *gross assets* [financial assets, equity in homes, and other real property] and *liabilities* [consumer credit, mortgage debt, and other debts]. The estimates exclude the value of consumer durables, the cash value of life insurance, equity in small businesses and farms, and the present value of expected future benefits from pensions or social security.)

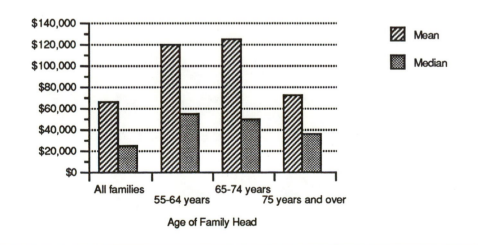

Source: Board of Governors of the Federal Reserve System, *Federal Reserve Bulletin*, December 1984; and 1983 *Survey of Consumer Finances*.

Table 2–20. Distribution of Household Net Worth, by Selected Characteristics: 1984

(Excludes persons in group quarters)

Characteristic	Number of households (thousands)	Zero or negative	$1 to $4,999	$5,000 to $9,999	$10,000 to $24,999	$25,000 to $49,999	$50,000 to $99,999	$100,000 to $249,999	$250,000 to $499,999	$500,000 or over	Median (dollars)	Standard error (dollars)
Total	86,790	11.0	15.3	6.4	12.4	14.5	19.3	15.3	4.0	1.9	$32,667	$683
Age of Householder												
55 to 64	12,920	5.3	7.7	3.3	7.8	13.3	25.3	25.7	7.6	4.0	73,664	1,965
65 years and over	18,151	6.7	8.7	4.0	9.1	15.5	24.7	23.1	5.9	2.3	60,266	1,630
65 to 69 years	5,668	6.8	6.8	2.9	8.2	15.1	25.7	24.9	6.6	3.0	66,621	2,873
70 to 74 years	5,014	7.2	9.8	3.4	9.4	14.5	25.0	21.9	6.0	2.7	60,573	3,092
75 years and over	7,468	6.4	9.4	5.1	9.5	16.6	23.8	22.5	5.2	1.6	55,178	2,517
Type of Household												
Married-couple households	50,606	6.0	10.5	5.6	12.2	15.6	22.7	19.5	5.3	2.7	50,166	1,072
Age of spouse:												
55 to 64 years	7,974	2.0	4.4	2.2	6.2	11.5	27.8	32.0	9.0	3.1	91,227	3,084
65 years and over	6,015	2.1	4.6	2.9	6.2	12.7	27.2	31.0	9.0	4.8	90,313	3,270
Other household type:												
Male householder	12,588	15.5	25.1	9.7	13.3	11.6	13.0	8.0	2.6	1.4	9,883	825
55 to 64 years	1,398	11.9	10.5	4.7	13.9	19.6	18.7	15.7	4.3	1.4	37,166	4,247
65 years and over	2,233	11.7	13.0	4.5	10.4	15.8	21.1	15.7	4.9	3.0	41,208	3,969
Female householder	23,596	19.3	20.3	6.4	12.2	13.5	15.3	10.3	2.0	0.6	13,885	998
55 to 64 years	3,148	11.9	10.5	4.7	13.9	19.6	18.7	15.7	4.3	0.7	35,879	2,721
65 years and over	8,055	9.6	11.6	4.9	10.8	17.5	23.9	17.9	3.1	0.7	42,885	2,365

Source: U.S. Bureau of the Census. *Current Population Reports.* Series 70, No. 7.

Table 2–21. Median Net Worth, by Age of Householder and Monthly Household Income

(Excludes group quarters)

Monthly household income	Total (All ages)	65 years and over			
		Total	65 to 69 years	70 to 74 years	75 years and over
All households (thousands)	86,790	18,151	5,668	5,014	7,468
Median income	$ 1,677	$ 1,021	$ 1,306	$ 1,022	$ 828
Median net worth	32,667	60,266	66,621	60,573	55,178
Excluding home equity	7,783	18,790	21,502	18,455	17,025
Net worth by income of less than $900:					
Households (thousands)	22,297	7,934	1,702	2,167	4,064
Median net worth	$ 5,080	$ 25,863	$ 23,257	$ 23,578	$ 28,986
Excluding home equity	1,386	3,727	2,468	3,488	4,634
$900 to $1,999:					
Households (thousands)	26,599	6,672	2,428	1,933	2,310
Median net worth	$ 24,647	$ 74,775	$ 68,509	$ 75,188	$ 80,044
Excluding home equity	6,329	29,849	22,412	27,718	41,343
$2,000 to $3,999:					
Households (thousands)	27,173	2,802	1,185	696	921
Median net worth	$ 46,744	$162,900	$151,450	$164,048	$175,949
Excluding home equity	11,437	80,327	73,618	81,060	97,146
$4,000 or more:					
Households (thousands)	10,720	743	354	217	172
Median net worth	$123,474	$344,518	$247,105	$410,252	(B)
Excluding home equity	44,860	212,710	156,751	268,515	(B)

Note: (B) Base is less than 200,000.

Source: U.S. Bureau of the Census, Current Population Reports, Series P. 70, No. 7.

Table 2–22. Assets by Age of Householder and Type of Household: 1984

(excludes persons in group quarters) (in percent)

| Characteristic | Number of households (thousands) | Percent owning | | | | | | | | | | | | |
		Interest-earning assets at financial institutions[1]	Other interest-earning assets[2]	Regular checking accounts	Stocks and mutual fund shares	Own business or profession	Motor vehicles	Own home	Rental property	Other real estate	Mortgages	U.S. savings bonds	IRA or KEOGH accounts	Other assets[3]
Total	86,790	71.8	8.5	53.9	20.0	12.9	85.8	64.3	9.8	10.0	2.9	15.0	19.5	3.5
Age of Householder														
65 years and over	18,151	77.5	11.6	48.5	21.1	5.1	71.4	73.0	10.8	8.4	5.2	11.3	8.5	2.9
65 to 69 years	5,668	78.2	13.5	49.0	22.9	7.0	83.7	78.7	11.8	12.0	5.3	13.7	17.5	3.7
70 to 74 years	5,014	75.7	10.0	49.5	19.3	5.7	76.6	72.1	10.2	7.9	6.3	11.7	5.5	2.9
75 years and over	7,468	78.3	11.2	47.3	20.8	3.2	58.6	69.3	10.5	6.1	4.3	9.2	3.8	2.2
Type of Household														
Married-couple households	50,606	78.2	9.6	59.5	24.4	17.6	95.9	77.2	11.8	13.3	3.4	18.9	25.1	4.4
Age of spouse:														
65 years and over	6,015	84.8	14.7	51.9	26.9	7.6	91.7	84.3	12.5	12.5	6.7	14.7	11.2	3.1
Other household type:														
Male householder	12,588	65.0	8.1	46.7	15.4	10.4	81.9	41.5	7.4	6.9	1.8	10.3	14.4	3.0
65 years and over	2,233	72.9	12.8	42.8	19.2	5.3	68.3	58.5	8.0	7.2	4.6	9.5	6.1	2.2
Female householder	23,596	61.5	6.2	45.9	13.1	4.0	66.1	48.8	6.6	4.6	2.6	9.2	10.3	1.9
65 years and over	8,055	73.0	8.3	47.6	15.8	2.1	51.7	65.5	9.6	4.5	3.9	8.3	3.8	1.9

Notes: 1. Includes passbook savings accounts, money market deposit accounts, certificates of deposit, and interest-earning checking accounts.
2. Includes money market funds, U.S. Government securities, municipal and corporate bonds, and other interest-earning assets.
3. Includes unit trusts and other financial investments.
4. Persons of Spanish origin may be of any race.

Source: U.S. Bureau of the Census, *Current Population Reports*, Series P-70, No. 7.

Table 2–23. Interest-Earning Assets, Householder Age 65 and Over, and Type of Household: 1984

(excludes persons in group quarters) (by percent)

| Characteristic | Number of households (thous.) | Percent owning interest-earning financial assets | | | | | | | | | | |
| | | | Held at financial institutions | | | | | Other interest-earning assets | | | | |
		Total[1]	Total[1]	Passbook savings accounts	Money market deposit accounts	Certificates of deposit	Interest-earning checking account	Total[1]	Money market funds	U.S. Government securities	Municipal and corporate bonds	Other assets
Total	86,790	72.4	71.8	62.9	15.7	19.1	24.9	8.5	3.8	1.4	2.6	2.8
Age of Householder												
65 years and over	18,151	78.2	77.5	62.5	23.9	36.0	30.0	11.6	4.7	3.1	4.7	3.0
65 to 69 years	5,668	78.9	78.2	60.8	27.3	34.5	33.1	13.5	5.7	3.3	4.5	3.5
70 to 74 years	5,014	76.4	75.7	62.6	24.4	37.6	28.7	10.0	4.0	2.9	4.7	2.3
75 years and over	7,468	79.0	78.3	63.7	21.1	36.0	28.5	11.2	4.5	3.1	4.8	3.0
Type of Household												
Married-couple households	50,606	78.8	78.2	69.6	18.2	20.9	27.9	9.6	4.3	1.4	3.0	3.3
Age of spouse												
65 years and over	6,015	85.5	84.8	70.7	30.2	44.6	37.2	14.7	5.5	3.5	6.4	4.3
Other household type												
Male householder	12,588	66.0	65.0	55.3	12.7	11.9	23.3	8.1	4.0	1.8	2.7	2.2
65 years and over	2,233	73.3	72.9	57.0	22.1	28.2	28.4	12.8	6.6	4.6	5.5	2.4
Female householder	23,596	62.2	61.5	52.7	12.1	18.9	19.2	6.2	2.6	1.1	1.8	1.9
65 years and over	8,055	73.8	73.0	59.3	19.0	32.0	23.7	8.3	3.6	2.0	2.8	2.1

Note: 1. Detail does not add to total because some households have more than one of the types of interest-earning assets specified.
Source: U.S. Bureau of the Census, *Current Population Reports*, Series P-70, No. 7.

Table 2–24. Median Value of Holdings for Asset Owners Age 65 and Over, by Selected Characteristics: 1984

(Excludes persons in group quarters)

Characteristic	Net worth	Interest-earning deposits at financial institutions[1]	Other interest-earning assets[2]	Regular checking accounts	Stock and mutual fund shares	Equity in own home	Rental property equity	Other real estate equity	Equity in business or profession	Equity in motor vehicles	U.S. savings bonds	IRA or KEOGH accounts	Other assets[3]
Total	$32,667	$3,066	$9,471	$449	$3,892	$40,597	$34,556	$14,791	$6,298	$4,104	$300	$4,805	$12,789
Age of Householder													
65 years and over	60,266	13,255	18,144	651	6,882	46,192	42,527	17,329	5,019	3,372	1,113	6,369	19,557
65 to 69 years	66,621	12,574	14,454	611	6,852	48,117	49,989	19,813	3,379	4,316	1,332	7,389	19,895
70 to 74 years	60,573	14,220	17,350	652	7,081	47,607	43,260	14,500	7,319	3,473	762	5,699	24,857
75 years and over	55,178	13,113	21,060	686	6,749	44,066	33,609	10,874	5,009	2,825	2,061	4,618	12,837
Type of Household													
Married-couple households	50,116	3,336	9,150	477	3,488	42,634	38,119	15,944	8,087	4,942	300	5,499	16,677
Age of spouse													
65 years and over	90,313	19,337	20,331	707	9,059	52,871	54,284	20,673	7,314	4,189	984	6,789	21,647
Other household type													
Male householder	9,883	2,091	8,368	481	4,098	30,238	32,676	10,933	5,157	3,102	283	4,262	5,448
65 years and over	41,208	12,946	14,358	914	13,717	38,567	(B)	(B)	(B)	3,111	2,178	(B)	10,774
Female householder	13,885	2,941	10,083	358	4,277	38,009	26,414	10,849	1,733	2,731	315	3,976	10,034
65 years and over	42,885	10,727	15,856	511	6,461	42,083	28,789	10,158	(B)	2,589	997	4,292	(B)

Notes: 1. Includes passbook savings accounts, money market deposit accounts, certificates of deposit, and interest-earning checking accounts.

2. Includes money market funds, U.S. Government securities, municipal and corporate bonds, and other interest-earning assets.

3. Includes mortgages held from sale of real estate, amount due from sale of a business, unit trusts, and other financial investments.

(B) Base is less than 200,000.

Source: U.S. Bureau of the Census, *Current Population Reports*, Series P-70, No. 7.

EXPENDITURES

Table 2–25. Selected Characteristics and Annual Expenditures of Urban Consumer Units Classified by Age of Reference Person: 1984

(Based on Consumer Expenditure Interview Survey)

Item	All consumer units*	65–74	75 and over
Total expenditures	$21,788	$15,873	$11,196
Food	3,391	2,831	1,912
Food at home	2,342	2,065	1,517
Food away from home	1,048	766	394
Alcoholic beverages	299	179	90
Housing	6,626	4,848	3,972
Shelter	3,747	2,386	2,014
Owned dwellings	2,188	1,378	1,009
Mortgage interest	1,342	272	119
Property taxes	433	569	428
Maintenance, repairs, insurance, other expenses	413	537	462
Rented dwellings	1,171	632	884
Other lodging	388	377	122
Utilities, fuels, and public services	1,679	1,644	1,311
Natural gas	342	379	301
Electricity	618	575	425
Fuel oil and other fuels	111	167	188
Telephone	453	358	269
Water and other public services	156	165	127
Household operations	333	269	356
Domestic services	270	184	314
Other household expenses	63	85	42
Housefurnishings and equipment	868	549	291
Household textiles	86	70	38
Furniture	275	129	70
Floor coverings	59	39	29
Major appliances	145	121	65
Small appliances, misc. housewares	64	45	20
Miscellaneous household equipment	239	145	68
Apparel and services	1,192	715	346
Men and boys	306	148	70
Men, 16 and over	248	133	65
Boys, 2 to 15	58	15	6
Women and girls	484	347	160
Women, 16 and over	407	328	152
Girls, 2 to 15	77	18	8
Children under 2	44	19	8
Footwear	130	84	39
Other apparel products and services	227	117	68
Transportation	$4,385	$3,041	$1,450
Cars and trucks, new (net outlay)	1,079	877	254
Cars and trucks, used (net outlay)	767	297	116
Other vehicles	27	(1)	2 14
Vehicle finance charges	219	77	30
Gasoline and motor oil	1,047	764	354
Maintenance and repairs	452	334	203
Vehicle insurance	358	298	197
Public transportation	288	302	238
Vehicle rental, licenses, other charges	147	92	44

Table 2–25. (continued)

Item	All consumer units*	65–74	75 and over
Health care	899	1,340	1,487
Health insurance	281	604	657
Medical services	466	484	555
Prescription drugs, medical supplies	153	251	275
Entertainment	1,040	604	291
Fees and admissions	348	266	139
Television, radios, sound equipment	326	173	107
Other equipment and services	366	165	44
Personal care	205	211	148
Reading	140	130	93
Education	312	88	[2]101
Tobacco and smoking supplies	225	173	65
Miscellaneous	311	172	135
Cash contributions	740	762	878
Personal insurance and pensions	2,023	778	229
Life and other personal insurance	302	220	86
Retirement, pensions, Social Security	1,721	558	142

Notes: *Definition of "Consumer Unit"*—A consumer unit, the basic reporting unit for the Diary survey, is comprised of either: (1) All members of a particular household who are related by blood, marriage, adoption, or other legal arrangement such as a foster child; (2) a person living alone or sharing a household with others or living as a roomer in a private home or lodging house or in permanent living quarters in a hotel or motel, but who is financially independent; or (3) two or more persons living together who pool their income to make joint expenditure decisions.

Financial independence is determined by the three major expense categories: housing, food, and other living expenses. To be considered financially independent, at least two of the three major expense categories have to be provided by the respondent.

1. No data reported.

2. Data are likely to have large sampling errors.

Source: U.S. Department of Labor. Bureau of Labor Statistics. *Consumer Expenditure Survey: Interview Survey, 1984.* Bulletin 2267 (1986)

Table 2–26. Expenditures and Income for Age Groups 60–64, 65–74, and 75 and Over: Interview Survey, 1972–73 and 1982–83

Item	1972–73			1982–83		
	60–64	65–74	75 and over	60–64	65–74	75 and over
Income before taxes	$12,362	$7,633	$5,491	$21,461	$15,515	$10,409
Income after taxes	n.a.	n.a.	n.a.	19,319	14,568	9,735
Total expenditures	8,699	6,410	4,551	18,148	14,127	9,411
Food, total	1,598	1,282	1,021	3,166	2,586	1,797
Food at home	1,261	1,050	888	2,190	1,876	1,409
Food away from home	337	232	134	976	710	388
Alcoholic beverages	73	46	23	243	172	70
Housing	2,252	1,900	1,568	5,199	4,470	3,550
Shelter	1,209	1,057	876	2,631	2,237	1,802
Fuels, utilities, and public services	572	491	407	1,657	1,464	1,141
Household operations	145	122	165	205	235	322
House furnishings and equipment	327	231	120	707	534	286
Apparel and services	619	425	236	944	643	304
Transportation	1,568	1,059	456	3,528	2,526	1,059
Vehicles	579	329	111	1,168	834	82
Gasoline and motor oil	376	252	109	1,042	752	356
Other vehicle expenses	496	369	165	1,016	704	363
Public transportation	117	109	71	301	236	111
Health care	506	459	438	1,139	1,274	1,154
Entertainment	299	189	100	802	511	189
Personal care	129	100	72	207	187	131
Reading	47	36	27	137	120	84
Education	116	31	12	120	67	11
Tobacco	122	80	32	204	147	64
Miscellaneous	84	36	29	280	224	157
Cash contributions	521	503	430	716	643	702
Personal insurance and pensions	766	265	107	1,462	559	141
Life and other personal insurance	365	147	68	276	204	71
Retirement, pensions, Social Security	401	118	39	1,186	354	69

Notes: n.a. – not available

Source: U.S. Department of Labor, Bureau of Labor Statistics, *Consumer Expenditure Survey: Interview Survey, 1984*, Bulletin 2267 (1986).

Table 2–27. Selected Characteristics and Weekly Expenditures of Urban Consumer Units for Food Items by Age of Reference Person

(Based on Consumer Expenditure Diary Survey)

Item	All consumer units*	65–74	75 and over
Number of consumer units (in thousands)	74,283	7,249	6,050
Number of sample diaries	10,589	1,047	818
Consumer unit characteristics:			
Income before taxes[1]	$23,389	$15,971	$11,284
Size of consumer unit	2.6	1.8	1.5
Age of reference person	46.0	69.7	80.6
Number in consumer unit			
Earners	1.3	.5	.2
Vehicles	1.4	1.2	.7
Children under 18	.7	.1	(2)
Persons 65 and over	.3	1.4	1.3
Percent homeowner	58	77	62
Average weekly expenditures			
Food, total	$57.71	$47.80	$31.84
Food at home, total	37.08	32.26	23.65
Cereals and cereal products	1.57	1.33	1.01
Bakery products	3.42	3.30	2.51
Beef	3.89	3.05	2.30
Pork	2.20	1.86	1.23
Other meats	1.53	1.27	.88
Poultry	1.62	1.34	1.01
Fish and seafood	1.30	1.25	.70
Eggs	.67	.59	.46
Fresh milk and cream	2.40	1.88	1.59
Other dairy products	2.40	2.11	1.48
Fresh fruits	1.86	1.99	1.54
Fresh vegetables	1.82	1.83	1.31
Processed fruits	1.39	1.38	1.12
Processed vegetables	1.08	.95	.71
Sugar and other sweets	1.39	1.26	.98
Fats and oils	1.02	.83	.72
Miscellaneous foods	4.14	3.19	2.03
Nonalcoholic beverages	3.38	2.85	2.08
Food away from home	20.63	15.55	8.19

Notes: * *Definition of "Consumer Unit"*—A consumer unit, the basic reporting unit for the Diary survey, is comprised of either: (1) All members of a particular household who are related by blood, marriage, adoption, or other legal arrangement such as a foster child; (2) a person living alone or sharing a household with others or living as a roomer in a private home or lodging house or in permanent living quarters in a hotel or motel, but who is financially independent; or (3) two or more persons living together who pool their income to make joint expenditure decisions.

Financial independence is determined by the three major expense categories: housing, food, and other living expenses. To be considered financially independent, at least two of the three major expense categories have to be provided by the respondent.

1. Income values are derived from "complete income reporters only." Represents the combined income of all consumer unit members 14 years old or over during the 12 months preceding the interview. A complete reporter is a consumer unit who provided at least one of the major sources of its income.

2. Value less than .05

Source: U.S. Department of Labor, Bureau of Labor Statistics, *Consumer Expenditure Diary Survey: Results From 1984* (BLS News Release USDL 86-258).

Figure 2-7. Charitable Contributions by Age

(Covers population 18 years and over. Data exclude those respondents who (1) reported giving, but did not report a specific amount; (2) did not respond at all; and (3) reported "not sure or no answer" to particular questions. Based on a sample survey of 1,151 persons and subject to sampling variability.)

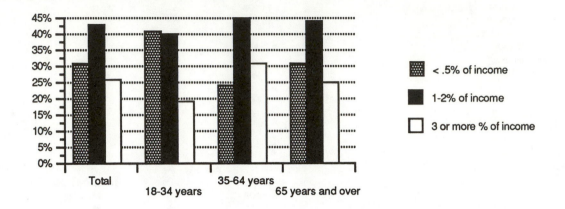

Source: Independent Sector, Washington, D.C. *The Charitable Behavior of Americans,* 1986 (copyright by the Rockefeller Brothers Fund.)

CREDIT AND DEBT

Table 2-28. Families Using Selected Financial Services, 1983

(In percent)

AGE OF HEAD AND 1982 FAMILY INCOME	CREDIT CARDS						Money market deposit account	Money market mutual fund account	Brokerage account
	At least one	Gasoline	Bank	Travel and entertainment	Any retail	Other[1]			
All families	62	26	40	9	54	4	8	6	7
55–64 years	72	37	50	11	62	5	12	7	9
65–74 years	60	26	37	5	53	2	14	7	9
75 years and over	35	15	16	(²)	26	1	10	4	2

Notes: 1. Comprises airline and automobile rental cards, and other miscellaneous credit cards.

2. Less than .5 percent.

Source: Board of Governors of the Federal Reserve System, *Federal Reserve Bulletin,* monthly; *Annual Statistical Digest;* and unpublished data.

Table 2–29. Average Consumer Debt for Households With Householder Age 65 or Over

(Average consumer debt for all households with debt, percent of households with consumer debt; by household income and age of householder, 1983)

Age of household head	All households		Household income												
			Under $10,000		$10,000–19,999		$20,000–29,999		$30,000–39,999		$40,000–49,999		$50,000–and over	
	Average consumer debt	Percent with debt	Average consumer debt	Percent with debt	Average consumer debt	Percent with debt	Average consumer debt	Percent with debt	Average consumer debt	Percent with debt	Average consumer debt	Percent with debt	Average consumer debt	Percent with debt
65 and over	$3,000	24%	$1,305	21%	$1,718	34%	$3,324	34%	$4,881	42%	$17,031	16%	$11,826	35%
All	6,053	59	3,205	39	3,723	61	4,725	73	5,687	78	7,432	78	15,629	73

Note: Consumer debt consists of credit card and other open-end debt, installment debt, and noninstallment debt from various sources. Consumer debt does not include mortgages. Average debt is for all households with debt.

Source: 1983 Survey of Consumer Finances, Federal Reserve Board.

Figure 2–8. Percent of Householders Age 65 and Over Who Believe It Is All Right to Use Installment Debt for Different Purchases: 1983

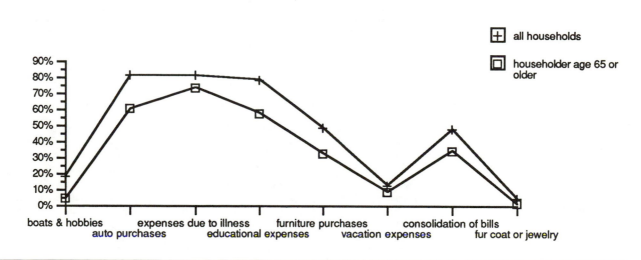

Source: Federal Reserve Board. *1983 Survey of Consumer Finances.*

Table 2–30. Mortgage and Consumer Debt Outstanding— Families With Debt and Amount, Family Head Age 65 and Over: 1983

(Families include one-person units. Based on a sample survey of 3,024 families residing in the coterminous United States, excluding those on military reservations. Data are subject to sampling variability.)

	Mortgage Debt[1]					Consumer Debt					
	Percent of homeowners with debt[2]			Amount outstanding [3, 4] (dollars)		Per-cent of fami-lies with debt[5]	Amount outstanding[4, 5] (dollars)		Percent of families with installment debt		
		Ratio of monthly debt payments to monthly income								Ratio of monthly debt payments to monthly income	
Age of Family Head and 1982 Family Income	Total	1–9 per-cent	10–19 per-cent	20 per-cent or more	Mean	Medi-an		Mean	Medi-an	Total	1–9 per-cent	10–19 per-cent	20 per-cent or more
All families	57%	29%	18%	10%	$27,147	$21,010	62%	$5,400	$2,382	41%	25%	11%	5%
65–74 years	20	10	6	3	14,703	10,067	31	3,537	943	14	7	4	3
75 years and over	5	3	1	1	11,029	9,981	15	1,117	308	6	2	2	2

Notes: 1. Includes farm families and owners of mobile homes.
   2. Represents homeowners with regular monthly mortgage payments.
   3. Consists of first and second mortgage debt outstanding.
   4. Values are for families with outstanding debt.
   5. Consists of credit card and other open-end debt, installment debt, and noninstallment consumer debt from all sources for all families.

Source: Board of Governors of the Federal Reserve System, *Federal Reserve Bulletin*, December 1984.

POVERTY LEVEL

Table 2–31. Persons 65 Years Old and Over Below Poverty Level, by Selected Characteristics: 1970 to 1985

(Persons as of March of following year)

| Characteristic | Number Below Poverty Level (1,000) | | | | | Percent Below Poverty Level | | | | |
	1970	1979[1]	1983	1984	1985	1970	1979[1]	1983	1984	1985
Persons, 65 yr. and over[2]	4,793	3,682	3,730	3,330	3,456	24.6	15.2	14.2	12.4	12.6
White	4,011	2,911	2,875	2,579	2,698	22.6	13.3	12.1	10.7	11.0
Black	735	740	796	710	717	47.7	36.3	36.2	31.7	31.5
Spanish origin[3]	(NA)	154	178	176	219	(NA)	26.8	22.7	21.5	23.9
In families	2,013	1,380	1,439	1,205	1,173	14.8	8.4	8.1	6.7	6.4
Householder	1,188	822	844	713	708	16.5	9.1	8.7	7.3	7.0
Male	980	629	581	489	498	15.9	8.4	7.3	6.0	6.0
Female	209	193	263	224	210	20.1	13.0	15.5	13.0	12.1
Other members	825	559	595	493	465	13.0	7.6	7.4	6.0	5.6
Unrelated individuals	2,779	2,299	2,279	2,123	2,281	47.2	29.4	26.6	24.2	25.6
Male	549	428	426	401	402	38.9	25.3	22.6	20.8	20.5
Female	2,230	1,871	1,853	1,722	1,879	49.8	30.5	27.7	25.2	27.0
Persons, 60 yr. and over	5,977	4,753	4,973	4,496	4,677	21.3	13.9	13.4	12.0	12.3

Notes: (NA) Not available.
   1. Population controls based on 1980 census.
   2. Beginning 1979, includes members of unrelated subfamilies not shown separately. For earlier years, unrelated subfamily members are included in the "in families" category.
   3. Persons of Spanish origin may be of any race.

Source: U.S. Bureau of the Census, *Current Population Reports*, Series P-60, No. 154, and unpublished data.

Table 2–32. Selected Characteristics of the Aged—Poverty Status in 1984 of Persons 65 Years and Over, by Age and Sex

(Numbers in thousands, persons as of March 1985)

Characteristic	All Income Levels 65 Years Old and Over			Below Poverty Level 65 Years Old and Over		
	Total	65 to 71 years	72 Years and over	Total	65 to 71 years	72 Years and over
Both Sexes						
Family status and composition						
Total	26,818	12,511	14,307	3,330	1,208	2,122
In families	18,038	9,390	8,647	1,205	559	646
Householder	9,806	5,098	4,708	713	325	388
With related children under 18 years	621	410	212	178	106	72
Mean number of children	1.66	1.70	1.59	2.07	2.33	(B)
Mean size of family	2.38	2.45	2.30	2.84	3.21	2.53
Spouse of householder	6,096	3,661	2,435	371	191	179
Other family members	2,136	631	1,504	122	42	79
In related subfamilies	154	74	80	37	18	20
Married, spouse present	151	74	77	35	18	17
Other	3	—	3	3	—	3
In unrelated subfamilies	17	4	13	1	—	1
Unrelated Individuals	8,763	3,117	5,647	2,123	649	1,475
Living alone	8,111	2,833	5,278	1,913	556	1,357
Living with nonrelatives	652	284	368	210	93	118
In households	537	249	289	176	83	93
In group quarters	115	35	80	34	10	24
Marital status						
Total	26,818	12,511	14,307	3,330	1,208	2,122
Single	1,392	607	785	257	93	165
Married, spouse present	14,317	8,085	6,232	855	414	441
Married, spouse absent	494	282	213	145	81	63
Separated	295	194	101	89	55	34
Other	199	88	112	56	27	29
Widowed	9,535	2,906	6,629	1,817	481	1,336
Divorced	1,081	632	448	256	139	117
Work Experience						
Persons[1]	26,818	12,511	14,307	3,330	1,208	2,122
Worked last year	4,059	2,853	1,206	151	88	63
50 to 52 weeks	2,089	1,522	567	63	39	24
Full time	1,140	890	249	37	27	11
49 weeks or less	1,970	1,331	639	87	49	38
Full time	646	493	153	28	18	11
Main reason for working part year:						
Ill or disabled	245	159	86	22	8	14
Keeping house	215	153	61	13	6	6
Unable to find work	121	82	40	8	4	4
Retired	1,113	749	365	32	22	10
Other	276	189	87	13	9	3
Mean number of weeks worked	38.1	38.5	37.1	33.2	33.9	(B)
Did not work last year	22,759	9,658	13,101	3,179	1,120	2,059
Main reason for not working:						
Ill or disabled	3,374	1,263	2,111	879	318	561
Keeping house	4,691	2,367	2,324	582	238	343
Unable to find work	56	35	22	19	12	7
Retired	14,432	5,912	8,519	1,653	535	1,118
Other	206	80	125	46	16	30

Table 2–32. (continued)

Characteristic	All Income Levels 65 Years Old and Over			Below Poverty Level 65 Years Old and Over		
	Total	65 to 71 years	72 Years and over	Total	65 to 71 years	72 Years and over
Family householders[1]	9,806	5,098	4,708	713	325	388
Worked last year	2,143	1,553	590	67	43	23
50 to 52 weeks	1,150	881	269	33	24	8
Full time	679	553	126	18	15	3
49 weeks or less	993	672	321	34	19	15
Full time	347	276	71	14	10	4
Main reason for working part year:						
Ill or disabled	116	74	42	8	3	5
Keeping house	45	33	13	3	1	1
Unable to find work	57	40	17	4	2	2
Retired	666	450	216	13	8	4
Other	109	75	33	6	5	2
Mean number of weeks worked	38.7	39.6	36.3	(B)	(B)	(B)
Did not work last year	7,663	3,545	4,118	646	282	364
Main reason for not working:						
Ill or disabled	1,063	455	608	189	82	107
Keeping house	463	235	228	59	34	25
Unable to find work	19	14	5	2	1	2
Retired	6,105	2,833	3,271	394	165	229
Other	13	7	6	2	—	2
Unrelated individuals[1]	8,763	3,117	5,647	2,123	649	1,475
Worked last year	1,107	666	441	70	34	35
50 to 52 weeks	548	342	206	26	11	15
Full time	252	174	78	17	9	8
49 weeks or less	560	325	235	44	23	21
Full time	156	94	62	11	6	5
Main reason for working part year:						
Ill or disabled	87	50	37	13	5	9
Keeping house	51	28	23	6	2	5
Unable to find work	54	32	22	3	2	2
Retired	257	144	112	14	10	4
Other	112	71	41	6	5	2
Mean number of weeks worked	38.5	38.9	37.9	(B)	(B)	(B)
Did not work last year	7,656	2,450	5,206	2,054	614	1,440
Main reason for not working:						
Ill or disabled	1,389	465	924	573	179	395
Keeping house	1,203	390	813	330	107	223
Unable to find work	26	12	14	12	9	3
Retired	4,914	1,530	3,384	1,098	303	795
Other	125	54	71	40	16	24
Source of Income						
Persons	26,818	12,511	14,307	3,330	1,208	2,122
Earnings only	148	126	22	15	14	1
Wage or salary income only	132	114	18	12	11	1
Self-employment income only	16	12	4	4	3	1
Wage or salary and self-employment income	—	—	—	—	—	—
Earnings and income other than earnings	3,892	2,712	1,181	134	73	61
Earnings and social security income only	516	365	151	39	22	17
Earnings and supplemental security income only	16	11	6	4	3	2
Earnings, social security, and supplemental security income only	17	8	9	6	6	—
Earnings and other income only	3,338	2,323	1,015	85	43	42
Other combinations	5	5	—	—	—	—

Table 2–32. (continued)

Characteristic	All Income Levels 65 Years Old and Over			Below Poverty Level 65 Years Old and Over		
	Total	65 to 71 years	72 Years and over	Total	65 to 71 years	72 Years and over
Income other than earnings only	22,482	9,515	12,967	3,063	1,067	1,996
Social security income only	3,889	1,563	2,326	1,076	390	686
Supplemental security income only	328	104	224	171	61	110
Other income only	346	181	165	74	39	35
Other transfer payments only[2]	38	22	16	17	12	5
Social security and supplemental security income only	1,025	316	709	602	195	407
Social security and other income only	16,348	7,126	9,222	1,067	354	714
Social security income and other transfer payments only[2]	417	169	248	71	14	57
Social security and "all other" income only[3]	15,931	6,957	8,974	997	340	657
Other combinations	547	226	321	72	28	44
No income	296	158	137	117	54	63
Family householders	9,806	5,098	4,708	713	325	388
Earnings only	71	66	6	9	9	—
Wage or salary income only	59	55	4	6	6	—
Self-employment income only	12	11	2	3	3	—
Wage or salary and self-employment income	—	—	—	—	—	—
Earnings and income other than earnings	2,067	1,483	583	58	35	23
Earnings and social security income only	226	158	69	17	10	7
Earnings and supplemental security income only	3	2	1	2	1	1
Earnings, social security, and supplemental security income only	5	1	4	—	—	—
Earnings and other income only	1,832	1,323	509	39	23	15
Other combinations	—	—	—	—	—	—
Income other than earnings only	7,622	3,530	4,092	619	272	347
Social security income only	1,044	465	579	219	105	115
Supplemental security income only	82	23	59	35	12	23
Other income only	81	47	33	20	9	11
Other transfer payments only[2]	12	8	4	6	2	4
Social security and supplemental security income only	255	76	179	109	37	72
Social security and other income only	5,960	2,817	3,144	219	100	119
Social security income and other transfer payments only[2]	152	87	65	9	4	4
Social security and "all other" income only[3]	5,808	2,729	3,079	210	96	114
Other combinations	200	102	97	16	9	7
No income	46	19	27	27	9	17
Unrelated Individuals	8,763	3,117	5,647	2,123	649	1,475
Earnings only	26	19	7	4	2	1
Wage or salary income only	26	19	7	3	2	1
Self-employment income only	1	—	1	1	—	1
Wage or salary and self-employment income	—	—	—	—	—	—
Earnings and income other than earnings	1,080	648	432	66	32	34
Earnings and social security income only	154	100	54	18	9	8
Earnings and supplemental security income only	11	6	5	2	1	1
Earnings, social security, and supplemental security income only	12	7	5	6	6	—
Earnings and other income only	897	529	369	40	15	25
Other combinations	5	5	—	—	—	—
Income other than earnings only	7,614	2,432	5,182	2,011	596	1,415
Social security income only	1,186	357	829	675	206	469

Table 2–32. (continued)

Characteristic	All Income Levels 65 Years Old and Over			Below Poverty Level 65 Years Old and Over		
	Total	65 to 71 years	72 Years and over	Total	65 to 71 years	72 Years and over
Supplemental security income only	118	45	72	108	41	67
Other income only	88	41	47	37	19	18
Other transfer payments only[2]	17	12	5	10	9	—
Social security and supplemental security income only	551	162	389	422	122	299
Social security and other income only	5,461	1,767	3,694	723	192	531
Social security income and other transfer payments only[2]	220	61	158	60	10	50
Social security and "all other" income only[3]	5,242	1,706	3,536	663	182	480
Other combinations	210	59	151	46	16	31
No income	43	18	25	43	18	25
Type of Income						
Persons	26,818	12,511	14,307	3,330	1,208	2,122
Earnings[4]	4,040	2,838	1,202	149	87	63
Wage and salary income	3,296	2,382	913	98	57	41
Nonfarm self-employment income	665	412	253	27	14	14
Farm self-employment income	244	157	88	30	21	10
Income other than earnings	26,375	12,227	14,147	3,197	1,140	2,057
Social security income	24,569	11,185	13,384	2,859	998	1,860
Supplemental security income	1,811	611	1,200	984	337	647
Other transfer payments[2]	1,410	699	711	254	91	163
Dividends, interest, and rent	18,406	8,795	9,612	968	315	653
Private pensions, government employee pensions, alimony, annuities, etc.	8,382	4,227	4,155	234	123	110
No income	296	158	137	117	54	63
Family householders	9,806	5,098	4,708	713	325	388
Earnings[4]	2,138	1,549	589	67	43	23
Wage and salary income	1,629	1,219	410	35	20	14
Nonfarm self-employment income	435	286	149	11	8	3
Farm self-employment income	183	119	63	25	17	8
Income other than earnings[4]	9,688	5,013	4,675	677	307	370
Social security income	8,966	4,496	4,470	595	271	324
Supplemental security income	422	144	278	169	64	105
Other transfer payments[2]	610	394	216	59	33	27
Dividends, interest, and rent	7,136	3,735	3,401	203	86	117
Private pensions, government employee pensions, alimony, annuities, etc.	4,254	2,364	1,890	77	43	33
No income	46	19	27	27	9	17
Unrelated individuals	8,763	3,117	5,647	2,123	649	1,475
Earnings[4]	1,106	666	440	70	34	35
Wage and salary income	963	596	367	52	29	23
Nonfarm self-employment income	146	74	72	14	4	11
Farm self-employment income	37	26	11	6	4	2
Income other than earnings[4]	8,694	3,080	5,615	2,077	628	1,449
Social security income	8,166	2,845	5,321	1,878	545	1,332
Supplemental security income	966	317	648	704	227	477
Other transfer payments[2]	635	231	404	179	48	131
Dividends, interest, and rent	5,808	2,068	3,740	634	167	467
Private pensions, government employee pensions, alimony, annuities, etc.	2,769	1,143	1,626	138	63	75
No income	43	18	25	43	18	25
Tenure and living arrangements						
All persons	26,818	12,511	14,307	3,330	1,208	2,122

Table 2–32. (continued)

Characteristic	All Income Levels 65 Years Old and Over			Below Poverty Level 65 Years Old and Over		
	Total	65 to 71 years	72 Years and over	Total	65 to 71 years	72 Years and over
Living with relatives	18,038	9,390	8,647	1,205	559	646
Owner-occupied units	15,561	8,208	7,353	917	421	496
Renter-occupied units	2,476	1,182	1,294	289	138	150
Public	203	104	99	48	27	21
Private	2,274	1,078	1,195	241	111	130
Subsidized	101	29	73	6	2	3
Family householders	9,806	5,098	4,708	713	325	388
Owner-occupied units	8,465	4,456	4,009	543	240	302
Renter-occupied units	1,341	642	699	170	85	85
Public	115	59	56	36	20	16
Private	1,226	583	643	134	65	69
Subsidized	56	12	44	3	2	2
Living with nonrelatives only	669	288	381	211	93	119
Owner-occupied units	405	168	237	110	44	66
Renter-occupied units	264	120	144	101	49	52
Public	9	6	4	5	3	2
Private	255	114	141	96	46	51
	11	6	5	6	4	3
Living alone	8,111	2,833	5,278	1,913	556	1,357
Owner-occupied units	5,046	1,812	3,233	978	275	703
Renter-occupied units	3,065	1,021	2,045	935	281	655
Public	652	181	471	274	71	204
Private	2,413	840	1,574	661	210	451
Subsidized	323	91	232	126	37	89
Female						
Family status and composition						
Total	15,804	6,963	8,841	2,370	825	1,545
In families	8,964	4,617	4,347	647	304	343
Householder	1,721	784	937	224	106	117
With related children under 18 years	270	164	106	94	52	42
Mean number of children	1.73	1.88	1.49	2.05	(B)	(B)
Mean size of family	2.74	2.85	2.65	3.30	3.72	2.92
Spouse of householder	5,728	3,464	2,264	340	171	169
Other family members	1,514	369	1,145	84	27	57
In related subfamilies	60	26	34	16	7	9
Married, spouse present	57	26	32	14	7	6
Other	3	—	3	3	—	3
In related subfamilies	8	—	8	1	—	1
Unrelated individuals	6,832	2,346	4,486	1,722	521	1,201
Living alone	6,497	2,224	4,274	1,599	470	1,129
Living with nonrelative	335	122	213	123	50	73
In households	278	116	162	103	48	55
In group quarters	57	6	51	20	2	18
Marital status						
Total	15,804	6,963	8,841	2,370	825	1,545
Single	811	298	514	146	52	95
Married, spouse present	6,057	3,666	2,392	358	183	175
Married, spouse absent	250	145	106	90	51	39
Separated	139	89	50	52	30	22
Other	112	55	56	38	21	17
Widowed	8,012	2,452	5,560	1,609	448	1,161
Divorced	674	404	270	167	91	75

Table 2–32. (continued)

Characteristic	All Income Levels 65 Years Old and Over			Below Poverty Level 65 Years Old and Over		
	Total	65 to 71 years	72 Years and over	Total	65 to 71 years	72 Years and over
Work experience						
Persons	15,804	6,963	8,841	2,370	825	1,545
Worked last year	1,656	1,165	491	67	36	31
50 to 52 weeks	791	563	227	23	9	13
Full-time	338	264	73	11	5	6
49 weeks or less	866	602	264	45	27	18
Full-time	250	196	54	11	6	5
Main reason for working part year:						
Ill or disabled	90	57	33	11	7	4
Keeping house	207	150	56	13	6	6
Unable to find work	52	37	14	2	2	—
Retired	373	255	118	14	9	5
Other	144	103	41	5	3	2
Mean number of weeks worked	37.1	37.0	37.2	(B)	(B)	(B)
Did not work last year	14,147	5,798	8,350	2,303	789	1,514
Main reason for not working:						
Ill or disabled	2,316	798	1,518	650	224	426
Keeping house	4,642	2,334	2,308	576	234	342
Unable to find work	23	13	10	10	5	5
Retired	6,984	2,584	4,400	1,024	310	714
Other	182	69	113	44	16	28
Family householders	1,721	784	937	224	106	117
Worked last year	218	162	56	12	7	5
50 to 52 weeks	120	92	28	6	4	2
Full-time	50	43	7	2	2	—
49 weeks or less	98	71	28	6	3	3
Full-time	33	25	8	1	—	1
Main reason for working part year:						
Ill or disabled	10	5	4	4	2	2
Keeping house	37	30	8	3	1	1
Unable to find work	5	4	2	—	—	—
Retired	33	20	13	—	—	—
Other	13	12	1	—	—	—
Mean number of weeks worked	39.2	39.7	(B)	(B)	(B)	(B)
Did not work last year	1,503	622	881	211	99	112
Main reason for not working:						
Ill or disabled	356	122	234	68	25	43
Keeping house	436	218	218	55	31	23
Unable to find work	6	5	1	—	—	—
Retired	696	270	427	89	43	46
Other	9	7	2	—	—	—
Unrelated individuals	6,832	2,346	4,486	1,722	521	1,201
Worked last year	780	477	303	43	21	22
50 to 52 weeks	365	232	133	12	2	10
Full-time	139	98	41	6	—	6
49 weeks or less	415	245	170	31	19	12
Full-time	105	68	38	7	4	2
Main reason for working part year:						
Ill or disabled	51	26	24	7	5	2
Keeping house	51	28	23	6	2	5
Unable to find work	38	25	12	2	2	—

Table 2–32. (continued)

Characteristic	All Income Levels 65 Years Old and Over			Below Poverty Level 65 Years Old and Over		
	Total	65 to 71 years	72 Years and over	Total	65 to 71 years	72 Years and over
Retired	187	106	80	11	8	3
Other	90	59	30	5	3	2
Mean number of weeks worked	38.3	38.9	37.3	(B)	(B)	(B)
Did not work last year	6,052	1,869	4,183	1,679	500	1,179
Main reason for not working:						
Ill or disabled	1,168	379	789	484	149	335
Keeping house	1,192	383	809	329	106	223
Unable to find work	12	4	8	7	4	3
Retired	3,564	1,055	2,509	819	225	594
Other	116	48	68	40	16	24
Source of Income						
Persons	15,804	6,963	8,841	2,370	825	545
Earnings only	59	51	8	6	5	1
Wage or salary income only	58	50	8	6	5	1
Self-employment income only	—	—	—	—	—	—
Wage or salary and self-employment income	—	—	—	—	—	—
Earnings and income other than earnings	1,586	1,102	484	61	30	30
Earnings and social security income only	240	180	59	13	5	8
Earnings and supplemental security income only	5	4	—	1	1	—
Earnings, social security, and supplemental security income only	12	5	7	3	3	—
Earnings and other income only	1,327	909	418	42	20	22
Other combinations	3	3	—	—	—	—
Income other than earnings only	13,939	5,694	8,245	2,227	753	1,473
Social security income only	2,749	1,097	1,652	803	293	510
Supplemental security income only	246	81	166	127	46	81
Other income only	241	117	125	40	15	25
Other transfer payments only[2]	19	8	11	12	8	4
Social security and supplemental security income only	761	242	519	446	154	292
Social security and other income only	9,635	4,046	5,589	771	236	535
Social security income and other transfer payments only[2]	227	64	164	54	10	43
Social security and "all other" income only[3]	9,408	3,982	5,426	717	226	491
Other combinations	307	112	195	41	11	30
No income	220	117	103	77	36	41
Family householders	1,721	784	937	224	106	117
Earnings only	13	12	1	4	4	—
Wage or salary income only	13	12	1	4	4	—
Self-employment income only	—	—	—	—	—	—
Wage or salary and self-employment income	—	—	—	—	—	—
Earnings and income other than earnings	203	149	54	9	4	5
Earnings and social security income only	34	32	2	2	—	2
Earnings and supplemental security income only	—	—	—	—	—	—
Earnings, social security, and supplemental security income only	5	1	4	—	—	—
Earnings and other income only	164	116	49	7	4	3
Other combinations	—	—	—	—	—	—
Income other than earnings only	1,480	614	866	203	98	105
Social security income only	373	163	210	85	47	38
Supplemental security income only	54	20	35	20	11	9

Table 2–32. (continued)

Characteristic	All Income Levels 65 Years Old and Over			Below Poverty Level 65 Years Old and Over		
	Total	65 to 71 years	72 Years and over	Total	65 to 71 years	72 Years and over
Other income only	18	6	11	5	—	5
Other transfer payments only[2]	3	—	3	3	—	3
Social security and supplemental security income only	123	43	80	38	15	23
Social security and other income only	867	362	506	53	23	30
Social security income and other transfer payments only[2]	35	13	22	2	2	—
Social security and "all other" income only[3]	832	348	484	51	21	30
Other combinations	44	20	24	2	2	—
No income	25	9	16	8	2	7
Unrelated individuals	6,832	2,346	4,486	1,722	521	1,201
Earnings only	16	13	3	1	—	1
Wage or salary income only	16	13	3	1	—	1
Self-employment income only	—	—	—	—	—	—
Wage or salary and self-employment income	—	—	—	—	—	—
Earnings and income other than earnings	764	464	300	42	20	21
Earnings and social security income only	101	64	37	7	3	4
Earnings and supplemental security income only	5	4	—	1	1	—
Earnings, social security, and supplemental security income only	7	4	3	3	3	—
Earnings and other income only	649	389	260	29	12	17
Other combinations	3	3	—	—	—	—
Income other than earnings only	6,022	1,856	4,166	1,650	487	1,162
Social security income only	951	282	670	560	179	382
Supplemental security income only	94	34	60	84	29	55
Other income only	60	23	37	22	7	15
Other transfer payments only[2]	10	7	3	7	7	—
Social security and supplemental security income only	447	134	313	342	104	238
Social security and other income only	4,312	1,348	2,964	607	162	445
Social security income and other transfer payments only[2]	164	39	125	49	8	41
Social security and "all other" income only[3]	4,148	1,309	2,839	558	154	404
Other combinations	157	35	122	35	7	28
No income	30	13	17	30	13	17
Type of income						
Persons	15,804	6,963	8,841	2,370	825	1,545
Earnings[4]	1,645	1,152	492	66	35	31
Wage and salary income	1,471	1,056	415	58	32	26
Nonfarm self-employment income	184	106	78	11	4	7
Farm self-employment income	33	18	15	—	—	—
Income other than earnings[4]	15,525	6,796	8,729	2,287	784	1,503
Social security income	14,549	6,327	8,223	2,070	705	1,365
Supplemental security income	1,336	452	884	738	263	475
Other transfer payments[2]	643	223	420	172	44	128
Dividends, interest, and rent	10,515	4,773	5,742	693	212	481
Private pensions, government employee pensions, alimony, annuities, etc.	3,462	1,595	1,867	128	62	66
No income	220	117	103	77	36	41
Family householders	1,721	784	937	224	106	117
Earnings[4]	217	161	56	12	7	5
Wage and salary income	190	143	48	12	7	5

Table 2–32. (continued)

Characteristic	All Income Levels 65 Years Old and Over			Below Poverty Level 65 Years Old and Over		
	Total	65 to 71 years	72 Years and over	Total	65 to 71 years	72 Years and over
Nonfarm self-employment income	35	24	11	2	—	2
Farm self-employment income	4	2	2	—	—	—
Income other than earnings[4]	1,683	763	920	212	101	110
Social security income	1,536	688	848	183	87	96
Supplemental security income	217	85	132	69	33	37
Other transfer payments[2]	116	52	64	25	9	16
Dividends, interest, and rent	933	415	517	45	21	24
Private pensions, government employee pensions, alimony, annuities, etc.	396	196	201	9	6	4
No income	25	9	16	8	2	7
Unrelated individuals	6,832	2,346	4,486	1,722	521	1,201
Earnings[4]	780	477	303	43	21	22
Wage and salary income	703	440	263	36	19	17
Nonfarm self-employment income	82	40	42	7	1	5
Farm self-employment income	12	10	2	—	—	—
Income other than earnings[4]	6,786	2,321	4,466	1,691	508	1,183
Social security income	6,413	2,173	4,239	1,545	460	1,086
Supplemental security income	779	249	530	572	187	385
Other transfer payments[2]	427	131	296	134	29	106
Dividends, interest, and rent	4,608	1,586	3,022	532	139	394
Private pensions, government employee pensions, alimony, annuities, etc.	2,005	821	1,184	108	45	62
No income	30	13	17	30	13	17
Tenure and living arrangements						
All persons	15,804	6,963	8,841	2,370	825	1,545
Living with relatives	8,904	4,817	4,047	847	304	343
Owner-occupied units	7,586	3,954	3,632	479	221	258
Renter-occupied units	1,378	663	715	168	83	85
Public	119	66	54	30	19	11
Private	1,259	597	662	138	64	74
Subsidized	57	18	39	3	—	3
Family householders	1,721	784	937	224	106	117
Owner-occupied units	1,330	588	742	151	66	85
Renter-occupied units	391	196	195	72	40	32
Public	42	28	14	18	12	6
Private	349	168	182	54	28	26
Subsidized	15	1	14	1	—	1
Living with nonrelatives only	343	122	220	124	50	74
Owner-occupied units	212	74	138	66	27	40
Renter-occupied units	131	49	82	57	23	34
Public	6	2	4	2	—	2
Private	125	46	78	56	23	32
Subsidized	8	3	5	5	3	3
Living alone	6,497	2,224	4,274	1,599	470	1,129
Owner-occupied units	4,094	1,454	2,639	840	249	591
Renter-occupied units	2,404	769	1,634	759	221	538
Public	540	152	388	240	64	176
Private	1,864	617	1,247	519	157	362
Subsidized	282	74	207	109	31	78

Notes: 1. Includes members of the armed forces, not shown separately.

2. "Other transfer payments" includes public assistance, unemployment compensation, workmen's compensation, and veterans' payments.

3. "All Other" income includes dividends, interest, rent, private pensions, government employee pensions, alimony, and annuity income.

4. Detail does not add to total because some persons receive more than one of the specified types of income.

Source: U.S. Bureau of the Census. *Current Population Reports,* Series P-60, No. 152.

III

EMPLOYMENT AND UNEMPLOYMENT

EMPLOYMENT

Figure 3-1. Civilian Labor Force by Age: 1985

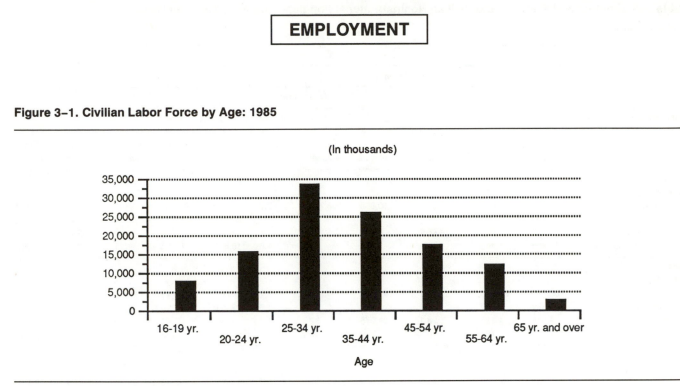

(In thousands)

Age

Source: U.S. Bureau of Labor Statistics. *Employment and Earnings,* monthly.

Table 3-1. Civilian Labor Force and Participation Rates, Sex, and Age 65 and Over, 1970 to 1985, and Projections, 1990 and 1995

(For civilian noninstitutional population 16 years old and over. Annual averages of monthly figures. Rates are based on annual average civilian noninstitutional population of each specified group and represent proportion of each specified group in the civilian labor force. Based on Current Population Survey.)

Sex and Age	Civilian Labor Force (millions)							Participation Rate (percent)						
	1970	1975	1980	1984	1985	1990	1995	1970	1975	1980	1984	1985	1990	1995
Total	**82.8**	**93.8**	**106.9**	**113.5**	**115.5**	**122.7**	**129.2**	**60.4**	**61.2**	**63.8**	**64.4**	**64.8**	**65.7**	**66.6**
Male	51.2	56.3	61.5	63.8	64.4	67.1	69.3	79.7	77.9	77.4	76.4	76.3	75.8	75.3
65 years and over	2.2	1.9	1.9	1.8	1.8	1.6	1.4	26.8	21.6	19.0	16.3	15.8	13.2	11.0
Female	31.5	37.5	45.5	49.7	51.1	55.5	59.9	43.3	46.3	51.5	53.6	54.5	56.6	58.9
65 years and over	1.1	1.0	1.2	1.2	1.2	1.1	1.0	9.7	8.2	8.1	7.5	7.3	6.4	5.5

Source: U.S. Bureau of Labor Statistics, *Employment and Earnings,* monthly; *Monthly Labor Review,* November 1985; and unpublished data.

Table 3-2. Employment Status of the Civilian Noninstitutional Population by Age, Sex, and Race

(Numbers in thousands)

Age, sex, and race	Civilian noninstitutional population	June 1986									
		Civilian labor force					Not in labor force				
					Unemployed						
		Total	Percent of population	Employed	Number	Percent of labor force	Total	Keeping house	Going to school	Unable to work	Other reasons
TOTAL											
Total employed,											
16 years and over	180,503	119,644	66.3	110,869	8,775	7.3	60,859	29,838	4,101	2,780	24,140
65 years and over	27,481	3,071	11.2	2,978	93	3.0	24,410	9,554	9	1,089	13,758
65 to 69 years	9,525	1,925	20.2	1,854	71	3.7	7,600	3,098	8	236	4,257
70 years and over	17,955	1,145	6.4	1,124	21	1.8	16,811	6,456	1	852	9,502
Men											
Total employed,											
16 years and over	85,763	66,678	77.7	61,960	4,718	7.1	19,085	491	2,073	1,575	14,947
65 years and over	11,337	1,852	16.3	1,784	67	3.6	9,486	214	2	412	8,857
65 to 69 years	4,318	1,127	26.1	1,075	52	4.7	3,191	61	3	129	2,998
70 years and over	7,019	724	10.3	710	15	2.0	6,295	153	–	283	5,859
Women											
Total employed,											
16 years and over	94,740	52,966	55.9	48,909	4,057	7.7	41,774	29,347	2,028	1,206	9,193
65 years and over	16,143	1,219	7.6	1,193	26	2.1	14,924	9,340	6	677	4,901
65 to 69 years	5,207	798	15.3	779	19	2.4	4,409	3,037	5	107	1,259
70 years and over	10,936	421	3.8	414	6	1.5	10,516	6,303	1	569	3,643
WHITE											
Total employed,											
16 years and over	155,376	103,253	66.5	96,823	6,430	6.2	52,123	26,148	2,937	2,214	20,824
65 years and over	24,757	2,787	11.3	2,707	80	2.9	21,970	8,741	7	894	12,328
65 to 69 years	8,503	1,726	20.3	1,666	60	3.5	6,778	2,768	7	201	3,802
70 years and over	16,252	1,061	6.5	1,041	21	2.0	15,192	5,973	1	693	8,526
Men											
Total employed,											
16 years and over	74,367	58,246	78.3	54,739	3,507	6.0	16,121	376	1,487	1,271	12,987
65 years and over	10,218	1,704	16.7	1,643	61	3.6	8,514	171	3	335	8,004
65 to 69 years	3,862	1,019	26.4	972	47	4.6	2,843	42	3	112	2,686
70 years and over	6,355	685	10.8	671	14	2.1	5,671	129	–	223	5,319
Women											
Total employed,											
16 years and over	81,009	45,007	55.6	42,084	2,923	6.5	36,002	25,772	1,450	943	7,837
65 years and over	14,539	1,083	7.4	1,064	19	1.8	13,456	8,569	4	559	4,323
65 to 69 years	4,641	707	15.2	694	13	1.8	3,935	2,726	4	89	1,116
70 years and over	9,897	376	3.8	370	7	1.7	9,521	5,844	1	470	3,207
BLACK											
Total employed,											
16 years and over	19,974	12,981	65.0	10,936	2,046	15.8	6,993	2,935	807	519	2,732
65 years and over	2,297	238	10.4	228	10	4.1	2,059	721	2	177	1,159
65 to 69 years	834	168	20.1	158	10	6.0	667	290	2	32	342
70 years and over	1,463	70	4.8	70	1	(¹)	1,392	431	–	145	817

Table 3–2. (continued)

	June 1986										
Age, sex, and race	Civilian labor force						Not in labor force				
					Unemployed						
	Civilian noninsti- tutional population	Total	Percent of population	Employed	Number	Percent of labor force	Total	Keeping house	Going to school	Unable to work	Other reasons
Men											
Total employed,											
16 years and over	8,951	6,582	73.5	5,547	1,035	15.7	2,369	92	380	280	1,616
65 years and over	924	123	13.3	118	5	4.3	801	42	–	72	687
65 to 69 years	361	90	24.8	85	5	5.2	272	19	–	15	237
70 years and over	563	33	5.9	32	1	(1)	530	23	–	57	450
Women											
Total employed,											
16 years and over	11,023	6,399	58.1	5,389	1,011	15.8	4,624	2,842	427	238	1,116
65 years and over	1,373	115	8.4	111	4	3.9	1,258	679	2	105	472
65 to 69 years	473	78	16.4	73	5	6.0	395	271	2	17	105
70 years and over	900	37	4.2	38	–	(1)	862	408	–	88	367

Note: 1. Data not shown where base is less than 75,000.

Source: Monthly Labor Review, July 1986.

Table 3–3. Persons 65 Years of Age or Over at Work in Nonagricultural Industries, by Full– or Part–Time Status: 1977–1985

(Numbers in thousands)

| | | | | On full–time schedules | | | Average hours | |
Year	Total at work	On part- time for economic reasons	On voluntary part-time	Total	40 hours or less	41 hours or more	All workers	Workers on full–time schedules
1977	2,201	87	1,071	1,043	707	336	29.1	43.1
1978	2,334	98	1,151	1,085	736	349	28.6	42.8
1979	2,404	102	1,169	1,133	798	335	29.0	42.4
1980	2,391	99	1,164	1,128	786	342	29.0	42.5
1981	2,377	99	1,151	1,127	806	321	28.9	42.0
1982	2,389	121	1,146	1,122	801	321	29.1	42.5
1983	2,408	118	1,154	1,136	803	333	29.2	42.7
1984	2,348	107	1,116	1,125	798	327	29.2	42.2
1985	2,328	104	1,127	1,097	777	320	28.9	42.2

Source: U.S. Department of Labor. Bureau of Labor Statistics. *Employment and Earnings* (January issues—national averages).

Figure 3–2. Employment by Industry of Persons Age 65 Years and Over: 1984

(Distribution in percent)

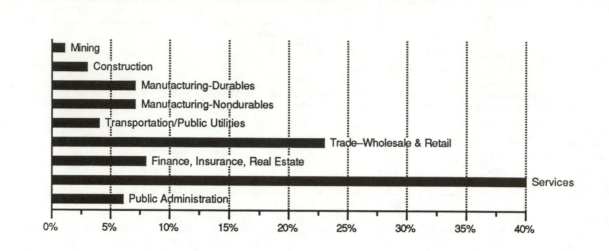

Note: Figures do not total to 100 percent due to rounding.

Source: U.S. Department of Labor. Bureau of Labor Statistics. *Current Population Survey,* unpublished.

Figure 3–3. Employment of Persons Age 65 Years and Over by Occupation: 1984

(Distribution in percent)

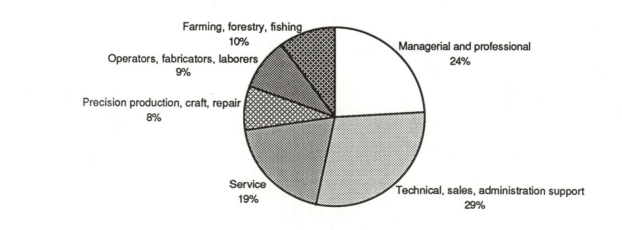

Note: Figures do not total to 100 percent due to rounding.

Source: U.S. Department of Labor. Bureau of Labor Statistics. *Current Population Survey,* unpublished.

Figure 3–4. Projected Growth of Occupations and Current Elderly Participation

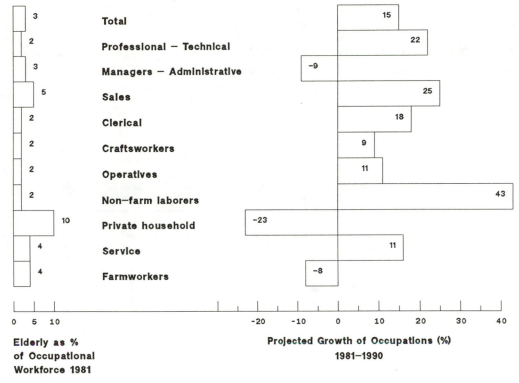

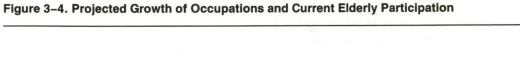

Elderly as % of Occupational Workforce 1981	Projected Growth of Occupations (%) 1981–1990

Source: Carey Max, "Occupational Employment Growth Through 1990," *Monthly Labor Review,* August 1981.

Table 3–4. Employed Persons 65 Years of Age or Over, By Class of Worker: United States, 1977–1985

(Numbers in thousands)

		Nonagricultural industries						Agriculture		
		Wage and salary workers								
Year	Total	Total	Private household workers	Govern-ment	Other	Self employed	Unpaid family workers	Wage and salary workers	Self employed	Unpaid family workers
1977	2,763	1,895	172	302	1,421	503	25	63	257	20
1978	2,919	2,018	181	303	1,534	522	25	76	262	16
1979	2,969	2,076	173	337	1,566	540	26	78	233	16
1980	2,928	2,071	150	358	1,564	533	19	59	232	13
1981	2,913	2,044	141	337	1,567	547	19	50	237	15
1982	2,922	2,051	140	337	1,574	556	19	45	239	12
1983	2,926	2,054	130	337	1,587	566	21	45	224	16
1984	2,835	2,003	126	339	1,538	546	16	47	208	15
1985	2,812	2,026	119	344	1,564	518	12	50	192	14

Source: U.S. Department of Labor. Bureau of Labor Statistics. *Employment and Earnings* (January issues—national averages).

UNEMPLOYMENT

Table 3–5. Unemployed Workers Age 65 and Over: 1972 to 1985

(In thousands, except as indicated. For civilian noninstitutional population. Annual averages of monthly figures.)

Item and Characteristic	1972	1975	1979	1980	1981	1982	1983	1984	1985
Unemployed									
Total	**4,882**	**7,929**	**6,137**	**7,637**	**8,273**	**10,678**	**10,717**	**8,539**	**8,312**
65 years and over	111	155	104	94	98	107	114	97	93
Male	2,659	4,442	3,120	4,267	4,577	6,179	6,260	4,744	4,521
65 years and over	73	103	67	58	55	69	73	53	55
Female	2,222	3,486	3,018	3,270	3,696	4,499	4,457	3,794	3,791
65 years and over	38	52	38	36	43	38	41	45	39
Unemployment Rate (percent)[1]									
Total	**5.6**	**8.5**	**5.8**	**7.1**	**7.6**	**9.7**	**9.6**	**7.5**	**7.2**
65 years and over	3.6	5.2	3.4	3.1	3.2	3.5	3.7	3.3	3.2
Male	5.0	7.9	5.1	6.9	7.4	9.9	9.9	7.4	7.0
65 years and over	3.6	5.4	3.4	3.1	2.9	3.7	3.9	3.0	3.1
Female	6.6	9.3	6.8	7.4	7.9	9.4	9.2	7.6	7.4
65 years and over	3.5	5.0	3.3	3.1	3.6	3.2	3.4	3.8	3.3

Note: 1. Unemployed as percent of civilian labor force in specified group.

Source: U.S. Bureau of Labor Statistics, *Employment and Earnings,* monthly; and unpublished data.

Figure 3–5. Unemployment Rates by Age

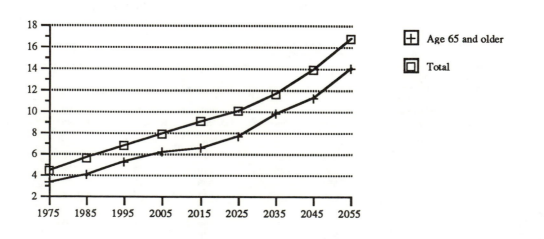

Source: U.S. Department of Health and Human Services. National Institute on Aging. *National Institute on Aging Macroeconomic-Demographic Model,* 1984.

Table 3–6. Persons 60 Years of Age or Over Not in the Labor Force, By Job Desire and Reasons Not Seeking Work: 1977–1983

Item	1977	1978	1979	1980	1981	1982	1983
				Numbers in thousands			
Total not in labor force	24,270	24,725	25,294	26,082	26,845	28,176	28,747
Do not want a job now	23,672	24,132	24,749	25,546	26,302	27,573	28,195
Current activity:							
Going to school	18	11	22	15	12	10	21
Ill, disabled	2,177	2,183	2,196	2,076	2,044	1,985	1,898
Keeping house	12,176	12,177	12,188	12,352	12,291	12,845	12,962
Retired	8,769	9,158	9,728	10,505	11,335	12.043	12,679
Other	532	603	615	598	620	690	635
Want a job now	588	594	544	537	543	601	556
Reason for not looking:							
School attendance	3	3	4	6	4	3	7
Ill health, disability	174	177	170	155	164	168	147
Home responsibilities	38	41	33	38	34	32	37
Think cannot get a job:	214	180	152	176	181	238	212
Job market factors	93	74	68	74	88	131	109
Personal factors	122	106	83	103	92	107	103
Other reasons	159	193	185	162	160	160	153
				Percent distribution			
Total not in labor force	100.0	100.0	100.0	100.0	100.0	100.0	100.0
Do not want a job now	97.5	97.6	97.8	97.9	98.0	97.9	98.1
Current activity:							
Going to school	0.1	.0	0.1	0.1	.0	.0	0.1
Ill, disabled	9.0	8.8	8.7	8.0	7.6	7.0	6.6
Keeping house	50.2	49.2	48.2	47.4	45.8	45.6	45.1
Retired	36.1	37.0	38.5	40.3	42.2	42.7	44.1
Other	2.2	2.4	2.4	2.3	2.3	2.4	2.2
Want a job now	2.4	2.4	2.2	2.1	2.0	2.1	1.9
Reason for not looking:							
School attendance	.0	.0	.0	.0	.0	.0	.0
Ill health, disability	0.7	0.7	0.7	0.6	0.6	0.6	0.5
Home responsibilities	0.2	0.2	0.1	0.1	0.1	0.1	0.1
Think cannot get a job:	0.9	0.7	0.6	0.7	0.7	0.8	0.7
Job market factors	0.4	0.3	0.3	0.3	0.3	0.5	0.4
Personal factors	0.5	0.4	0.3	0.4	0.3	0.4	0.4
Other reasons	0.7	0.8	0.7	0.6	0.6	0.6	0.5

Source: Bureau of Labor Statistics. Household data from the Current Population Survey, 1977–1984.

IV

HEALTH AND HEALTH CARE

HEALTH STATUS

Table 4–1. General Health Status of the Elderly as Reported By the National Health Interview Survey: January–June 1984

| Health characteristic | Total | 65–74 years | | | 75 years and over | | | Age | |
		Both sexes	Men	Women	Both sexes	Men	Women	75–84 years	85 years and over
					Number				
Sample	5,982	3,731	1,625	2,106	2,251	822	1,429	1,803	448
					Number in thousands				
Estimated population	26,290	16,227	7,048	9,178	10,063	3,685	6,378	8,073	1,990
					Percent distribution				
Total	100.0	100.0	100.0	100.0	100.0	100.0	100.0	100.0	100.0
Perceived health status[1]									
Excellent	15.6	15.5	16.3	14.8	15.8	16.3	15.4	15.9	15.4
Very good	19.2	19.6	19.2	20.0	18.6	17.7	19.0	18.3	19.6
Good	31.9	32.5	31.2	33.5	30.8	30.2	31.2	32.0	26.3
Fair	21.4	21.4	20.6	22.1	21.3	21.3	21.2	20.8	23.0
Poor	11.5	10.6	12.5	9.2	13.0	13.8	12.5	12.4	15.3
Bed days in year									
0	62.2	63.5	64.4	62.8	60.2	61.6	59.4	61.3	55.8
1–6 days	13.8	14.5	13.9	15.0	12.7	11.8	13.2	12.9	12.1
7–13 days	7.1	6.7	6.8	6.6	7.7	7.3	7.9	7.4	8.7
14–27 days	6.6	6.5	6.1	6.7	6.9	7.0	6.8	7.0	6.3
28–365 days	8.9	7.8	7.8	7.8	10.7	10.8	10.6	9.9	13.9
Always	1.4	1.0	1.0	1.0	1.9	1.5	2.2	1.6	3.4
Limitation of activity									
None	59.8	61.5	60.0	62.6	57.0	59.3	55.6	61.3	39.6
Outside activities only	15.2	14.5	14.2	14.8	16.2	20.2	13.9	16.8	13.8
Kind or amount of activity	13.6	12.4	9.9	14.4	15.6	10.7	18.5	13.4	24.6
Unable to perform usual activity	11.4	11.6	15.9	8.2	11.2	9.8	12.0	8.6	22.0

Notes: 1. Health status was unknown for 0.5 percent.

Source: National Center for Health Statistics. *Advancedata*, No. 115 (May 1, 1986).

Table 4–2. Selected Health Habits of Elderly Americans, 1985

	All Ages	65 Years and Over
Consider themselves "very" or "somewhat" overweight	25%	21%
Use seat belt all or most of the time	30	26
Exercise or play sports regularly	41	27
Current smoker	30	16
Eat breakfast almost every day	55	87
Have felt "a lot" or a "moderate" amount of stress in past 2 weeks	52	28

Source: National Center for Health Statistics, *Advancedata*, No. 113 (November 15, 1985), p. 14.

Figure 4–1. Percent of People Age 60 Years and Older Who Have No Difficulty in Performing Daily Activities

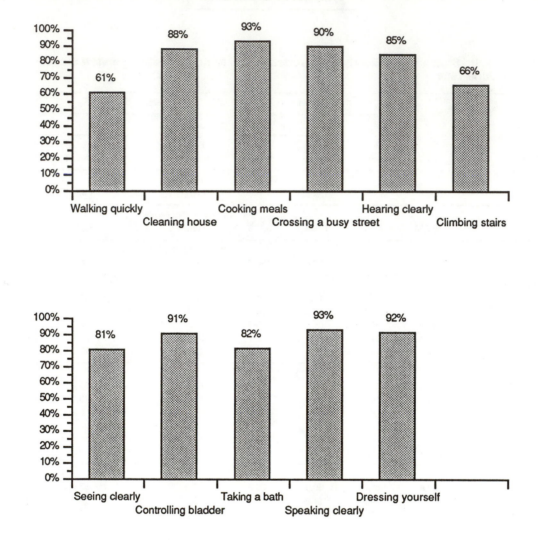

Note: Sample size = 481 adults 60 years and older.

Source: Survey by Research & Forecasts, Inc., for Americana Health Care Corporation, March–April 1980.

Figure 4–2. Health Impairment of the Elderly Population

(in percent)

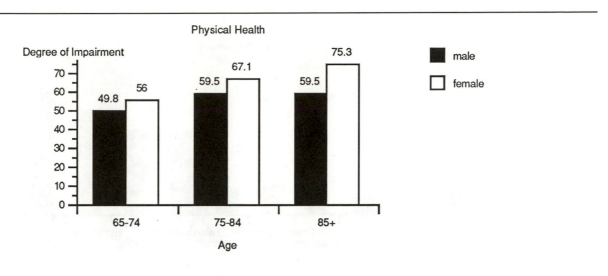

Physical Health

Degree of Impairment

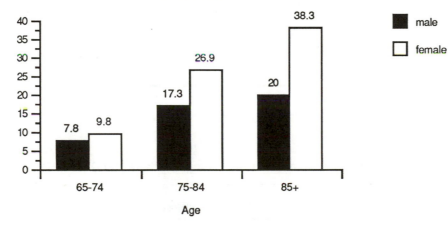

Mental Health

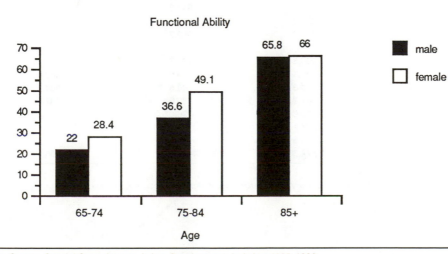

Functional Ability

Source: U.S. Congress. Senate. Special Committee on Aging. *Developments in Aging: 1985,* 1986.

Figure 4–3. Prevalence of Top Ten Chronic Conditions in Persons Age 65 Years and Over: 1983

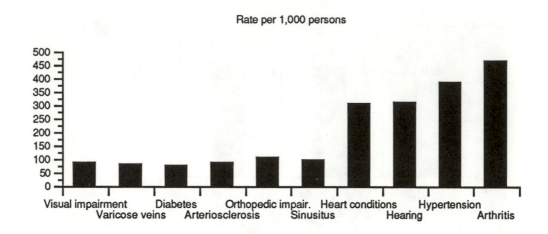

Rate per 1,000 persons

Source: National Center for Health Statistics. Division of Health Interview Statistics.

MORTALITY RATES

Table 4–3. Death Rates for 10 Leading Causes of Death for Persons 65 Years and Over, 1983

	Death Rate*			Percent of Total Deaths 65 Years and Over
	65–74 Years	75–84 Years	85 Years and Over	
Diseases of heart	1,139.2	2,816.3	7,335.5	43.6
Malignant neoplasms	829.3	1,254.7	1,583.4	20.1
Cerebrovascular diseases	182.2	652.7	1,912.5	9.5
Chronic obstructive pulmonary diseases	139.8	260.7	309.2	3.7
Pneumonia and influenza	51.1	205.8	859.9	3.4
Atherosclerosis	19.3	98.5	530.8	1.8
Diabetes mellitus	61.7	130.0	207.6	1.9
Accidents	50.5	106.0	257.5	1.7
Nephritis and nephrosis	25.5	74.6	186.6	1.1
Chronic liver disease and cirrhosis	38.5	31.8	18.5	.7
All causes	2,874.3	6,441.5	15,168.0	100.0

Notes: * Rates per 100,000 population in age group.
Source: U.S. National Center for Health Statistics, *Monthly Vital Statistics Report*, Vol. 33, No. 9. Supplement.

Table 4-4. Death Rates From Accidents and Violence: 1970 to 1983

(Rates are per 100,000 population. Excludes deaths of nonresidents of the U.S. Beginning 1979, deaths classified according to the ninth revision of the *International Classification of Diseases.* For earlier years, classified according to the revision in use at the time.)

Cause of Death and Age	White						Black					
	Male			Female			Male			Female		
	1970	1980	1983	1970	1980	1983	1970	1980	1983	1970	1980	1983
Total, All Ages	**101.9**	**97.1**	**84.8**	**42.4**	**36.3**	**32.7**	**183.2**	**154.0**	**124.5**	**51.7**	**42.6**	**37.0**
55–64 years	101.5	92.3	84.6	36.3	33.8	30.9	242.4	188.5	155.3	56.0	47.3	38.5
65 years and over	216.9	163.9	151.8	122.4	87.2	80.5	220.0	215.8	194.2	107.9	102.9	85.6
65–74 years	128.0	116.7	103.7	57.7	46.4	43.7	217.4	182.2	158.6	81.5	68.7	57.5
75–84 years	229.3	209.2	198.3	149.0	101.5	91.3	236.0	261.4	243.7	140.1	137.5	114.3
85 years old and over	466.7	438.5	418.6	391.4	268.1	233.3	271.8	379.2	336.5	214.3	235.7	176.7

Source: U.S. National Center for Health Statistics, *Vital Statistics of the United States*, Annual.

Table 4-5. Suicide Rates, By Sex and Race: 1970 to 1983

(Rates are per 100,000 population. Excludes deaths of nonresidents of the U.S. Beginning 1979, deaths classified according to the ninth revision of the *International Classification of Diseases.* For earlier years, classified according to the revision in use at the time.)

Age	Total[1]			Male						Female					
				White			Black			White			Black		
	1970	1980	1983	1970	1980	1983	1970	1980	1983	1970	1980	1983	1970	1980	1983
All ages[2]	**11.6**	**11.9**	**12.1**	**18.0**	**19.9**	**20.6**	**8.0**	**10.3**	**9.9**	**7.1**	**5.9**	**5.9**	**2.6**	**2.2**	**2.0**
65 years and over	20.8	17.8	19.2	41.1	37.5	40.2	8.7	11.4	14.2	8.5	6.5	7.2	2.6	1.4	1.4

Notes: 1. Includes other races not shown separately.
2. Includes other age groups not shown separately.
Source: U.S. National Center for Health Statistics, *Vital Statistics of the United States*, annual.

HEALTH CARE

Table 4–6. Frequency of Physician and Dental Visits of Persons Age 65 and Over: United States, 1964, 1978, and 1983

(Data are based on household interviews of a sample of the civilian noninstitutionalized population)

| | Interval Since Last Physician Visit | | | | | | | | |
| | Less than 1 year | | | 1 year–less than 2 years | | | 2 years or more | | |
Selected characteristic	1964	1978	1983	1964	1978	1983	1964	1978	1983
	Percent of population[1]								
Total (all ages)[1]	66.0	75.3	74.0	13.8	11.0	10.8	17.6	12.3	13.5
65 years and over	68.8	79.8	81.4	9.2	6.2	5.9	20.3	13.3	11.7

| | Interval Since Last Dental Visit | | | | | | | | | | | |
| | Dental visits | | | Less than 1 year | | | 2 years or more | | | Never visited dentist | | |
Selected characteristic	1964	1978	1983	1964	1978	1983	1964	1978	1983	1964	1978	1983
	Number per person			Percent of population[1]								
Total, (all ages)[1]	1.6	1.6	1.8	42.0	49.9	51.8	28.1	25.1	23.7	15.6	10.5	10.8
65 years and over	0.8	1.2	1.5	20.8	32.3	37.8	66.8	58.2	51.3	1.5	0.6	0.9

Notes: 1. Includes unknown interval since last physician or dental visit.

Source: National Center for Health Statistics. Data from National Health Interview Survey.

Figure 4–4. Number of Prescribed Medicines Used in a Year

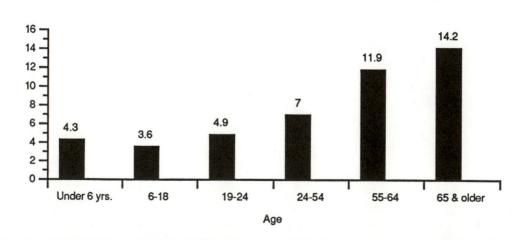

Source: U.S. Congress. Senate, Special Committee on Aging; and U.S. Congress, House, Select Committee on Aging. *Drug Use and Misuse: A Growing Concern for Older Americans: Joint Hearings,* 98th Congress, first session, 1983.

Table 4–7. Hospital Discharges and Days of Care, By Sex and Diagnosis: 1984

(Represents estimates of inpatients discharged from noninstitutional, short-stay hospitals, exclusive of federal hospitals. Excludes newborn. Based on sample data collected from the National Hospital Discharge Survey, a sample survey of hospital records of patients discharged in year shown; subject to sampling variability.)

Age and First–Listed Diagnosis	Discharges Number (1,000)	Discharges Per 1,000 persons[1]	Days of care per 1,000 persons[1]	Average stay (days)	Age and First-Listed Diagnosis	Discharges Number (1,000)	Discharges Per 1,000 persons[1]	Days of care per 1,000 persons[1]	Average stay (days)
Male					**Female**				
All ages[2]	**14,899**	**131.6**	**923.9**	**7.0**	All ages[2]	**22,263**	**183.6**	**1,155.2**	**6.3**
Diseases of heart	1,905	16.8	125.8	7.5	Delivery	3,853	31.8	109.1	3.4
Malignant neoplasms	943	8.3	84.3	10.1	Diseases of heart	1,694	14.0	113.1	8.1
Fracture	541	4.8	39.4	8.2	Malignant neoplasms	1,117	9.2	87.1	9.5
Pneumonia	424	3.7	27.3	7.3	Fracture	573	4.7	48.7	10.3
Cerebrovascular disease	420	3.7	36.4	9.8	Cerebrovascular disease	476	3.9	42.5	10.8
65 years and over[2]	4,799	424.8	3,757.3	8.8	65 years and over[2]	6,427	383.9	3,451.6	9.0
Diseases of heart	949	84.0	675.9	8.1	Diseases of heart	1,161	69.3	598.6	8.6
Malignant neoplasms	534	47.2	503.8	10.7	Malignant neoplasms	536	32.0	344.9	10.8
Cerebrovascular disease	298	26.4	261.7	9.9	Cerebrovascular disease	369	22.0	236.1	10.7
Hyperplasia of prostate	190	16.8	131.0	7.8	Eye diseases, conditions	328	19.6	52.1	2.7
Pneumonia	177	15.6	146.8	9.4	Fracture	321	19.2	251.4	13.1

Notes: 1. Based on Bureau of the Census estimated civilian population as of July 1.
2. Includes other first-listed diagnoses, not shown separately.
Source: U.S. National Center for Health Statistics, *Vital and Health Statistics,* series 13, and unpublished data.

Table 4–8. Distributions of Caregivers by Relationship to 65 Plus Individual with Activity Limitations

(percent distribution)

Age of recipient and relationship of caregiver	Care recipient Male	Care recipient Female	Age of recipient and relationship of caregiver	Care recipient Male	Care recipient Female
65 to 74:			85 + :		
Spouse	45	18	Spouse	20	2
Offspring	21	29	Offspring	34	39
Other relative	21	33	Other relative	27	36
Formal	13	20	Formal	19	23
75 to 84:			All 65 + :		
Spouse	35	8	Spouse	37	10
Offspring	23	35	Offspring	24	34
Other relative	25	36	Other relative	23	35
Formal	19	23	Formal	16	21

Source: Preliminary data from the 1982 National Long-Term Care Survey.

HEALTH CARE COSTS

Table 4–9. Personal Health Care Expenditures for People 65 Years of Age or Over, By Source of Funds and Type of Service: United States, 1984

Year and source of funds	Type of service (in millions of dollars)				
	Total care	Hospital	Physician	Nursing home	Other care
1984:					
Total	$119,872	$54,200	$24,770	$25,105	$15,798
Private	39,341	6,160	9,827	13,038	10,316
Consumer	38,875	5,964	9,818	12,856	10,237
Out–of–pocket*	30,198	1,694	6,468	12,569	9,467
Insurance	8,677	4,270	3,350	287	770
Other private	466	196	9	182	79
Government	80,531	48,040	14,943	12,067	5,482
Medicare	58,519	40,524	14,314	539	3,142
Medicaid	15,288	2,595	467	10,418	1,808
Other government	6,724	4,920	162	1,110	532
Population (in millions)	**28.5**				

Note: * Out of pocket funds exclude premium payments for Medicare Part B and private health insurance.

Source: Waldo, Daniel R. and Lazenby, Helen C. "Demographic Characteristics and Health Care Use and Expenditures by the Aged in the United States: 1977–1984." *Health Care Financing Review* 6 (Fall 1984).

Table 4–10. Personal Health Care Expenditures Per Capita for People 65 Years of Age or Over, By Source of Funds and Type of Service: United States, 1984

Year and source of funds	Type of service				
	Total care	Hospital	Physician	Nursing home	Other care
1984:					
Total	$4,202	$1,900	$868	$880	$554
Private	1,379	216	344	457	362
Consumer	1,363	209	344	451	359
Out–of–pocket*	1,059	59	227	441	332
Insurance	304	150	117	10	27
Other private	16	7	1	6	3
Government	2,823	1,684	524	423	192
Medicare	2,051	1,420	502	19	110
Medicaid	536	91	16	365	63
Other government	236	172	6	39	19

Note: * Out-of-pocket funds exclude premium payments for Medicare Part B and private health insurance.

Source: Waldo, Daniel R. and Lazenby, Helen C. "Demographic Characteristics and Health Care Use and Expenditures by the Aged in the United States: 1977–1984." *Health Care Financing Review* 6 (Fall 1984).

Figure 4–5. Aged Income and Health Cost Increases

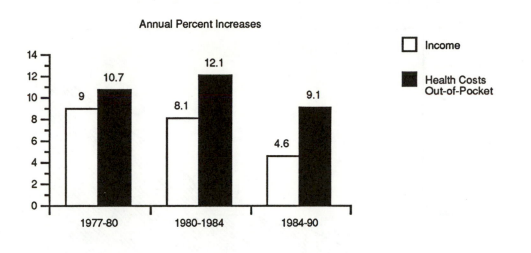

Annual Percent Increases

Source: U.S. Congress, House, Select Committee on Aging, July 1985; Health Care Financing Administration, July 1985; and U.S. Census Bureau, July 1985.

Figure 4–6. Personal Health Care Expenditures as a Percentage of Income for People Age 65 and Older in 1977, 1980, 1984, and 1990

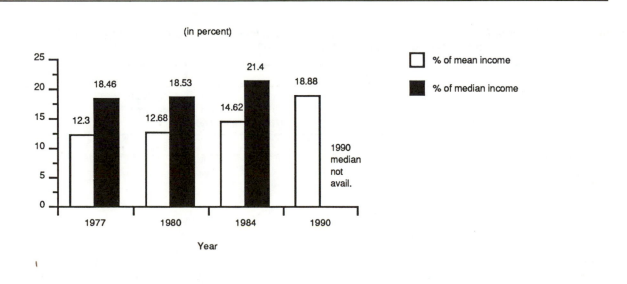

(in percent)

Year

Source: U.S. Congress, House, Select Committee on Aging, July 1985; U.S. Census Bureau, July 1985; and Health Care Financing Administration, July 1985.

Figure 4–7. Out-of-Pocket Health Care Expenditures for Persons Age 65 and Older: Per Capita, 1966-1984

(Includes private insurance and premiums for supplementary medical insurance paid by the elderly)

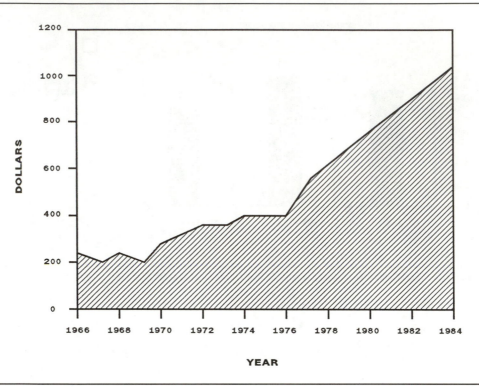

Source: Health Care Financing Administration, Bureau of Data Management and Strategy. *Health Care Spending Bulletin,* July 1984; Robert Gibson and Marjorie Mueller, "Differences by Age Group in Health Care Spending," *Social Security Bulletin,* June 1976; Office of Financial and Actuarial Analysis, Bureau of Data Management and Strategy, Health Care Financing Administration, July 1984.

Table 4–11. Projected Expenditures for Physicians' Services, Hospital Care, and Nursing Home Care, and Percent Distribution by Age: United States, 1978 and 2003

	Physicians' Services			Hospital Care			Nursing Home Care		
	1978	2003 constant mortality	2003 declining mortality	1978	2003 constant mortality	2003 declining mortality	1978	2003 constant mortality	2003 declining mortality
Expenditures (in billions of dollars)	$36.3	$47.2	$49.6	$73.9	$97.5	$105.8	$14.5	$22.6	$30.3
Percent **Distribution**									
Under 20 years	15.4%	12.7%	12.3%	9.6%	7.8%	7.3%	–	–	–
20–64 years	62.5	64.2	61.9	62.7	62.4	59.2	–	–	–
Under 65 years	–	–	–	–	–	–	16.6%	13.3%	9.9%
65 years and over	22.3	23.1	25.8	27.7	29.8	33.6	83.4	86.7	90.1

Source: U.S. Department of Health and Human Services; *Changing Mortality Patterns, Health Services Utilization and Health Care Expenditures:* United States 1978–2003. Washington, D.C.: U.S. Government Printing Office, 1983.

NURSING HOMES

Table 4–12. Nursing and Related Care Facilities—Selected Characteristics: 1982

(Excludes hospital-based nursing homes. Based on National Master Facility Inventory.)

Characteristic	Total Facilities		Nursing Homes[1]							Residential facilities[3]	
				Beds		Registered nurses[2]		Licensed nurses[2]			
	Homes	Beds (1,000)	Homes	Number (1,000)	Average beds per home	Number (1,000)	Per 100 beds	Number (1,000)	Per 100 beds	Homes	Beds (1,000)
Total	**25,849**	**1,642**	**17,819**	**1,509**	**84.7**	**64**	**4.3**	**86**	**5.7**	**8,030**	**133**
Northeast	3,866	330	3,866	330	85.3	21	6.4	19	5.6	–	–
Midwest	8,137	540	5,894	523	88.7	20	3.8	25	4.8	2,243	17
South	6,225	463	5,423	450	83.0	12	2.7	30	6.6	802	13
West	7,621	309	2,636	206	78.2	11	5.4	13	6.1	4,985	103
Government	1,111	113	916	111	121.1	6	5.4	8	6.8	195	2
Proprietary	21,132	1,194	13,410	1,066	79.5	41	3.9	61	5.7	7,722	128
Nonprofit	3,606	336	3,493	332	94.9	17	5.2	18	5.3	113	4
3–9 beds	6,955	40	1,399	8	5.4	(Z)	.8	(Z)	1.5	5,556	33
10–24 beds	3,450	58	1,855	32	17.1	1	2.8	1	3.8	1,595	26
25–49 beds	3,083	113	2,718	101	37.1	4	3.7	5	5.3	365	12
50–74 beds	3,465	208	3,332	200	60.0	8	3.8	11	5.5	133	8
75–99 beds	2,472	216	2,366	208	87.9	9	4.2	13	6.1	106	8
100–199 beds	5,293	690	5,094	666	130.7	29	4.3	39	5.9	199	24
200–299 beds	832	192	788	183	231.9	8	4.6	11	5.8	44	10
300–499 beds	241	87	212	77	361.4	4	4.8	4	5.0	29	10
500 beds or more	58	37	55	35	642.8	2	6.6	2	6.1	3	2
Certification:											
Medicare or Medicaid (skilled nursing facility)[4]	7,032	855	7,032	855	121.6	49	5.7	55	6.4	–	–
Medicaid (intermediate care facility)[4]	5,564	442	5,564	442	79.5	11	2.5	25	5.7	–	–
Not certified	5,643	213	4,841	200	30.9	4	2.1	5	2.7	802	13
Unknown	7,610	132	382	12	41.2	(Z)	1.7	(Z)	2.4	7,228	120

Notes: – Represents zero.

Z Fewer than 500 nurses.

1. These facilities have three or more beds and provide to adults who require it either (a) nursing care or (b) personal care (such as help with bathing, eating, using toilet facilities, or dressing) and/or supervision over such activities as money management, walking, and shopping.

2. Estimated full–time equivalent.

3. These facilities offer no nursing services and provide only personal care or supervisory care. Only those residential facilities in Florida, Michigan, Kentucky, and California are included in this category. Facilities meeting this definition also exist in the other states, but because they cannot be identified precisely as residential, they appear in the counts of nursing homes.

4. Facilities certified as skilled nursing facilities and intermediate care facilities have been classified as skilled nursing facilities.

Source: U.S. National Center for Health Statistics, Advancedata from Vital and Health Statistics, No. 111.

Figure 4–8. Nursing Home Population Projections—Persons 65 Years and Older by Age Group: 1980–2040

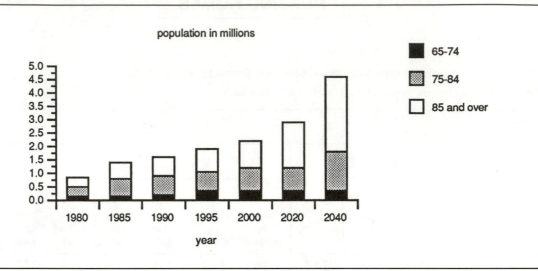

Source: U.S. Congress, Senate, Special Committee on Aging. *Developments in Aging: 1985,* 1986.

Table 4–13. Nursing Home Care Expenditures Aggregate, Per Capita, and Percent Distribution, by Source of Funds: Selected Calendar Years 1965–85

| | | | | | | Third parties | | | | |
| | | | | | | | Government | | | |
Year	Total	Direct patient payments	All third parties	Private health insurance	Other private funds	Total	Federal	State and local	Medicare[1]	Medicaid[2]
				Amount in billions						
1965	$2.1	$1.3	$0.7	$0.0	$0.0	$0.7	$0.5	$0.3	–	–
1970	4.7	2.4	2.3	0.0	0.0	2.3	1.3	0.9	0.3	$1.4
1975	10.1	4.3	5.8	0.1	0.1	5.6	3.2	2.5	0.3	4.8
1980	20.4	8.9	11.5	0.2	0.1	11.2	6.0	5.2	0.4	9.8
1985	35.2	18.1	17.1	0.3	0.3	16.5	9.4	7.1	0.6	14.7
				Per capita amount						
1965	$10	$7	$4	$0	$0	$3	$2	$1	–	–
1970	22	11	11	0	0	11	6	4	(3)	(3)
1975	45	19	26	0	0	25	14	11	(3)	(3)
1980	87	38	49	1	1	48	26	22	(3)	(3)
1985	143	73	69	1	1	67	38	29	(3)	(3)
				Percent distribution						
1965	100.0	64.5	35.5	0.1	1.0	34.3	22.2	12.1	–	–
1970	100.0	50.3	49.7	0.4	0.7	48.6	28.6	20.0	5.6	30.3
1975	100.0	42.7	57.3	0.7	0.6	56.0	31.4	24.6	2.9	47.9
1980	100.0	43.6	56.4	0.9	0.6	54.9	29.6	25.3	1.9	48.0
1985	100.0	51.4	48.6	1.0	0.7	46.9	26.8	20.2	1.7	41.8

Notes: $0.0 denotes less than $50 million for aggregate amounts, and $0 denotes less than $.50 per capita amounts. Per capita amounts are based on July 1 social security area population estimates.

    1. Subset of Federal funds.

    2. Subset of Federal and State and local funds.

    3. Calculation of per capita estimates is inappropriate.

Source: Health Care Financing Administration, Office of the Actuary. Data from the Division of National Cost Estimates.

Table 4-14. Nursing Home Care Per Capita Expenditures and Average Annual Percent Change, According to Geographic Division and State: United States, Selected Years 1966–82

(Data are compiled by the Health Care Financing Administration)

Geographic Division and State	1966	1969	1972	1976	1980	1982	Average annual percent change 1966–82
				Per capita amount			
United States	$12	$19	$31	$52	$ 90	$114	15.1
New England	20	28	47	85	145	185	15.0
Maine	15	23	40	70	134	176	16.6
New Hampshire	16	20	35	43	71	90	11.4
Vermont	19	27	39	75	121	149	13.7
Massachusetts	22	32	52	94	152	192	14.5
Rhode Island	15	21	34	78	169	214	18.1
Connecticut	19	29	49	90	156	206	16.1
Middle Atlantic	14	21	36	66	108	145	15.7
New York	16	26	46	85	135	184	16.5
New Jersey	10	15	24	45	77	97	15.3
Pennsylvania	12	18	28	48	88	116	15.2
East North Central	12	19	31	54	97	125	15.8
Ohio	12	18	27	53	99	143	16.8
Indiana	12	20	33	57	102	129	16.0
Illinois	13	20	33	52	90	109	14.2
Michigan	10	17	27	48	86	106	15.9
Wisconsin	14	22	39	71	120	150	16.0
West North Central	18	28	44	69	131	172	15.2
Minnesota	22	33	57	91	175	235	16.0
Iowa	22	36	51	81	143	168	13.5
Missouri	12	19	29	47	95	139	16.5
North Dakota	19	33	47	60	112	154	14.0
South Dakota	18	30	49	69	132	165	14.9
Nebraska	17	27	42	68	112	140	14.1
Kansas	18	26	42	65	130	163	14.8
South Atlantic	8	12	20	33	59	77	15.2
Delaware	8	12	20	42	67	86	16.0
Maryland	9	17	24	46	75	102	16.4
District of Columbia	6	10	18	22	43	55	14.9
Virginia	6	9	16	30	63	85	18.0
West Virginia	3	5	12	20	41	62	20.8
North Carolina	6	11	16	30	58	75	17.1
South Carolina	6	9	16	28	62	76	17.2
Georgia	8	13	23	37	67	79	15.4
Florida	11	15	25	31	48	65	11.7
East South Central	7	11	20	35	67	86	17.0
Kentucky	9	14	23	40	81	104	16.5
Tennessee	6	10	17	28	56	76	17.2
Alabama	8	14	22	40	62	79	15.4
Mississippi	4	7	15	30	71	90	21.5
West South Central	12	19	31	48	79	94	13.7
Arkansas	13	21	34	50	95	112	14.4
Louisiana	8	13	22	38	68	89	16.3
Oklahoma	19	31	47	58	91	111	11.7
Texas	11	18	30	48	78	88	13.9

Table 4–14. (continued)

Geographic Division and State	1966	1969	1972	1976	1980	1982	Average annual percent change 1966–82
				Per capita amount			
Mountain	10	15	23	35	59	74	13.3
Montana	12	17	33	43	66	92	13.6
Idaho	12	17	26	45	69	84	12.9
Wyoming	6	12	23	24	38	49	14.0
Colorado	15	21	33	54	86	104	12.9
New Mexico	5	9	15	16	34	49	15.3
Arizona	8	13	17	22	41	53	12.5
Utah	9	12	17	30	55	63	12.9
Nevada	7	10	20	29	60	82	16.6
Pacific	12	18	31	48	82	97	14.0
Washington	16	21	43	61	109	137	14.4
Oregon	17	24	37	57	94	113	12.6
California	11	18	30	47	78	91	14.1
Alaska	1	2	9	17	14	26	22.6
Hawaii	6	10	18	28	36	63	15.8

Note: Per capita spending estimates are the expenditure level of services rendered in a geographic area per resident population. Per capita figures cannot be interpreted directly as spending per resident unless substantially all of the services provided in a state are consumed by residents of that state.

Source: Office of the Actuary. Personal health care expenditures by state, selected years 1966–1982, by K. R. Levit, *Health Care Financing Review*. HCFA Pub. No. 03199. Washington, D.C.: Health Care Financing Administration. U.S. Government Printing Office, summer 1985.

V

HOUSING AND HOMEOWNERSHIP

HOMEOWNERSHIP
AND HOUSEHOLD CHARACTERISTICS
BY GEOGRAPHIC LOCATION

Figure 5–1. Homeownership by Age of Householder: 1983

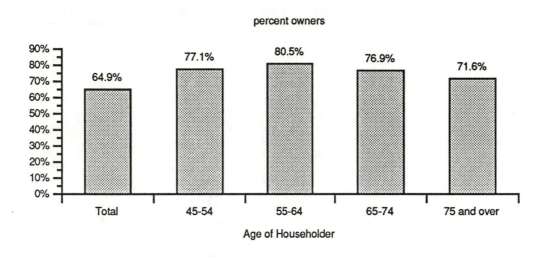

Source: U.S. Bureau of the Census, *Current Population Reports,* Series P-20, no. 388.

Table 5–1. Housing Tenure by Household Composition, Sex of Householder, and Urban/Rural Location: United States, 1983

(in thousands)

| Characteristics | Total 1983 | Urban | | | Rural | | | | |
		Total 1983	Inside SMSA's 1983	Outside SMSA's 1983	Total 1983	Nonfarm 1983	Farm 1983	Inside SMSA's 1983	Outside SMSA's 1983
All Occupied Housing Units									
Total	84,638	58,654	48,855	9,800	25,984	23,543	2,440	8,943	17,041
Household Composition by Age of Householder									
Owner occupied	54,724	34,353	28,127	6,227	20,371	18,292	2,079	7,039	13,332
2-or-more-person households	45,895	28,432	23,368	5,064	17,463	15,614	1,848	6,155	11,307
Married-couple families, no nonrelatives	39,073	23,726	19,415	4,310	15,347	13,646	1,701	5,409	9,938
65 years and over	6,926	4,297	3,356	942	2,629	2,212	416	685	1,943
Other male householder	2,325	1,530	1,299	231	794	718	76	291	504
65 years and over	406	264	207	57	142	113	29	45	97
Other female householder	4,497	3,176	2,654	522	1,321	1,250	71	455	866
65 years and over	1,027	726	578	148	301	263	37	81	220
1-person households	8,829	5,921	4,758	1,163	2,908	2,677	231	884	2,024
Male householder	3,071	1,996	1,719	277	1,075	966	109	351	724
65 years and over	1,063	675	551	124	388	336	52	87	302
Female householder	5,758	3,925	3,039	886	1,833	1,711	122	533	1,300
65 years and over	3,645	2,457	1,831	626	1,188	1,098	89	309	878
Renter occupied	29,914	24,301	20,728	3,573	5,613	5,251	361	1,904	3,709
2-or-more-person households	19,757	15,538	13,252	2,286	4,219	3,900	319	1,463	2,756
Married-couple families, no nonrelatives	11,448	8,486	7,125	1,361	2,963	2,681	281	1,037	1,925
65 years and over	1,115	862	760	102	252	225	27	79	174
Other male householder	2,515	2,109	1,864	245	405	383	22	153	252
65 years and over	124	98	77	21	26	22	3	6	20
Other female householder	5,794	4,943	4,262	680	851	836	15	272	579
65 years and over	403	318	263	56	84	79	6	22	62
1-person households	10,157	8,763	7,477	1,287	1,394	1,351	43	441	953
Male householder	4,584	3,910	3,345	565	674	642	32	203	471
65 years and over	734	595	512	83	140	133	7	23	116
Female householder	5,573	4,853	4,131	722	720	709	11	237	482
65 years and over	2,332	1,967	1,638	329	366	356	9	96	270
Persons 65 Years Old and Over									
Owner occupied	54,724	34,353	28,127	6,227	20,371	18,292	2,079	7,039	13,332
None	40,183	24,908	20,732	4,176	15,276	13,876	1,400	5,664	9,612
1 person	9,402	6,216	4,916	1,300	3,186	2,819	368	887	2,300
2 persons or more	5,138	3,230	2,479	751	1,909	1,598	311	489	1,420
Renter occupied	29,914	24,301	20,728	3,573	5,613	5,251	361	1,904	3,709
None	24,866	20,169	17,230	2,939	4,696	4,390	306	1,662	3,035
1 person	4,089	3,364	2,834	530	725	689	36	180	545
2 persons or more	960	768	664	104	192	172	19	62	130

Source: U.S. Bureau of the Census and U.S. Department of Housing and Urban Development, *Annual Housing Survey: 1983.*

Table 5-2. Housing Tenure by Household Composition, Sex of Householder, and Urban/Rural Location: Northeast Region, 1983

(in thousands)

Characteristics	Total 1983	Urban			Rural				
		Total 1983	Inside SMSA's 1983	Outside SMSA's 1983	Total 1983	Nonfarm 1983	Farm 1983	Inside SMSA's 1983	Outside SMSA's 1983
All Occupied Housing Units									
Total	**18,221**	**13,986**	**12,389**	**1,597**	**4,235**	**4,090**	**145**	**1,939**	**2,296**
Household Composition by Age of Householder									
Owner occupied	**11,009**	**7,592**	**6,583**	**1,009**	**3,418**	**3,290**	**128**	**1,572**	**1,845**
2-or-more-person households	9,340	6,355	5,519	836	2,985	2,866	119	1,388	1,597
Married-couple families, no nonrelatives	7,884	5,278	4,584	694	2,606	2,503	104	1,230	1,376
65 years and over	1,369	965	853	113	404	388	16	167	236
Other male householder	516	347	294	53	169	160	9	70	99
65 years and over	117	87	72	15	30	25	5	14	16
Other female householder	940	730	641	89	210	204	6	87	122
65 years and over	237	192	169	23	45	45	–	20	26
1-person households	1,670	1,237	1,064	173	433	423	9	185	248
Male householder	590	428	362	66	162	158	5	69	93
65 years and over	259	191	159	33	68	66	2	23	44
Female householder	1,080	809	702	108	271	266	5	116	155
65 years and over	652	493	424	69	159	155	4	60	98
Renter occupied	**7,212**	**6,395**	**5,806**	**588**	**817**	**800**	**17**	**367**	**451**
2-or-more-person households	4,569	4,020	3,648	372	549	535	14	253	296
Married-couple families, no nonrelatives	2,530	2,153	1,944	209	377	368	10	184	193
65 years and over	372	331	317	14	40	40	–	16	24
Other male householder	523	470	429	41	52	51	2	22	30
65 years and over	28	27	25	2	1	1	–	–	1
Other female householder	1,516	1,396	1,275	122	120	117	3	46	73
65 years and over	126	115	108	7	11	10	1	3	8
1-person households	2,643	2,375	2,158	217	268	265	3	113	155
Male householder	1,029	922	826	96	107	105	2	42	65
65 years and over	212	187	176	11	25	25	–	6	19
Female householder	1,614	1,453	1,332	121	161	160	1	71	89
65 years and over	746	662	607	55	84	84	–	25	59
Persons 65 Years Old and Over									
Owner occupied	**11,009**	**7,592**	**6,583**	**1,009**	**3,418**	**3,290**	**128**	**1,572**	**1,845**
None	7,968	5,343	4,636	707	2,625	2,528	97	1,238	1,387
1 person	1,979	1,494	1,292	203	485	467	18	211	274
2 persons or more	1,062	754	655	100	307	294	13	123	184
Renter occupied	**7,212**	**6,395**	**5,806**	**588**	**817**	**800**	**17**	**367**	**451**
None	5,623	4,975	4,480	494	648	632	16	314	334
1 person	1,263	1,124	1,043	82	139	139	–	39	100
2 persons or more	326	296	283	12	30	29	1	14	17

Source: U.S. Bureau of the Census and U.S. Department of Housing and Urban Development, *Annual Housing Survey: 1983.*

Table 5–3. Housing Tenure by Household Composition, Sex of Householder, and Urban/Rural Location: Midwest Region, 1983

(in thousands)

Characteristics	Total 1983	Urban Total 1983	Urban Inside SMSA's 1983	Urban Outside SMSA's 1983	Rural Total 1983	Rural Nonfarm 1983	Rural Farm 1983	Rural Inside SMSA's 1983	Rural Outside SMSA's 1983
All Occupied Housing Units									
Total	**21,618**	**14,896**	**11,944**	**2,952**	**6,722**	**5,648**	**1,074**	**2,248**	**4,474**
Household Composition by Age of Householder									
Owner occupied	**14,935**	**9,592**	**7,610**	**1,982**	**5,343**	**4,415**	**928**	**1,789**	**3,554**
2-or-more-person households	12,550	8,006	6,370	1,637	4,544	3,731	812	1,577	2,967
Married-couple families, no nonrelatives	10,902	6,811	5,368	1,443	4,091	3,334	757	1,401	2,690
65 years and over	1,902	1,172	849	323	729	534	195	174	555
Other male householder	555	353	290	62	203	169	34	70	133
65 years and over	96	54	38	16	42	30	12	10	33
Other female householder	1,093	842	711	131	250	229	22	105	145
65 years and over	238	181	138	43	56	46	11	15	41
1-person households	2,385	1,586	1,240	345	799	683	116	212	587
Male householder	854	532	445	87	321	267	55	96	225
65 years and over	267	154	120	34	113	85	28	20	93
Female householder	1,531	1,053	796	258	478	417	61	116	362
65 years and over	1,023	683	495	188	341	293	48	72	269
Renter occupied	**6,683**	**5,304**	**4,334**	**971**	**1,379**	**1,233**	**146**	**459**	**920**
2-or-more-person households	4,163	3,141	2,608	533	1,022	892	130	346	677
Married-couple families, no nonrelatives	2,434	1,692	1,371	321	743	621	122	247	496
65 years and over	232	179	151	28	52	43	9	19	33
Other male householder	463	377	327	50	86	82	4	35	51
65 years and over	19	14	12	2	5	5	-	1	4
Other female householder	1,266	1,072	910	162	194	190	4	64	130
65 years and over	92	73	61	12	20	17	2	7	12
1-person households	2,520	2,163	1,725	438	356	341	16	113	243
Male householder	1,081	920	739	182	161	153	8	54	107
65 years and over	161	124	103	21	37	35	2	8	29
Female householder	1,438	1,243	987	256	195	188	7	59	136
65 years and over	654	547	439	108	107	99	7	26	81
Persons 65 Years Old and Over									
Owner occupied	**14,935**	**9,592**	**7,610**	**1,982**	**5,343**	**4,415**	**928**	**1,789**	**3,554**
None	11,106	7,139	5,792	1,347	3,967	3,351	615	1,465	2,502
1 person	2,428	1,580	1,214	366	848	673	175	203	645
2 persons or more	1,401	873	604	269	528	390	138	121	407
Renter occupied	**6,683**	**5,304**	**4,334**	**971**	**1,379**	**1,233**	**146**	**459**	**920**
None	5,471	4,324	3,531	793	1,147	1,022	125	393	754
1 person	999	811	664	147	188	174	14	53	135
2 persons or more	213	169	138	31	44	37	7	13	31

Source: U.S. Bureau of the Census and U.S. Department of Housing and Urban Development, *Annual Housing Survey: 1983.*

Table 5–4. Housing Tenure by Household Composition, Sex of Householder, and Urban/Rural Location: South Region, 1983

(in thousands)

Characteristics	Total 1983	Urban			Rural				
		Total 1983	Inside SMSA's 1983	Outside SMSA's 1983	Total 1983	Nonfarm 1983	Farm 1983	Inside SMSA's 1983	Outside SMSA's 1983
All Occupied Housing Units									
Total	**27,931**	**16,482**	**12,642**	**3,839**	**11,449**	**10,532**	**917**	**3,311**	**8,139**
Household Composition by Age of Householder									
Owner occupied	**18,825**	**9,847**	**7,428**	**2,419**	**8,978**	**8,193**	**784**	**2,600**	**6,377**
2-or-more-person households	15,734	8,039	6,121	1,918	7,695	6,995	699	2,266	5,429
Married-couple families, no nonrelatives	13,325	6,650	5,056	1,594	6,675	6,037	638	1,957	4,718
65 years and over	2,330	1,211	833	378	1,119	956	163	228	891
Other male householder	726	418	336	82	308	284	24	107	201
65 years and over	123	69	46	22	55	45	10	15	40
Other female householder	1,683	971	730	242	712	674	37	202	509
65 years and over	424	250	178	72	174	150	23	39	135
1-person households	3,091	1,808	1,307	502	1,283	1,198	85	335	948
Male householder	919	490	408	82	428	391	38	111	318
65 years and over	321	159	114	45	162	144	18	27	135
Female householder	2,173	1,318	898	420	855	807	47	224	631
65 years and over	1,399	847	539	308	552	521	31	132	419
Renter occupied	**9,106**	**6,635**	**5,214**	**1,420**	**2,472**	**2,339**	**133**	**711**	**1,761**
2-or-more-person households	6,363	4,456	3,453	1,003	1,907	1,791	116	562	1,344
Married-couple families, no nonrelatives	3,784	2,463	1,860	603	1,321	1,224	98	394	927
65 years and over	287	168	123	45	119	108	12	28	91
Other male householder	758	583	482	101	175	164	11	53	122
65 years and over	54	39	25	14	15	11	3	3	11
Other female householder	1,820	1,410	1,111	299	411	404	7	116	295
65 years and over	141	93	60	33	48	45	3	9	39
1-person households	2,744	2,179	1,762	417	565	548	17	148	417
Male householder	1,295	1,009	835	174	286	270	15	76	210
65 years and over	170	130	97	33	40	37	3	3	37
Female householder	1,449	1,170	927	243	279	277	2	73	207
65 years and over	585	448	319	130	137	135	2	26	111
Persons 65 Years Old and Over									
Owner occupied	**18,825**	**9,847**	**7,428**	**2,419**	**8,978**	**8,193**	**784**	**2,600**	**6,377**
None	13,766	7,061	5,526	1,536	6,705	6,190	515	2,093	4,612
1 person	3,311	1,845	1,261	584	1,467	1,326	140	344	1,123
2 persons or more	1,747	941	642	300	806	677	129	164	642
Renter occupied	**9,106**	**6,635**	**5,214**	**1,420**	**2,472**	**2,339**	**133**	**711**	**1,761**
None	7,774	5,683	4,540	1,143	2,090	1,983	108	635	1,456
1 person	1,084	793	566	228	290	275	15	53	237
2 persons or more	249	158	109	49	91	81	10	23	69

Source: U.S. Bureau of the Census and U.S. Department of Housing and Urban Development, *Annual Housing Survey: 1983.*

Table 5–5. Housing Tenure by Household Composition, Sex of Householder, and Urban/Rural Location: West Region, 1983

(in thousands)

| Characteristics | Total 1983 | Urban | | | Rural | | | | |
		Total 1983	Inside SMSA's 1983	Outside SMSA's 1983	Total 1983	Nonfarm 1983	Farm 1983	Inside SMSA's 1983	Outside SMSA's 1983
All Occupied Housing Units									
Total	**16,868**	**13,290**	**11,880**	**1,410**	**3,578**	**3,273**	**304**	**1,446**	**2,132**
Household Composition by Age of Householder									
Owner occupied	19,955	7,323	6,506	817	2,633	2,394	239	1,078	1,555
2-or-more-person households	8,271	6,032	5,358	674	2,239	2,021	218	925	1,314
Married-couple families, no nonrelatives	6,962	4,987	4,408	579	1,975	1,773	202	821	1,155
65 years and over	1,326	949	821	128	376	334	43	116	260
Other male householder	528	413	378	35	115	106	9	44	71
65 years and over	69	54	51	4	15	12	3	6	9
Other female householder	781	632	572	60	149	143	7	60	89
65 years and over	128	102	93	9	26	22	3	7	18
1-person households	1,684	1,291	1,148	143	393	373	21	153	241
Male householder	709	546	504	42	163	151	12	75	88
65 years and over	217	171	159	12	46	42	4	16	30
Female householder	975	744	643	101	230	222	9	78	153
65 years and over	570	434	373	61	136	130	6	45	92
Renter occupied	**6,912**	**5,968**	**5,374**	**594**	**945**	**879**	**66**	**368**	**577**
2-or-more-person households	4,661	3,921	3,543	379	740	681	59	302	438
Married-couple families, no nonrelatives	2,700	2,178	1,950	228	521	469	52	212	309
65 years and over	224	183	169	14	40	34	6	15	25
Other male householder	770	678	625	53	92	87	5	43	48
65 years and over	24	19	16	4	5	5	–	2	4
Other female householder	1,191	1,064	967	97	127	125	2	46	80
65 years and over	43	37	34	4	6	6	–	3	3
1-person households	2,251	2,046	1,831	215	205	198	7	66	138
Male householder	1,179	1,059	945	113	120	114	6	32	88
65 years and over	191	154	136	18	37	35	2	6	31
Female householder	1,073	988	886	102	85	84	1	34	50
65 years and over	347	309	273	36	38	38	–	20	18
Persons 65 Years Old and Over									
Owner occupied	9,955	7,323	6,506	817	2,633	2,394	239	1,078	1,555
None	7,343	5,365	4,778	587	1,979	1,806	173	869	1,110
1 person	1,684	1,297	1,150	147	387	352	35	129	258
2 persons or more	928	661	578	83	267	236	31	80	187
Renter occupied	**6,912**	**5,968**	**5,374**	**594**	**945**	**879**	**66**	**368**	**577**
None	5,998	5,188	4,679	509	811	753	58	320	490
1 person	743	635	561	74	108	101	6	35	73
2 persons or more	171	145	134	11	26	25	2	13	14

Source: U.S. Bureau of the Census and U.S. Department of Housing and Urban Development, *Annual Housing Survey: 1983.*

Table 5–6. Housing Tenure by Household Composition, Sex of Householder, and Urban/Rural Location: Black Householder—United States, 1983

(in thousands)

Characteristics	Total 1983	Urban Total 1983	Urban Inside SMSA's 1983	Urban Outside SMSA's 1983	Rural Total 1983	Rural Nonfarm 1983	Rural Farm 1983	Rural Inside SMSA's 1983	Rural Outside SMSA's 1983
All Occupied Housing Units									
Total	**9,163**	**7,640**	**6,752**	**888**	**1,523**	**1,464**	**59**	**377**	**1,146**
Household Composition by Age of Householder									
Owner occupied	**4,123**	**3,081**	**2,661**	**420**	**1,042**	**1,008**	**35**	**255**	**787**
2-or-more-person households	3,417	2,542	2,222	320	875	849	26	218	657
Married-couple families, no nonrelatives	2,300	1,691	1,474	217	608	591	17	168	440
65 years and over	358	234	190	44	124	117	8	23	101
Other male householder	254	197	180	17	57	55	2	13	44
65 years and over	57	50	42	8	7	7	1	3	5
Other female householder	864	654	568	86	210	203	7	37	173
65 years and over	175	124	109	16	50	46	4	5	45
1-person households	706	539	439	100	167	158	9	37	130
Male householder	280	207	181	26	73	66	7	18	55
65 years and over	95	67	54	13	28	26	2	6	22
Female householder	426	332	258	74	94	92	2	19	75
65 years and over	246	178	125	52	69	67	2	12	56
Renter occupied	**5,040**	**4,559**	**4,091**	**468**	**481**	**456**	**25**	**122**	**359**
2-or-more-person households	3,581	3,220	2,884	336	361	342	19	95	266
Married-couple families, no nonrelatives	1,341	1,181	1,040	141	160	146	14	49	112
65 years and over	123	101	96	5	22	21	2	5	17
Other male householder	387	359	326	33	28	25	3	4	24
65 years and over	39	34	23	11	5	3	2	-	5
Other female householder	1,853	1,680	1,519	161	173	171	2	42	131
65 years and over	106	83	68	16	23	22	1	5	18
1-person households	1,459	1,339	1,206	132	120	114	6	27	93
Male householder	704	637	583	53	67	63	4	14	53
65 years and over	76	64	58	7	12	11	1	-	12
Female householder	755	702	623	79	53	51	2	13	39
65 years and over	249	220	192	28	29	28	2	4	26
Persons 65 Years Old and Over									
Owner occupied	**4,123**	**3,081**	**2,661**	**420**	**1,042**	**1,008**	**35**	**255**	**787**
None	3,055	2,315	2,036	279	739	722	18	200	539
1 person	774	559	460	98	215	205	10	44	171
2 persons or more	295	207	165	42	88	81	6	11	77
Renter occupied	**5,040**	**4,559**	**4,091**	**468**	**481**	**456**	**25**	**122**	**359**
None	4,399	4,017	3,616	401	382	364	18	108	274
1 person	523	448	387	60	75	69	6	12	63
2 persons or more	118	94	87	7	24	23	1	3	21

Source: U.S. Bureau of the Census and U.S. Department of Housing and Urban Development, *Annual Housing Survey: 1983.*

Table 5–7. Housing Tenure by Household Composition, Sex of Householder, and Urban/Rural Location: Spanish Origin Householder—United States, 1983

(in thousands)

Characteristics	Total 1983	Urban 1983	Rural 1983
All Occupied Housing Units			
Total	**4,594**	**3,954**	**640**
Household Composition			
by Age of Householder			
Owner occupied	**1,977**	**1,585**	**392**
2-or-more-person households	1,802	1,448	354
Married-couple families, no nonrelatives	1,525	1,217	307
65 years and over	137	112	26
Other male householder	89	70	18
65 years and over	15	8	7
Other female householder	189	160	29
65 years and over	29	25	5
1-person households	175	137	38
Male householder	71	59	12
65 years and over	23	18	5
Female householder	104	78	26
65 years and over	49	36	13
Renter occupied	**2,617**	**2,369**	**247**
2-or-more-person households	2,161	1,946	215
Married-couple families, no nonrelatives	1,282	1,121	161
65 years and over	65	54	11
Other male householder	243	221	23
65 years and over	8	7	1
Other female householder	636	605	31
65 years and over	28	27	1
1-person households	456	423	33
Male householder	244	225	19
65 years and over	31	27	3
Female householder	211	197	14
65 years and over	68	59	9
Persons 65 Years Old and Over			
Owner occupied	**1,977**	**1,585**	**392**
None	1,644	1,313	331
1 person	245	205	40
2 persons or more	88	67	21
Renter occupied	**2,617**	**2,369**	**247**
None	2,367	2,149	218
1 person	200	176	24
2 persons or more	50	44	6

Source: U.S. Bureau of the Census and U.S. Department of Housing and Urban Development, *Annual Housing Survey: 1983.*

9999999999

9999999999999

9999999999

99999999999999999

Table 5–8. Presence of Persons 65 Years Old and Over by Age of Householder, and Location of Present Unit by Tenure of Present Unit and Previous Unit: United States, 1983

(in thousands)

| Characteristics | Present unit: Age of householder and presence of persons 65 years old and over | | | | | | | | | |
| | Age of householder | | | | | | | Units with persons 65 years old and over | | |
	Total	Under 25 years	25 to 29 years	30 to 34 years	35 to 44 years	45 to 64 years	65 years and over	Total	None	1 or more
United States										
Units Occupied by Recent Movers										
Total	13,531	3,261	3,116	2,258	2,345	1,873	679	13,531	12,722	809
Same householder in present and previous unit	10,319	1,831	2,393	1,908	1,978	1,624	585	10,319	9,618	701
Previous unit owner occupied:										
Present unit owner occupied	1,649	62	228	334	435	452	139	1,649	1,476	174
Present unit renter occupied	1,384	173	258	233	329	281	111	1,384	1,258	126
Previous unit renter occupied:										
Present unit owner occupied	1,397	165	370	351	283	189	40	1,397	1,340	57
Present unit renter occupied	5,887	1,431	1,538	991	931	703	295	5,887	5,543	344
Different householder in present and previous unit	3,213	1,429	723	351	367	249	94	3,213	3,105	108
Inside standard metropolitan statistical areas										
Units Occupied by Recent Movers										
Total	9,613	2,319	2,292	1,668	1,683	1,230	421	9,613	9,100	513
Same householder in present and previous unit	7,252	1,285	1,734	1,397	1,408	1,068	360	7,252	6,810	442
Previous unit owner occupied:										
Present unit owner occupied	1,009	26	154	213	306	252	58	1,009	930	78
Present unit renter occupied	932	120	181	159	226	177	69	932	852	80
Previous unit renter occupied:										
Present unit owner occupied	980	104	250	290	197	114	23	980	947	32
Present unit renter occupied	4,332	1,035	1,149	735	678	525	210	4,332	4,080	252
Different householder in present and previous unit	2,361	1,033	558	271	275	162	61	2,361	2,290	71
In central city										
Units Occupied by Recent Movers										
Total	4,641	1,245	1,105	741	747	572	232	4,641	4,370	270
Same householder in present and previous unit	3,430	689	843	621	598	482	197	3,430	3,196	234
Previous unit owner occupied:										
Present unit owner occupied	267	10	43	50	70	72	23	267	237	30
Present unit renter occupied	435	68	86	84	94	73	30	435	403	31
Previous unit renter occupied:										
Present unit owner occupied	412	34	102	118	92	55	12	412	395	17
Present unit renter occupied	2,316	578	613	369	342	282	133	2,316	2,161	156
Different householder in present and previous unit	1,211	556	262	119	149	90	35	1,211	1,174	36
Not in central city										
Units Occupied by Recent Movers										
Total	4,972	1,074	1,187	928	937	658	190	4,972	4,730	243
Same householder in present and previous unit	3,822	596	891	776	810	586	163	3,822	3,614	208
Previous unit owner occupied:										
Present unit owner occupied	741	16	111	163	236	180	35	741	693	48
Present unit renter occupied	497	52	96	75	132	103	39	497	448	49
Previous unit renter occupied:										
Present unit owner occupied	568	71	148	172	105	60	12	568	552	15
Present unit renter occupied	2,016	458	536	366	336	243	77	2,016	1,920	96
Different householder in present and previous unit	1,150	478	296	152	127	72	27	1,150	1,116	34

Table 5–8. (continued)

Characteristics	Present unit: Age of householder and presence of persons 65 years old and over									
		Age of householder						Units with persons 65 years old and over		
	Total	Under 25 years	25 to 29 years	30 to 34 years	35 to 44 years	45 to 64 years	65 years and over	Total	None	1 or more
	Outside standard metropolitan statistical areas									
Units Occupied by Recent Movers										
Total	3,918	942	824	590	661	643	257	3,918	3,622	296
Same householder in present and previous unit	3,066	546	659	511	570	557	224	3,066	2,808	258
Previous unit owner occupied:										
Present unit owner occupied	641	36	74	121	129	200	81	641	545	95
Present unit renter occupied	453	53	77	74	103	104	42	453	407	46
Previous unit renter occupied:										
Present unit owner occupied	418	61	120	61	86	75	16	418	393	25
Present unit renter occupied	1,555	396	388	256	252	178	85	1,555	1,463	92
Different householder in present and previous unit	852	396	165	79	92	87	33	852	814	38

Source: Bureau of the Census and U.S. Department of Housing and Urban Development, *Annual Housing Survey: 1983.*

GEOGRAPHIC MOBILITY

Table 5–9. Housing Units Occupied by Recent Movers by Tenure, Household Composition, Sex of Householder, and Inside/Outside SMSA's: United States, 1983

(in thousands)

Characteristics	All occupied housing units					Housing units occupied by recent movers				
		Inside SMSA's					Inside SMSA's			
	Total	Total	In central city	Not In central city	Outside SMSA's	Total	Total	In central city	Not In central city	Outside SMSA's
All Occupied Housing Units										
Total	**84,638**	**57,798**	**25,161**	**32,637**	**26,840**	**13,531**	**9,613**	**4,641**	**4,972**	**3,918**
Household Composition										
by Age of Householder										
Owner occupied	**54,724**	**35,166**	**12,372**	**22,794**	**19,558**	**3,574**	**2,342**	**778**	**1,584**	**1,231**
2-or-more-person households	45,895	29,523	9,935	19,589	16,371	3,049	1,963	634	1,329	1,086
Married-couple families, no nonrelatives	39,073	24,825	7,979	16,846	14,248	2,551	1,613	486	1,127	938
65 years and over	6,926	4,041	1,456	2,585	2,885	107	48	13	35	59
Other male householder	2,325	1,590	609	981	735	247	173	71	102	74
65 years and over	406	252	106	147	154	2	-	-	-	2
Other female householder	4,497	3,109	1,347	1,762	1,388	252	177	77	100	74
65 years and over	1,027	659	340	319	368	13	6	3	2	7
1-person households	8,829	5,642	2,437	3,205	3,187	524	379	144	235	145
Male householder	3,071	2,070	868	1,202	1,001	302	218	79	140	84
65 years and over	1,063	638	286	352	426	19	11	6	4	8
Female householder	5,758	3,572	1,570	2,003	2,186	222	161	65	95	61
65 years and over	3,645	2,141	946	1,194	1,504	55	30	15	14	25
Renter occupied	**29,914**	**22,632**	**12,788**	**9,844**	**7,282**	**9,958**	**7,271**	**3,863**	**3,408**	**2,687**
2-or-more-person households	19,757	14,715	7,949	6,765	5,042	7,002	5,053	2,559	2,495	1,949
Married-couple families, no nonrelatives	11,448	8,162	3,990	4,172	3,286	3,831	2,651	1,184	1,467	1,179
65 years and over	1,115	839	435	404	276	101	74	32	42	27
Other male householder	2,515	2,018	1,112	906	497	1,187	939	499	440	248
65 years and over	124	83	56	27	41	24	16	15	1	8
Other female householder	5,794	4,534	2,847	1,688	1,259	1,985	1,464	876	588	521
65 years and over	403	285	188	97	117	27	18	9	9	9
1-person households	10,157	7,918	4,839	3,078	2,240	2,956	2,218	1,304	913	738
Male householder	4,584	3,549	2,187	1,362	1,035	1,648	1,231	716	515	417
65 years and over	734	535	364	172	199	99	68	42	26	30
Female householder	5,573	4,369	2,653	1,716	1,204	1,308	987	589	398	321
65 years and over	2,332	1,734	1,067	667	599	232	151	96	55	81

Source: U.S. Bureau of the Census and U.S. Department of Housing and Urban Development, *Annual Housing Survey: 1983.*

Table 5–10. General Mobility, by Region and Age

(Mobility data from March 1983 to March 1984. Numbers in thousands.)

United States and Regions	Total	Same House (Non-Movers)	Different House in the United States (Movers)									Movers from Abroad
			Total	Different County								
				Same County	Total	Same State	Different State					
							Total	North-east	Midwest	South	West	
NUMBER												
United States in 1984												
Total, 1 year old and over	228,232	188,853	38,300	23,659	14,641	8,198	6,444	985	1,552	2,235	1,672	1,079
55 to 64 years	22,033	20,597	1,415	808	607	335	272	61	65	80	67	21
65 years and over	26,291	25,073	1,200	717	484	283	201	31	29	74	67	17
Northeast in 1984												
Total, 1 year old and over	48,532	42,712	5,607	3,560	2,047	1,154	893	407	105	252	130	213
55 to 64 years	5,174	4,924	248	146	102	61	41	22	6	6	6	2
65 years and over	6,055	5,808	247	164	83	58	25	10	–	7	8	–
Midwest (Formerly North Central) in 1984												
Total, 1 year old and over	57,382	48,414	8,826	5,708	3,118	1,848	1,270	124	450	359	337	141
55 to 64 years	5,565	5,246	317	194	123	76	47	2	11	12	22	2
65 years and over	6,512	6,240	269	173	95	49	46	2	7	21	16	4
South in 1984												
Total, 1 year old and over	77,436	62,755	14,298	8,415	5,883	3,223	2,661	355	624	1,262	420	383
55 to 64 years	7,368	6,867	496	261	236	109	126	32	34	54	6	4
65 years and over	9,129	8,697	422	229	192	109	84	14	11	42	16	10
West in 1984												
Total, 1 year old and over	44,882	34,973	9,568	5,976	3,593	1,973	1,620	99	373	362	785	341
55 to 64 years	3,926	3,560	354	207	147	89	58	5	13	7	33	13
65 years and over	4,594	4,328	263	149	113	68	46	4	11	3	27	4
PERCENT DISTRIBUTION												
United States in 1984												
Total, 1 year old and over	100.0	82.7	16.8	10.4	6.4	3.6	2.8	0.4	0.7	1.0	0.7	0.5
55 to 64 years	100.0	93.5	6.4	3.7	2.8	1.5	1.2	0.3	0.3	0.4	0.3	0.1
65 years and over	100.0	95.4	4.6	2.7	1.8	1.1	0.8	0.1	0.1	0.3	0.3	0.1
Northeast in 1984												
Total, 1 year old and over	100.0	88.0	11.6	7.3	4.2	2.4	1.8	0.8	0.2	0.5	0.3	0.4
55 to 64 years	100.0	95.2	4.8	2.8	2.0	1.2	0.8	0.4	0.1	0.1	0.1	–
65 years and over	100.0	95.9	4.1	2.7	1.4	1.0	0.4	0.2	–	0.1	0.1	–
Midwest (Formerly North Central) in 1984												
Total, 1 year old and over	100.0	84.4	15.4	9.9	5.4	3.2	2.2	0.2	0.8	0.6	0.6	0.2
55 to 64 years	100.0	94.3	5.7	3.5	2.2	1.4	0.8	–	0.2	0.2	0.4	–
65 years and over	100.0	95.8	4.1	2.7	1.5	0.8	0.7	–	0.1	0.3	0.2	0.1
South in 1984												
Total, 1 year old and over	100.0	81.0	18.5	10.9	7.6	4.2	3.4	0.5	0.8	1.6	0.5	0.5
55 to 64 years	100.0	93.2	6.7	3.5	3.2	1.5	1.7	0.4	0.5	0.7	0.1	0.1
65 years and over	100.0	95.3	4.6	2.5	2.1	1.2	0.9	0.2	0.1	0.5	0.2	0.1
West in 1984												
Total, 1 year old and over	100.0	77.9	21.3	13.3	8.0	4.4	3.6	0.2	0.8	0.8	1.7	0.8
55 to 64 years	100.0	90.7	9.0	5.3	3.7	2.3	1.5	0.1	0.3	0.2	0.8	0.3
65 years and over	100.0	94.2	5.7	3.2	2.5	1.5	1.0	0.1	0.2	0.1	0.6	0.1

Source: U.S. Bureau of the Census. *Current Population Reports,* Series P-20, no. 407.

HOUSING CHARACTERISTICS

Figure 5–2. Year Housing Structure Built of Householders 65 Years and Older

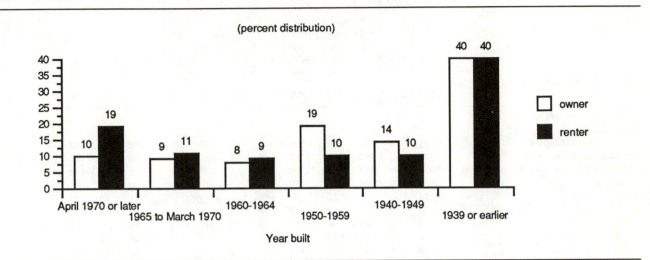

(percent distribution)

Source: U.S. Senate. Special Committee on Aging and the American Association of Retired Persons. *Aging in America: Trends and Projections,* 1984; U.S. Bureau of the Census, *America in Transition: An Aging Society,* 1983; and U.S. Bureau of the Census, Annual Housing Survey, 1980, unpublished.

Table 5–11. 1973 Characteristics of Housing Units Removed From the Inventory by Household Composition, Sex of Householder, and Inside/Outside SMSA's, Monitored in 1983: United States

(in thousands)

Characteristics	All units removed					Conventional units removed					Mobile homes and trailers				
		Inside SMSA's					Inside SMSA's					Inside SMSA's			
	Total	Total	In central city	Not in central city	Outside SMSA's	Total	Total	In central city	Not in central city	Outside SMSA's	Total	Total	In central city	Not in central city	Outside SMSA's
All Occupied Housing Units															
Total	**4,540**	**2,766**	**1,733**	**1,032**	**1,775**	**3,741**	**2,486**	**1,694**	**792**	**1,255**	**799**	**280**	**40**	**240**	**520**
Household Composition by Age of Householder															
Owner occupied	1,700	774	315	460	926	1,044	542	277	265	502	656	232	38	195	424
2-or-more-person households	1,272	565	215	350	707	778	395	185	209	383	494	171	30	141	323
Male head, wife present, no nonrelatives	1,050	451	157	294	599	604	298	129	169	306	445	153	28	125	292
65 years and over	152	73	29	44	79	129	63	29	34	66	23	10	–	10	13
Other male head	73	37	15	22	36	55	27	13	14	28	18	10	2	8	8
65 years and over	12	5	4	2	7	10	5	4	2	5	2	–	–	–	2
Female head	149	77	44	34	72	119	70	44	26	49	30	8	–	8	23
65 years and over	46	23	13	10	23	44	23	13	10	21	2	–	–	–	2
1-person households	428	209	99	110	219	266	148	92	56	118	162	62	8	54	101
65 years and over	233	114	47	67	119	166	84	47	37	83	67	30	–	30	37
Renter occupied	**2,840**	**1,991**	**1,419**	**572**	**849**	**2,697**	**1,944**	**1,417**	**527**	**754**	**143**	**47**	**2**	**46**	**96**
2-or-more-person households	1,805	1,226	855	371	579	1,706	1,193	854	340	513	99	33	2	31	66
Male head, wife present, no nonrelatives	1,133	709	441	268	424	1,059	683	439	244	376	74	26	2	24	48
65 years and over	112	63	38	25	50	111	63	38	25	48	2	–	–	–	2
Other male head	185	134	94	41	51	175	131	94	37	44	10	4	–	4	7
65 years and over	18	12	7	5	5	18	12	7	5	5	–	–	–	–	–
Female head	486	383	321	62	104	472	379	321	58	92	15	4	–	4	11
65 years and over	39	26	19	7	13	37	26	19	7	11	2	–	–	–	2
1-person households	1,035	765	563	201	271	991	750	563	187	241	44	14	–	14	30
65 years and over	320	203	137	66	118	305	201	137	64	104	16	2	–	2	14

Source: U.S. Bureau of the Census and U.S. Department of Housing and Urban Development, *Annual Housing Survey: 1983.*

Table 5–12. Selected Characteristics for New Construction Units by Household Composition, Sex of Householder, and Inside/Outside SMSA's: United States, 1983

(in thousands)

Characteristics	All new construction					Conventional new construction					Mobile homes and trailers				
		Inside SMSA's					Inside SMSA's					Inside SMSA's			
	Total	Total	In central city	Not in central city	Outside SMSA's	Total	Total	In central city	Not in central city	Outside SMSA's	Total	Total	In central city	Not in central city	Outside SMSA's
All Occupied Housing Units															
Total	**21,766**	**14,008**	**4,275**	**9,733**	**7,758**	**19,199**	**13,117**	**4,166**	**8,951**	**6,082**	**2,567**	**891**	**109**	**782**	**1,676**
Household Composition															
by Age of Householder															
Owner occupied	14,534	8,446	1,811	6,635	6,087	12,291	7,651	1,718	5,933	4,640	2,243	796	93	702	1,447
2-or-more-person households	12,892	7,430	1,566	5,865	5,462	11,120	6,858	1,500	5,359	4,262	1,772	572	66	506	1,200
Married-couple families, no nonrelatives	11,396	6,529	1,354	5,174	4,867	9,896	6,042	1,300	4,742	3,854	1,500	487	54	432	1,013
65 years and over	1,056	524	114	410	531	823	433	106	326	390	233	92	8	84	141
Other male householder	572	369	73	296	203	471	342	70	272	130	101	27	3	24	74
65 years and over	26	11	–	11	15	19	9	–	9	10	6	2	–	2	4
Other female householder	924	533	138	394	391	752	474	130	345	278	172	58	8	50	113
65 years and over	71	37	12	25	35	57	32	12	20	26	14	5	–	5	9
1-person households	1,641	1,016	245	771	626	1,171	792	218	574	378	471	224	27	196	247
Male householder	700	471	128	343	230	507	374	113	261	133	193	96	15	82	97
65 years and over	94	45	9	37	49	62	37	9	28	25	32	8	–	8	24
Female householder	941	545	117	428	396	664	418	105	314	245	278	127	13	115	150
65 years and over	394	199	42	156	195	254	136	35	101	118	139	63	8	55	77
Renter occupied	**7,232**	**5,561**	**2,464**	**3,098**	**1,671**	**6,908**	**5,466**	**2,448**	**3,018**	**1,442**	**324**	**95**	**16**	**80**	**229**
2-or-more-person households	4,688	3,558	1,455	2,103	1,130	4,431	3,480	1,445	2,035	951	257	78	10	68	179
Married-couple families, no nonrelatives	2,762	2,063	759	1,304	699	2,590	2,009	756	1,253	581	172	54	4	51	117
65 years and over	273	205	62	143	68	266	203	62	141	63	7	2	–	2	6
Other male householder	659	547	236	311	112	632	537	234	303	94	27	10	2	8	17
65 years and over	25	22	14	8	3	24	21	14	8	3	1	1	–	1	–
Other female householder	1,267	948	460	488	320	1,209	933	455	478	275	58	14	5	9	44
65 years and over	62	37	23	14	25	56	35	23	12	21	6	2	–	2	4
1-person households	2,544	2,003	1,009	995	541	2,477	1,986	1,003	983	491	67	17	6	11	50
Male householder	1,060	850	422	428	210	1,021	839	421	418	182	39	11	2	9	28
65 years and over	144	101	60	41	43	139	99	60	39	40	6	2	–	2	3
Female householder	1,484	1,153	586	567	331	1,456	1,147	582	565	309	28	6	4	2	22
65 years and over	651	465	259	206	187	641	461	257	204	179	11	4	2	2	7

Source: U.S. Bureau of the Census and U.S. Department of Housing and Urban Development, *Annual Housing Survey: 1983.*

HOUSING FINANCE

Table 5–13. The Value of Homes and Mortgage/Installment Debt by Age of Owner: 1983

Age	Net Equity of Homeowner[1]		Age of Household Head	Proportion of Households with	
	Mean	Median		Mortgage Debt[2]	Installment Debt
Under 25	$18,870	$13,780			
25-35	32,640	27,770	Total Households	57%	41%
35-45	52,070	40,600	Under 35	80	52
45-55	64,470	50,000	35-50	80	54
55-65	73,580	55,000	50-65	49	37
65-75	63,670	45,000	65-75	20	14
75 and over	47,760	40,000	75 and over	5	6

Notes: 1. Based on nonfarm homeowners
2. Percent of homeowners
Source: The Conference Board, *Midlife and Beyond: The $800 Billion Over-Fifty Market.* 1985.

Table 5–14. Mortgage Debt by Household Income and Age of Householder, 1983

| | All households | | Household Income | | | | | | | | | | | |
| | | | Under $10,000 | | $10,000–$19,999 | | $20,000–29,999 | | $30,000–39,999 | | $40,000–49,999 | | $50,000 and over | |
Age of household head	Average mortgage debt	Percent with debt	Average mortgage debt	Percent with debt	Average mortgage debt	Percent with debt	Average mortgage debt	Percent with debt	Average mortgage debt	Percent with debt	Average mortgage debt	Percent with debt	Average mortgage debt	Percent with debt
<25	$26,233	12%	$3,550	2%	$22,273	15%	$29,175	24%	*	*	*	*	*	*
25-34	33,520	40	28,560	10	19,514	28	26,924	45	$34,575	67%	$44,994	62%	$77,976	71%
35-44	33,878	58	29,815	20	27,386	38	24,779	54	30,983	72	38,344	78	52,508	80
45-54	29,106	53	18,522	18	20,032	38	21,824	54	24,717	60	29,117	78	40,692	77
55-64	22,347	34	11,755	11	17,166	29	18,493	27	21,291	46	26,741	63	36,036	56
65+	19,780	10	9,100	5	18,823	13	23,550	18	7,711	18	28,256	23	33,714	28
All	29,916	37	19,133	9	21,178	27	24,448	42	29,505	61	35,149	68	48,749	69

Note: Mortgage debt consists of total debt owed on first and second mortgages. Average debt is for householders that hold mortgage debt, including farm families and owners of mobile homes.
*Denotes a group size of less than 10.
Source: 1983 Survey of Consumer Finances, Federal Reserve Board.

Table 5–15. Housing Costs as a Percentage of Household Income, by Age and Sex of Householder

(Housing costs include gross rent or mortgage, basic utility costs [if not included in the rent], real estate taxes, and insurance for owners.)

	Median percentage by age							
	25 to 64	55 to 59	60 to 64	65 to 69	70 to 74	75 to 79	80 to 84	85 plus
Male:								
Rent	18.4	16.2	17.8	21.7	23.5	24.6	25.5	25.8
Own, with mortgage	18.1	13.9	15.6	20.5	24.0	27.6	30.5	33.4
Own, without mortgage	7.2	7.0	8.1	10.9	12.5	13.5	14.6	15.6
Female:								
Rent	27.2	25.9	27.2	29.8	30.8	31.4	31.7	31.8
Own, with mortgage	24.7	22.8	26.1	33.1	36.5	37.4	38.4	39.3
Own, without mortgage	13.1	12.8	14.6	17.5	19.1	20.5	21.4	22.3

Source: U.S. Bureau of the Census, 1980 Census of Population and Housing. Public Use Microdata Sample, special tabulations.

Table 5–16. Housing Conditions of Households Headed by a Person Aged 62 Years or Older, by Income and Type of Housing: 1981

	Income[1]			
	Very low Income	Low Income	Other	Total
Renters (thousands of households):				
Living in housing requiring rehabilitation[2]	530	90	100	730
Housing costs exceed:[3]				
30 percent of income	1,660	400	80	2,140
50 percent of income	830	70	20	920
Percent of all households in category:				
Living in housing requiring rehabilitation[2]	16	9	10	14
Housing costs exceed:[3]				
30 percent of income	54	40	9	43
50 percent of income	27	7	2	18
Homeowners (thousands of households):				
Living in housing requiring rehabilitation[2]	510	90	120	720
Housing costs exceed:[4]				
30 percent of income	1,460	240	120	1,820
50 percent of income	450	20	20	490
Percent of all households in category:[5]				
Living in housing requiring rehabilitation[4]	9	3	2	5
Housing costs exceed:[3]				
30 percent of income	39	9	3	17
50 percent of income	12	1	0	5

Notes: 1. Income classification corresponds to definition in housing assistance programs. Very low income households are those with family incomes ranging from 35 percent of the area median for a one-person household to 66 percent of the area median for a household with eight or more members. (For a four-person household, the threshold is 50 percent of area median.) Low-income designation ranges from 56 percent of area median for a one-person household to 100 percent of area median for a household with eight or more members. (For a four-person household, the threshold is 80 percent.)

2. Units in need of rehabilitation are defined here as those lacking complete plumbing or kitchen facilities, or with two or more of 11 different structural defects.

3. Housing costs for renters include rent payments due the landlord plus utility costs not included in the rent payment.

4. Housing costs for homeowners include mortgage payments, real estate taxes, property insurance, and utilities. Housing costs are not reported for homes on 10 or more acres, or with a business on the property.

5. Calculated as a percent of households for which data are available.

Source: Congressional Budget Office tabulations of the 1981 Annual Housing Survey.

Figure 5–3. Net Equity in Homes of Households, by Age of Household Head: 1983

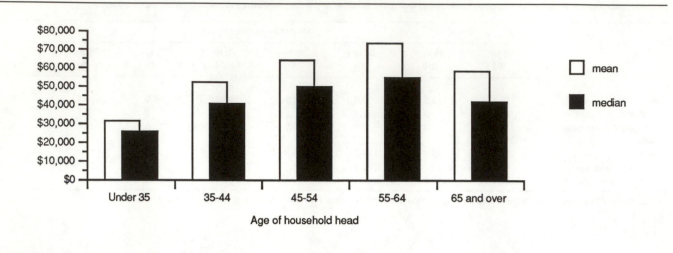

Note: Based on nonfarm homeowners, excluding owners of mobile homes.

Source: Robert A. Avery, Gregory E. Elliehausen, Glenn B. Canner, and Thomas A. Gustafson. "Survey of Consumer Finances, 1983." *Federal Reserve Bulletin,* September 1984.

Table 5–17. Equity Held by Elderly Homeowners With No Mortgage Debt

(Number of Households [000])

Equity ($000)	Age of Household Head		
	62–69	70 +	Total Elderly
<10	94	200	294
10–20	192	448	640
20–30	397	709	1,106
30–50	1,177	1,738	2,915
50–70	953	1,129	2,082
70–100	685	732	1,417
100 +	393	504	897
Total	3,892	5,460	9,351
Total Equity for Age Class* ($ billion)	243	305	548
Average Equity for Age Class* ($ thousand)	63	56	59

Note: *Total equity for each range is estimated by using the equity range mid-point for all units in the range.

Source: U.S. Bureau of the Census and U.S. Department of Housing and Urban Development. *Annual Housing Survey: 1983.*

HOUSING ALTERNATIVES

Figure 5–4. Estimates of the Number of Elderly Persons Residing in Alternative Housing and Living Arrangements: 1982

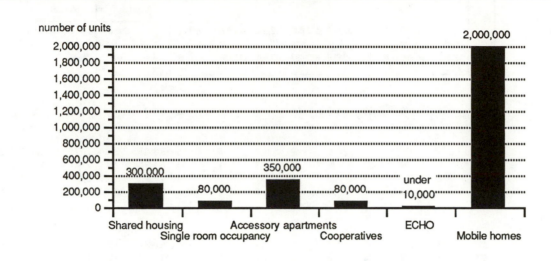

Note: *ECHO = a small, temporary unit (e.g., trailer or prefabricated unit) placed next to or behind a single-family home.

Source: Alternative Housing and Living Arrangements for Independent Living. Ann Arbor, MI: National Policy Center on Housing and Living Arrangements of Older Americans, 1982.

Table 5–18. Residence in Publicly Owned or Other Subsidized Renter-Occupied Housing—Households and Persons in Households, by Household Money Income and Poverty Status of the Primary Family or Individual: 1984

(Numbers in thousands. Households as of March 1985).

Characteristic	Total	Under $2,500	$2,500 to $4,999	$5,000 to $7,499	$7,500 to $9,999	$10,000 to $12,499	$12,500 to $14,999	$15,000 to $19,999	$20,000 and over	Median Income (dollars) Value	Median Income (dollars) Standard error	Mean Income (dollars) Value	Mean Income (dollars) Standard error	Below poverty Number	Below poverty Poverty rate
Householder 65 Years Old and Over															
Total	1,157	25	398	400	149	94	37	20	35	5,977	140	7,209	238	444	38.4
Region															
Northeast	406	4	123	137	50	49	20	8	16	6,389	239	7,774	414	129	31.7
Midwest	313	8	93	120	49	24	8	1	10	6,143	244	7,361	549	108	34.5
South	297	12	163	70	25	8	7	8	4	4,594	172	5,822	315	188	63.4
West	141	–	19	72	25	14	2	4	5	6,772	247	8,165	586	19	13.6
Race and Spanish Origin of Householder[1]															
White	953	17	316	337	129	75	34	16	30	6,066	150	7,322	277	342	35.8
Black	186	7	79	54	18	19	3	3	4	5,326	418	6,556	420	98	52.8
Spanish origin	63	1	30	19	6	1	4	1	1	(B)	(B)	(B)	(B)	36	(B)
Type of Household															
Family households	171	4	13	37	35	40	21	10	11	9,708	592	10,975	900	39	22.9
Married-couple families	118	2	7	27	22	27	19	5	10	10,170	713	11,668	1,235	19	16.4
Male householder, no wife present	3	–	–	–	1	–	–	–	2	(B)	(B)	(B)	(B)	–	(B)
Female householder, no husband present	50	3	6	10	12	13	2	4	–	(B)	(B)	(B)	(B)	19	(B)
Nonfamily households	986	20	385	363	114	54	16	11	23	5,608	142	6,556	221	405	41.1
Male householder	154	1	51	63	21	11	3	1	4	5,986	325	6,734	384	52	33.9
Female householder	833	19	334	300	93	43	13	10	20	5,529	158	6,523	252	353	42.4
Size of Household															
One person (living alone)	975	20	385	361	108	51	16	11	23	5,572	142	6,528	223	401	41.1
Two persons	153	4	13	33	38	31	20	5	8	9,205	535	10,569	980	31	20.6
Three persons	11	–	–	1	2	3	–	5	–	(B)	(B)	(B)	(B)	1	(B)
Four persons	11	–	–	1	–	5	1	–	3	(B)	(B)	(B)	(B)	4	(B)
Five persons	2	–	–	1	1	–	–	–	–	(B)	(B)	(B)	(B)	2	(B)
Six persons	5	–	–	3	–	3	–	–	–	(B)	(B)	(B)	(B)	5	(B)
Seven persons or more	–	–	–	–	–	–	–	–	–	(B)	(B)	(B)	(B)	–	(B)
Mean size of household	1.21	1.18	1.03	1.14	1.33	1.72	1.60	1.70	1.51	(X)	(X)	(X)	(X)	1.18	(X)
Presence of Children under 18 Years Old															
Households with children under 6 years old	30	–	3	6	6	10	1	3	2	(B)	(B)	(B)	(B)	16	(B)
Households with children under 18 years old	12	–	–	4	2	2	–	2	2	(B)	(B)	(B)	(B)	8	(B)
Households with no children under 18 years old	1,127	25	394	394	144	84	36	17	33	5,918	140	7,125	242	429	38.0

Table 5–18. (continued)

Characteristic	Total	Under $2,500	$2,500 to $4,999	$5,000 to $7,499	$7,500 to $9,999	$10,000 to $12,499	$12,500 to $14,999	$15,000 to $19,999	$20,000 and over	Median Income (dollars) Value	Median Income (dollars) Standard error	Mean Income (dollars) Value	Mean Income (dollars) Standard error	Below current poverty level Number	Below current poverty level Poverty rate
Work Experience in 1984 of Householder															
Total civilian hhldrs.	1,157	25	398	400	149	94	37	20	35	5,977	140	7,209	238	444	38.4
Worked	77	1	7	23	11	13	7	10	5	9,191	1,233	10,617	945	8	11.0
Worked at full-time jobs	28	–	–	5	3	6	5	3	5	(B)	(B)	(B)	(B)	–	(B)
40 weeks or more	16	–	–	1	3	3	1	3	4	(B)	(B)	(B)	(B)	–	(B)
27 to 39 weeks	2	–	–	2	–	–	–	–	1	(B)	(B)	(B)	(B)	–	(B)
26 weeks or less	10	–	–	3	–	3	4	–	–	(B)	(B)	(B)	(B)	–	(B)
Worked at part-time jobs	49	1	6	17	9	7	2	7	–	(B)	(B)	(B)	(B)	8	(B)
40 weeks or more	27	–	3	14	1	4	1	4	–	(B)	(B)	(B)	(B)	3	(B)
27 to 39 weeks	1	–	–	–	1	–	–	–	–	(B)	(B)	(B)	(B)	–	(B)
26 weeks or less	21	1	4	3	6	3	–	3	–	(B)	(B)	(B)	(B)	5	(B)
Did not work	1,081	24	391	377	138	81	30	10	29	5,832	143	6,967	243	436	40.3
Total Money Earnings in 1984[2]															
With earnings	77	1	7	23	11	13	7	10	5	9,191	1,233	10,617	945	8	11.0
Without earnings	1,081	24	391	377	138	81	30	10	29	5,832	143	6,967	243	436	40.3

Notes: 1. Persons of Spanish origin may be of any race.

2. Excludes a relatively small number of households reporting 'no income.'

B Base less than 75,000

X Not applicable

Source: U.S. Bureau of the Census. *Current Population Reports,* Series P-60, no. 150.

Table 5–19. Low-Income Public Housing Units, by Progress Stage: 1960 to 1985

(In thousands. As of Dec. 31. Housing for the elderly intended for persons 62 years old or over, disabled, or handicapped. Includes Puerto Rico and Virgin Islands. Covers units subsidized by HUD under annual contributions contracts. See also *Historical Statistics, Colonial Times to 1970.* Series N 186–191.)

Year	Total	Occupied units[1]	Under construction	Other[2]	Year	Total	Occupied units[1]	Under construction	Other[2]
1960	**593.3**	**478.2**	**36.4**	**78.8**	**1982**	**1,432.2**	**1,231.4**	**66.7**	**134.1**
Elderly	18.9	1.1	4.1	13.7	Elderly	392.0	328.4	27.7	35.9
1970	**1,155.3**	**893.5**	**126.8**	**135.0**	**1983**	**1,483.3**	**1,262.5**	**86.7**	**134.1**
Elderly	249.4	143.4	65.7	40.3	Elderly	410.0	338.4	35.7	35.9
1975	**1,316.7**	**1,180.4**	**52.9**	**83.4**	**1984**	**1,368.7**	**1,312.9**	**24.0**	**31.8**
Elderly	336.3	288.3	24.3	23.7	Elderly	373.0	351.4	9.4	12.2
1980	**1,321.1**	**1,195.6**	**20.9**	**104.6**	**1985**	**1,373.7**	**1,330.9**	**6.4**	**36.4**
Elderly	358.3	317.7	11.5	29.1	Elderly	373.4	359.1	1.8	12.4
1981	**1,404.0**	**1,229.3**	**51.5**	**123.2**					
Elderly	385.4	327.7	21.8	35.9					

Notes: 1. Under management or available for occupancy.

2. To be constructed or to go directly "under management" because no rehabilitation needed.

Source: U.S. Dept. of Housing and Urban Development, unpublished data.

Table 5–20. Summary of HUD Elderly Housing Program Activities

(Cumulative through Sept. 30, 1985)

Section and program	Status of program	Number of projects	Units or beds	Mortgages or loans	Elderly units	Percent of elderly units
Unassisted programs–Insurance written[1]						
231–Mortgage insurance of housing elderly	Active	498	66,164	$1,154,618,727	66,164	100
221(d)(3)–Multifamily rental housing	do	3,616	364,722	6,159,138,003	35,858	10
221(d)(4)–For low- and moderate-income families	do	6,904	752,056	20,113,648,217	115,962	15
232–Nursing home and intermediate care facilities	do	1,513	178,936	2,609,104,017	178,936	100
242–Mortgage insurance for hospitals	do	232	62,563	4,797,533,670	NA	NA
Assisted programs[2]						
202–Direct loans for housing for elderly and handicapped	do	3,358	188,071	7,761,806,605	169,264	90
202/236–202/236 conversions	Inactive	182	28,591	487,075,452	28,591	100
8[3]–Low-income rental assistance:						
New construction	Active	10,694	658,693	NA	342,453	52
Substantial rehabilitation	do	2,261	147,767	NA	53,981	37
Moderate rehabilitation	do	1,503	96,212	NA	20,932	22
Existing	do	NA	1,283,674	NA	340,824	27
Housing vouchers	do	NA	[4]52,468	NA	—	—

Notes: 1. Figures obtained from Management Information Systems Division. Housing. Department of HUD.

2. Figures for Assisted Programs indicate cumulative reservations. Figures were obtained from the HUD FY 1986 Budget Summary and preliminary FY 1985 actual data.

3. Excludes 202/8 reservations.

4. Figure obtained from Assisted Housing Accounting System, Office of Finance and Accounting, HUD.

Source: U.S. Senate, Special Committee on Aging. *Developments in Aging 1985. Volume 2–Appendixes.* A Report of the Special Committee on Aging. Washington, D.C.: U.S. Government Printing Office, 1986.

Table 5–21. Mobile Home/Trailer Tenure by Household Composition, Sex of Householder, and Urban/Rural Location

(in thousands)

Characteristics	Total	Urban	Rural
All Occupied Mobile Homes and Trailers			
Total	**3,999**	**1,041**	**2,958**
Household Composition by Age of Householder			
Owner occupied	**3,236**	**849**	**2,387**
2-or-more-person households	2,382	521	1,861
Married-couple families, no nonrelatives	1,974	430	1,544
65 years and over	345	143	202
Other male householder	156	36	120
65 years and over	11	–	11
Other female householder	253	55	198
65 years and over	25	6	19
1-person households	854	328	526
Male householder	397	141	256
65 years and over	110	48	62
Female householder	457	187	270
65 years and over	267	130	137
Renter occupied	**763**	**192**	**571**
2-or-more-person households	559	139	420
Married-couple families, no nonrelatives	345	77	267
65 years and over	12	2	11
Other male householder	78	23	54
65 years and over	6	2	4
Other female householder	137	38	99
65 years and over	9	5	5
1-person households	204	53	151
Male householder	123	32	92
65 years and over	21	3	18
Female householder	80	21	59
65 years and over	33	7	26

Source: U.S. Bureau of the Census and U.S. Department of Housing and Urban Development, *Annual Housing Survey: 1983.*

VI

FEDERAL PROGRAMS AND EXPENDITURES

GENERAL FEDERAL EXPENDITURES FOR THE ELDERLY

Figure 6–1. Federal Benefits for the Aged: 1971–1986

(For fiscal years ending in years shown)

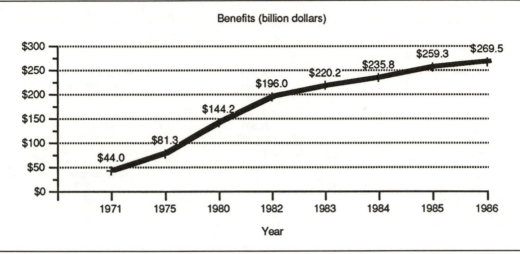

Benefits (billion dollars)

Source: U.S. Office of Management and Budget. *The Budget of the United States Government,* annual, and unpublished data.

Table 6–1. Federal Benefits for the Aged, by Type of Benefit: 1971 to 1986

(For fiscal years ending in year shown. Reflects outlays, including effects of proposed legislation, for recipients aged 65 and over in most cases. Other Federal programs that assist the elderly (e.g. consumer activities, USDA extension service, National Park Service) have been excluded due to data limitations. Estimates—mostly rough in nature—are based on Federal agency information—which may be administrative counts, samples, or less accurate estimates from Federal, State and program staff.)

Type of Benefit	Benefits (bil. dol.)								Percent		
	1971	1975	1980	1982	1983	1984	1985	1986	1971	1980	1986
Total outlays	**44.0**	**81.3**	**144.2**	**196.0**	**220.2**	**235.8**	**259.3**	**269.5**	**100.0**	**100.0**	**100.0**
Cash benefits	34.2	64.7	101.3	137.2	151.1	160.6	171.0	180.8	77.7	70.2	67.1
Social Security	27.1	51.8	81.2	111.2	122.5	129.3	137.9	146.2	61.6	56.3	54.2
Railroad employees	1.7	2.8	3.6	4.0	4.6	4.6	4.8	5.0	3.9	2.5	1.9
Federal civilian employees	2.3	5.5	7.8	11.1	11.8	13.0	13.7	14.2	5.2	5.4	5.3
Uniformed services members	.7	1.1	1.8	3.0	3.3	3.8	3.9	4.3	1.6	1.2	1.6
Coal miners[1]	.1	.2	1.3	1.3	1.6	1.4	1.4	1.3	.2	.9	.5
Supplemental Security Income	[2]1.4	1.8	2.3	2.7	2.9	3.5	3.6	3.7	[2]3.2	1.6	1.4
Veterans pensions[3]	.9	1.5	3.3	3.9	4.4	5.0	5.7	6.1	2.0	2.3	2.3
In–kind benefits	9.8	16.6	36.8	52.8	59.6	66.3	79.3	79.3	22.3	25.5	29.4
Medicare	7.5	12.8	29.3	42.6	48.4	53.3	60.9	64.4	17.0	20.3	23.9
Medicaid	1.9	2.6	4.7	6.0	7.0	7.4	8.1	8.9	4.3	3.3	3.3
Food stamps[4]	.2	1.0	.5	.9	.6	.6	.6	.6	.5	.3	.2
Subsidized public housing	.2	.4	2.3	3.3	3.6	5.0	[5]9.7	5.4	.5	1.6	2.0
Other[6]	(NA)	(NA)	6.1	6.0	9.5	8.9	9.0	9.4	(NA)	4.2	3.5

Notes: NA Not available.

1. Prior to 1980, represents benefit for coal miners' widows only.
2. Represents Federal grants to States for aid to the aged, blind, and disabled.
3. Includes other veterans' compensation for aged beginning 1980.
4. Includes nutrition assistance to Puerto Rico.
5. Financing was changed from loan guarantees to direct loans, resulting in a one–time outlay increase.
6. Includes Administration on Aging, National institute on Aging, ACTION, White House Conference on Aging, other Federal health programs, other Social Security benefits, Farmers Home Administration and Elderly Housing Loans programs, social services, energy assistance, unemployment compensation, and other miscellaneous program outlays.

Source: U.S. Office of Management and Budget, *The Budget of the United States Government,* annual, and unpublished data.

Table 6–2. Older Americans Act Appropriation Levels, Fiscal Years 1980–1987(a)

(In thousands of dollars)

Titles (1984 Amendments)	1980	1981	1982
Title II			
National Information and Resource			
Clearinghouse on Aging	$2,000	$1,800	$1,721
Federal Council on the Aging	450	481	191
Title III			
Grants for State and Community Programs			
on Aging (c)			
Supportive Services and Senior Centers	246,970	252,000	240,869
Nutrition Service (d)	320,000	350,000	344,099
Congregate	(270,000)	(295,000)	(286,749)
Home Delivered	(50,000)	(55,000)	(57,350)
State Administration and Other Activities	22,500	22,675	21,673
Title IV			
Training, Research, and Discretionary Projects			
and Programs	–	40,500	22,175
Education & Training	17,000	(f)	(f)
Research & Development Projects	8,500	(f)	(f)
Demonstration Projects	15,000	(f)	(f)
Title V			
Community Service Employment for Older			
Americans	266,900	277,100	277,100
Title VI			
Grants for Indian Tribes	6,000	6,000	5,735
TOTAL	908,320	950,556	913,563

Titles (1984 Amendments)	1983	1984	1985
Title II			
National Information and Resource			
Clearinghouse on Aging	(b)	(b)	(b)
Federal Council on the Aging	175	175	200
Title III			
Grants for State and Community Programs			
on Aging (c)			
Supportive Services and Senior Centers	240,869	250,869	265,000
Nutrition Service (d)	381,099	388,599	403,900
Congregate	(319,074)	(321,574)	(336,000)
Home Delivered	(62,025)	(67,025)	(67,900)
State Administration and Other Activities	21,673	21,673	(e)
Title IV			
Training, Research, and Discretionary Projects			
and Programs	22,175	22,175	25,000
Education & Training			
Research & Development Projects	(f)	(f)	(f)
Demonstration Projects (g)	(f)	(f)	(f)
Title V			
Community Service Employment for Older			
Americans	319,450	317,300	326,000
Title VI			
Grants for Indian Tribes	5,735	5,735	7,500
TOTAL	991,176	1,006,526	1,027,600

Table 6–2. (continued)

Titles (1984 Amendments)	1986	1987
Title II		
National Information and Resource		
Clearinghouse on Aging	(b)	(b)
Federal Council on the Aging	191	200
Title III		
Grants for State and Community Programs		
on Aging (c)		
Supportive Services and Senior Centers	253,605	270,000
Nutrition Service (d)	386,502	422,000
Congregate	(321,522)	(348,000)
Home Delivered	(64,980)	(74,000)
State Administration and Other Activities	(e)	(e)
Title IV		
Training, Research, and Discretionary Projects		
and Programs	23,925	25,000
Education & Training	(f)	(f)
Research & Development Projects	(f)	(f)
Demonstration Projects (g)	(f)	(f)
Title V		
Community Service Employment for Older		
Americans	312,002	326,000
Title VI		
Grants for Indian Tribes	7,178	7,500
TOTAL	983,403	1,050,700

Notes: a. Funds allocated for salaries and expenses. White House Conference on Aging, and federal administration are not included in these calculations.

b. Not authorized.

c. From 1966 to 1969. Title III funds were allocated to states for community planning and social services. There was no specific appropriation for state or area planning activities. Beginning in 1970 funds were appropriated for statewide planning. Beginning in 1973 funds were appropriated for area planning and social services; this appropriation was later termed social services. Funds for Area Agency planning are part of the services allotment. In 1977 and 1978 there was a separate appropriation for multipurpose senior centers under Title V of the Act: the 1978 amendments eliminated Title V and the appropriation for senior centers was incorporated under the appropriation for social services. The 1982 amendments changed reference to "supportive" services rather than "social" services.

d. Excludes U.S. Department of Agriculture commodities.

e. Public Law 98–459, the Older Americans Act Amendments of 1984, eliminated separate appropriations amount for State agency activities and included funds for this purpose in Title III services.

f. No separate appropriation: included in overall Title IV appropriation.

g. Funds were authorized under Title III for areawide demonstration model projects from fiscal year 1970 through fiscal year 1978. In 1979 and 1980 funds for this purpose were authorized under Title IV.

Source: National Association of State Units on Aging. *An Orientation to the Older Americans Act.* 1985 and unpublished material.

Table 6–3. Estimated Cost of Federal Tax Expenditures for the Elderly, 1984–1989

(in millions of dollars)

Tax Expenditure	1984	1985	1986	1987	1988	1989
Exclusion of Pension Contributions and Earnings						
—Employer Plans	$47,245	$52,670	$58,985	$66,065	$73,995	$82,875
—Plans for Self-Employed	1,475	1,530	1,645	1,725	1,770	1,890
—Individual Retirement Plans	9,190	9,840	10,945	11,890	12,705	13,870
Exclusion of Untaxed Social Security Benefits[a]						
—For retired persons	13,895	12,975	13,695	14,400	15,025	15,515
—For disabled persons	1,225	1,105	1,120	1,145	1,165	1,190
—For survivors and dependents	3,755	3,765	3,970	4,195	4,425	4,650
Additional Exemption for the Elderly	2,325	2,450	2,560	2,730	2,870	3,040
Child and Disabled Dependent Care Credit[b]	1,695	1,905	2,150	2,410	2,675	2,945
Exclusion of Capital Gains on Home Sales for Persons 55 and Older	1,630	1,875	2,000	2,100	2,345	2,515
Elderly Income Credit	145	210	200	190	180	170
Total	$82,580	$88,325	$97,270	$106,850	$117,155	$128,660

Notes: a. A portion of the social security benefits became taxable in 1984. The first full year of benefit taxation began in 1985. This accounts for the drop in level of revenue losses between 1984 and 1985.

b. An estimated 10% of the expenditures for the Child and Disabled Dependent Care Credit is related to the care of an elderly person.

Source: Joint Committee on Taxation, "Estimates of Federal Tax Expenditures for Fiscal Years 1984–1989," *Tax Notes* 25, no. 8 (November 19,1984).

MEDICARE/MEDICAID

Table 6–4. Elderly Persons With Health Care Coverage by Type of Coverage and Poverty Status: 1984

(In thousands. Persons as of March of following year who had coverage in year shown.)

Type of Coverage	Total	65 yr. old and over
Medicare, total[1]	28,423	25,710
Medicare only	22,513	20,855
Medicare and other health plans[2]	2,641	2,142
Below poverty level	3,772	3,132
Above poverty level	24,651	22,578
Medicaid, total	19,348	2,824
Medicaid only	14,077	–
Medicaid and Medicare only	3,270	2,712
Medicaid and group health plan only[3]	1,587	–
Medicaid and other health plans	415	111
Below poverty level	13,207	1,164
Above poverty level	6,141	1,660
Employer or union provided group plan	134,145	1,771
Employer or union helped pay for plan	127,792	1,663
Paid for all of plan	54,213	788
Paid for part of plan	73,579	875
Employer or union did not help pay	6,353	108
CHAMPUS[4], V.A.[5] or military health care	9,728	871

Notes: – Represents zero or rounds to zero.

     1. Includes Medicaid and Medicare only, shown under Medicaid.

     2. Excluding Medicaid.

     3. Employer or union provided.

     4. Civilian Health and Medical Program of the Uniformed Services. The Dept. of Defense operates this program to provide reimbursement (after payment of a deductible) for covered medical care rendered in civilian facilities to wives and children of active military personnel, to retired military personnel and their dependents, and to dependents of deceased personnel. Program is designed for those unable to use Government medical facilities for reasons of distance, overcrowding, or the unavailability of appropriate treatment at a military medical center.

     5. Veterans Administration.

Source: U.S. Bureau of the Census, Current Population Reports, series P-60, No. 150 and earlier reports.

Table 6–5. Medicare Program—Enrollment and Payments: 1970 to 1985

(Enrollment as of July 1; payments for calendar year. Benefit payments represent trust fund outlays. Includes Puerto Rico, outlying areas, and enrollees in foreign countries)

Type of insurance	Unit	1970	1975	1977	1978	1979	1980	1981	1982	1983	1984	1985
Hospital and/or												
Medical Insurance												
Enrollment, total	1,000	20,491	24,959	26,458	27,164	27,859	28,478	29,010	29,494	30,026	30,455	31,083
Benefit payments	Mil. dol	7,099	15,588	21,775	24,934	29,331	35,699	43,455	51,086	57,443	62,918	70,527
Hospital Insurance												
Enrollment, total	1,000	20,361	24,640	26,094	26,777	27,459	28,067	28,590	29,069	29,587	29,996	30,589
Persons 65 and over	1,000	20,361	22,472	23,475	23,984	24,548	25,104	25,591	26,115	26,670	27,112	27,683
Male	1,000	8,507	9,168	9,537	9,728	9,945	10,156	10,340	10,538	10,755	10,920	11,146
Female	1,000	11,855	13,304	13,937	14,256	14,604	14,948	15,250	15,577	15,915	16,192	16,536
Disabled persons[1]	1,000	(X)	2,168	2,619	2,793	2,911	2,963	2,999	2,954	2,918	2,884	2,907
Male	1,000	(X)	1,381	1,654	1,763	1,837	1,871	1,896	1,865	1,846	1,830	1,846
Female	1,000	(X)	788	965	1,030	1,073	1,093	1,103	1,089	1,072	1,054	1,061
Benefit payments	Mil. dol	5,124	11,315	15,737	17,682	20,623	25,064	30,342	35,631	39,337	43,257	47,580
Medical Insurance												
Enrollment, total	1,000	19,584	23,904	25,364	26,074	26,757	27,400	27,941	28,412	28,975	29,415	29,989
Persons 65 and over	1,000	19,584	21,945	22,991	23,531	24,098	24,680	25,182	25,707	26,292	26,764	27,311
Male	1,000	8,132	8,873	9,240	9,436	9,645	9,868	10,055	10,250	10,479	10,652	10,852
Female	1,000	11,452	13,073	13,751	14,094	14,454	14,813	15,127	15,457	15,813	16,112	16,459
Disabled persons[1]	1,000	(X)	1,959	2,373	2,543	2,659	2,719	2,759	2,705	2,682	2,651	2,678
Male	1,000	(X)	1,231	1,475	1,582	1,655	1,695	1,724	1,688	1,677	1,664	1,683
Female	1,000	(X)	729	897	961	1,004	1,025	1,036	1,018	1,005	987	995
Benefit payments	Mil. dol	1,975	4,273	6,038	7,252	8,708	10,635	13,113	15,455	18,106	19,661	22,947

Notes: X Not applicable.

1. Age under 65; includes persons enrolled because of end-stage renal disease (ESRD) only.

Source: U.S. Health Care Financing Administration. Published in U.S. Social Security Administration, *Annual Statistical Supplement* to the *Social Security Bulletin*.

Table 6–6. Medicare—Persons 65 Years Old and Over Served and Reimbursements: 1975 to 1983

(Persons served are enrollees who use covered services, incurred expenses greater than the applicable deductible amounts and for whom Medicare paid benefits. Reimbursements are amounts paid to providers for covered services. Excluded are retroactive adjustments resulting from end of fiscal year cost settlements and certain lump-sum interim payments. Also excluded are beneficiary (or third party payor) liabilities for applicable deductibles, coinsurance amounts, and charges for non-covered services. Includes data for enrollees living in outlying territories and foreign countries)

Types of Coverage and Service	Unit	Persons 65 Years Old and Over			
		1975	1980	1982	1983
Persons served, total[1]	**1,000**	**12,032**	**16,271**	**17,023**	**17,897**
Hospital insurance[1]	1,000	4,963	6,024	6,548	6,691
Inpatient hospital	1,000	4,913	5,951	6,338	6,441
Skilled-nursing services	1,000	260	248	244	257
Home health services[2]	1,000	329	675	1,074	1,228
Supplementary medical insurance[1]	1,000	11,762	16,099	16,807	17,675
Physicians' and other medical services	1,000	11,396	15,627	16,346	17,209
Outpatient services	1,000	3,768	6,629	7,465	8,065
Home health services[2]	1,000	161	302	17	20
Persons served per 1,000 enrollees, total[1]	**Rate**	**528**	**638**	**641**	**660**
Hospital insurance[1]	Rate	221	240	251	251
Inpatient hospital	Rate	219	237	243	242
Skilled-nursing services	Rate	12	10	9	10
Home health services[2]	Rate	15	27	41	46
Supplementary medical insurance[1]	Rate	536	652	654	672
Physicians' and other medical services	Rate	519	633	636	655
Outpatient services	Rate	172	269	290	307
Home health services[2]	Rate	7	12	1	1
Reimbursements, total	**Mil. dol**	**12,689**	**29,134**	**41,526**	**46,727**
Hospital insurance	Mil. dol	9,209	20,353	29,214	32,141
Inpatient hospital	Mil. dol	8,840	19,583	27,834	30,469
Skilled-nursing services	Mil. dol	233	331	388	413
Home health services[2]	Mil. dol	136	440	992	1,258
Supplementary medical insurance	Mil. dol	3,481	8,781	12,311	14,586
Physicians' and other medical services	Mil. dol	3,050	7,361	10,311	12,105
Outpatient services	Mil. dol	374	1,261	1,982	2,460
Home health services[2]	Mil. dol	56	159	19	22
Reimbursement, per person served, total	**Dollars**	**1,055**	**1,791**	**2,439**	**2,611**
Hospital insurance	Dollars	1,855	3,379	4,462	4,804
Inpatient hospital	Dollars	1,799	3,291	4,391	4,730
Skilled-nursing services	Dollars	896	1,336	1,591	1,612
Home health services[2]	Dollars	413	652	923	1,025
Supplementary medical insurance	Dollars	296	545	733	825
Physicians' and other medical services	Dollars	268	471	631	703
Outpatient services	Dollars	99	190	265	305
Home health services[2]	Dollars	347	526	1,091	1,098

Notes: 1. Persons are counted once for each type of covered service used, but are not double counted in totals.

2. Beginning 1982, a change in legislation resulted in virtually all home health services being paid under hospital insurance.

Source: U.S. Health Care Financing Administration, *Medicare Program Statistics,* annual; and unpublished data.

Table 6–7. Medicare—Hospital Utilization and Hospital and Physician Charges: 1970 to 1984

(Data reflect date claims approved for payment and cover only claims approved and recorded in Health Care Financing Administration central records before December 31, 1985. Includes Puerto Rico, outlying areas and enrollees in foreign countries.)

Item	Unit	Persons 65 years old and over				
		1970	1975	1980	1983	1984
Hospital inpatient care:						
Admissions	1,000	6,141	7,404	9,258	10,462	10,331
Per 1,000 enrollees[1]	Rate	304	332	369	392	381
Covered days of care	Millions	80	84	97	98	83
Per 1,000 enrollees[1]	Rate	3,949	3,786	3,861	3,690	3,043
Per admission	Days	13.0	11.4	10.5	9.4	8.0
Hospital charges	Mil. dol.	5,940	12,021	28,119	46,489	43,446
Per day	Dollars	74	142	290	472	527
Percent of charges reimbursed	Percent	77.1	75.2	69.6	64.9	68.8
Physician charges	Mil. dol.	[2]2,157	3,907	8,802	14,572	15,354
Percent reimbursed	Percent	[2]72.9	74.1	77.8	77.6	78.0

Notes: 1. Hospital insurance enrollment as of July 1.

　　　　2. Data reflect date paid claims were recorded in Health Care Financing Administration records.

Source: U.S. Health Care Financing Administration, *Health Care Financing Review*, quarterly; and unpublished data.

Figure 6-2. Where the Medicare Dollar for the Elderly Goes: 1984

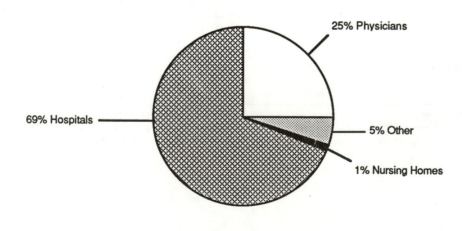

25% Physicians

69% Hospitals

5% Other

1% Nursing Homes

Source: U.S. Health Care Financing Administration, Office of Financial and Actuarial Analysis.

Figure 6–3. Medical Assistance (MEDICAID) — Recipients and Payments to Persons Age 65 and Over: 1975–1985

(For fiscal year ending in year shown. Includes Puerto Rico and outlying areas. Excludes Arizona, which has no Title XIX [Medicaid] Program.)

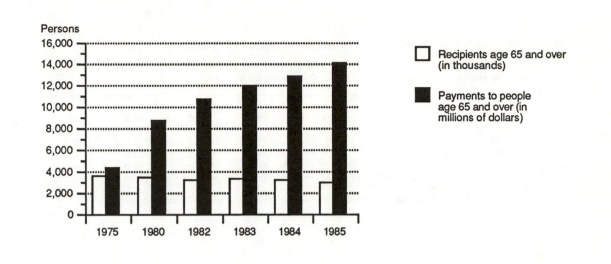

Source: U.S. Health Care Financing Administration. *Health Care Financing Review,* quarterly.

Figure 6–4. Where the Medicaid Dollar for the Elderly Goes: 1984

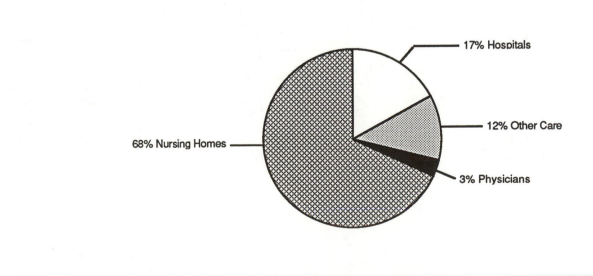

Source: U.S. Health Care Financing Administration. Office of Financial and Actuarial Analysis.

SOCIAL SECURITY

Table 6–8. Federal OASDI Fund Receipts, Outlays and Balances: 1975 to 1986

(In billions of dollars. For fiscal year ending in year shown. Receipts based on collections received and deposited. Outlays stated on a checks-issued basis less refunds collected. Balances: That portion of funds authorized for use which have not been spent.)

Type of Fund	1975	1979	1980	1981	1982	1983	1984	1985	1986, est.
OASDI[1] trust funds–receipts	66.7	102.1	117.4	134.6	148.0	172.5	181.1	200.3	214.5
OASDI[1] trust funds–outlays	64.7	104.1	118.6	139.6	156.0	172.3	180.9	191.0	201.3
OASDI[1] trust funds–balance	48.2	33.4	23.3	27.2	19.3	32.0	32.2	39.8	42.3

Notes: 1. Old-age, survivors, and disability insurance.

Source: U.S. Office of Management and Budget, *Special Analyses, Budget of the United States Government,* annual.

Table 6–9. Social Security (OASDI)—Retirement Benefits, by Sex: 1970 to 1985

(As of end of year. Benefits in current-payment status. OASDI = Old-age, survivors, and disability insurance. Persons who retire at age 65 or older receive full benefits; those who retire between ages 62 and 64 receive reduced benefits.)

Item	Unit	1970	1975	1979	1980	1981	1982	1983	1984	1985
Male										
Number receiving benefits[1]	1,000	7,688	9,164	10,192	10,461	10,767	11,030	11,358	11,573	11,817
Full benefits	1,000	4,930	4,699	4,607	4,587	4,586	4,647	4,751	4,703	4,651
Reduced benefits	1,000	2,758	4,465	5,586	5,874	6,181	6,383	6,607	6,870	7,166
Average monthly benefits, total	Dollars	131	228	327	380	431	470	495	518	538
Full	Dollars	139	247	359	420	480	528	565	598	628
Reduced[2]	Dollars	115	207	300	350	395	427	444	463	480
Female										
Number receiving benefits[1]	1,000	5,661	7,424	8,778	9,101	9,428	9,733	10,060	10,334	10,615
Full benefits	1,000	2,352	2,521	2,772	2,811	2,839	2,900	2,990	3,034	3,061
Reduced benefits	1,000	3,309	4,903	6,006	6,291	6,589	6,834	7,071	7,299	7,553
Average monthly benefits, total	Dollars	101	182	257	297	334	362	380	397	412
Full	Dollars	112	206	297	347	394	433	460	487	511
Reduced[2]	Dollars	94	169	238	275	309	332	345	359	372

Notes: 1. Includes disability beneficiaries who attained age 65.

2. After reduction.

Source: U.S. Social Security Administration, *Social Security Bulletin.*

Table 6–10. Social Security (OASDI)—Benefits, by Type of Beneficiary Age 62 or Older: 1970 to 1985

(OASDI = Old-age, survivors, and disability insurance.)

Type of Beneficiary	1970	1975	1978	1979	1980	1981	1982	1983	1984	1985
	Benefits in current–payment status[1] (end of year)									
Number of benefits (1,000)										
Retired workers[2] (1,000)	13,349	16,588	18,358	18,970	19,562	20,195	20,763	21,419	21,906	22,432
Special benefits[3] (1,000)	534	224	134	112	93	76	63	51	40	32
Average monthly benefit, current dollars:										
Retired workers[2]	118	207	263	294	341	386	419	441	461	479
Retired worker and wife[2]	199	344	438	489	567	(NA)	702	743	780	814
Special benefits[3]	45	69	83	92	105	116	125	129	134	138
Average monthly benefit, constant (1985) dollars:[4]										
Retired workers[2]	325	408	423	420	433	448	469	476	479	479
Retired worker and wife[2]	547	678	705	699	720	(NA)	786	802	811	814
	Benefits awarded during year (1,000)									
Number of benefits	**3,722**	**4,427**	**4,166**	**4,227**	**4,215**	**4,059**	**3,859**	**3,756**	**3,691**	**3,796**
Retired workers[2]	1,338	1,506	1,480	1,597	1,620	1,600	1,625	1,670	1,607	1,690
Special benefits[3]	30	4	3	2	1	1	1	1	1	1
	Benefit payments during year (mil. dol.)									
Total amount[5]	**31,863**	**66,923**	**92,865**	**104,263**	**120,472**	**140,995**	**156,137**	**167,033**	**175,762**	**186,195**
Monthly benefits	31,750	66,586	92,520	103,923	120,118	140,662	155,934	166,827	175,551	185,988
Retired workers[2]	18,437	38,078	53,255	60,379	70,359	83,614	95,123	103,578	109,957	116,823
Special benefits[3]	306	198	142	128	119	110	100	85	71	57

Notes: NA = Not available.

1. Benefit payment actually being made at a specified time with no deductions or with deductions amounting to less than a month's benefits; i.e., the benefits actually being received.

2. 62 years and over.

3. Benefits for persons aged 72 and over not insured under regular or transitional provisions of Social Security Act.

4. Constant dollar figures are based on the consumer price index published by the U.S. Bureau of Labor Statistics.

5. Represents total disbursements of benefit checks by the U.S. Dept. of the Treasury during the years specified.

Source: U.S. Social Security Administration, *Annual Statistical Supplement* to the *Social Security Bulletin*, and unpublished data.

Table 6–11. Social Security (OASDI)—Beneficiaries, Benefit Payments, and Average Monthly Benefits, 1970 to 1985, and by States and Other Areas, 1985

(Number of beneficiaries in current-payment status and average monthly benefit as of December. OASDI = old-age, survivors, and disability insurance.)

Year, Division, and State or Other Area	Number of beneficiaries (1,000)		Benefit payments (mil. dol.)		Average monthly benefits (dol.)
	Total[1]	Retired workers[2]	Total[1]	Retired workers[2]	Retired workers[3]
1970	26,229	16,559	31,863	20,770	118
1975	32,086	20,099	66,923	42,447	207
1979	35,125	22,501	104,263	66,947	294
1980	35,585	23,216	120,472	77,906	341
1981	36,006	23,859	140,995	92,478	386
1982	35,839	24,362	156,137	104,885	419
1983	36,085	24,970	167,033	114,048	441
1984	36,479	25,434	175,762	120,952	461
1985, total	37,058	25,989	186,195	128,479	479
U.S.	**36,166**	**25,474**	**183,269**	**126,877**	(NA)
New England	**2,050**	**1,525**	**10,753**	**7,857**	(NA)
Maine	203	144	962	667	442
New Hampshire	150	112	769	566	481
Vermont	82	59	411	288	471
Massachusetts	940	699	4,904	3,569	483
Rhode Island	175	130	905	658	480
Connecticut	500	381	2,802	2,109	525
Middle Atlantic	**6,132**	**4,424**	**33,417**	**23,704**	(NA)
New York	2,805	2,027	15,378	10,985	514
New Jersey	1,187	869	6,620	4,782	523
Pennsylvania	2,140	1,528	11,419	7,937	498
East North Central	**6,442**	**4,501**	**34,383**	**23,554**	(NA)
Ohio	1,699	1,156	8,901	5,896	494
Indiana	857	597	4,549	3,121	502
Illinois	1,682	1,203	9,121	6,435	511
Michigan	1,409	963	7,658	5,122	511
Wisconsin	795	582	4,154	2,980	492
West North Central	**2,891**	**2,106**	**14,408**	**10,251**	(NA)
Minnesota	634	474	3,146	2,285	465
Iowa	508	373	2,597	1,863	482
Missouri	871	613	4,303	2,962	465
North Dakota	107	78	505	359	432
South Dakota	123	89	565	399	440
Nebraska	259	192	1,294	940	471
Kansas	389	287	1,998	1,444	486
South Atlantic	**6,416**	**4,471**	**31,018**	**21,248**	(NA)
Delaware	94	67	500	348	501
Maryland	566	401	2,917	2,007	479
District of Columbia	81	57	364	253	414
Virginia	761	511	3,598	2,357	447
West Virginia	358	215	1,746	1,021	471
North Carolina	958	644	4,388	2,910	438
South Carolina	483	309	2,200	1,399	439
Georgia	805	508	3,655	2,278	434
Florida	2,310	1,759	11,655	8,675	478

Table 6–11. (continued)

Year, Division, and State or Other Area	Number of beneficiaries (1,000)		Benefit payments (mil. dol.)		Average monthly benefits (dol.)
	Total[1]	Retired workers[2]	Total[1]	Retired workers[2]	Retired workers[3]
East South Central	**2,463**	**1,555**	**10,978**	**6,808**	(NA)
Kentucky	610	378	2,754	1,665	433
Tennessee	762	500	3,483	2,243	438
Alabama	661	415	2,965	1,830	433
Mississippi	430	262	1,776	1,070	403
West South Central	**3,486**	**2,312**	**16,231**	**10,556**	(NA)
Arkansas	444	294	1,950	1,262	421
Louisiana	596	353	2,697	1,570	443
Oklahoma	497	346	2,363	1,607	452
Texas	1,949	1,319	9,221	6,117	458
Mountain	**1,662**	**1,193**	**8,226**	**5,795**	(NA)
Montana	127	90	625	432	468
Idaho	143	106	704	507	466
Wyoming	54	39	275	193	481
Colorado	363	257	1,792	1,233	468
New Mexico	189	125	860	569	452
Arizona	497	365	2,513	1,813	485
Utah	165	120	833	601	487
Nevada	124	91	624	447	481
Pacific	**4,624**	**3,387**	**23,855**	**17,104**	(NA)
Washington	640	477	3,368	2,455	497
Oregon	447	335	2,324	1,705	489
California	3,382	2,459	17,410	12,390	488
Alaska	26	16	127	78	487
Hawaii	129	100	626	476	476
Puerto Rico	548	290	1,641	822	300
Guam	4	2	12	7	358
American Samoa	3	1	7	3	290
Virgin Islands	9	6	35	24	429
Foreign	329	213	1,226	749	376

Notes: 1. Includes special benefits for persons aged 72 and over not insured under regular or transitional provisions of the Social Security Act.

2. Includes benefits payable to dependents.

3. Excludes persons with special benefits.

Source: U.S. Social Security Administration. *Social Security Bulletin.*

Table 6–12. Income from Social Security Benefits by Age, Sex, and Marital Status: Percentage Distribution of Aged Units, 1984.

(Note: An aged unit is a married couple living together or a nonmarried person. The concept of the aged unit allows one to measure incomes of the entire aged population either separately from or in combination with the income of other members of the families in which they live.)

Income (recipients only)[1]	Married couples			Nonmarried persons								
				Total			Men			Women		
	55–61	62–64	65 and older	55–61	62–64	65 and older	55–61	62–64	65 and older	55–61	62–64	65 and older
Number (in thousands)	702	1,288	7,585	588	1,043	11,086	165	275	2,395	423	768	8,692
Total percent	100.0	100.0	100.0	100.0	100.0	100.0	100.0	100.0	100.0	100.0	100.0	100.0
$1–$499	.8	1.6	.2	4.9	2.1	.4	0	3.4	.1	6.9	1.7	.5
$500–$999	3.3	4.5	.7	2.9	1.6	.5	1.7	1.1	.8	3.4	1.8	.4
$1,000–$1,499	3.2	4.0	.9	6.2	3.7	1.0	2.2	5.0	.9	7.8	3.2	1.0
$1,500–$1,999	5.8	3.5	1.1	3.1	5.9	2.4	0	5.8	2.6	4.4	6.0	2.4
$2,000–$2,499	5.6	4.6	1.0	8.2	7.3	6.4	7.5	7.9	6.0	8.5	7.1	6.5
$2,500–$2,999	4.2	3.7	1.5	9.1	8.0	5.1	12.4	5.5	5.7	7.9	8.9	5.0
$3,000–$3,499	5.1	4.7	2.0	11.4	10.8	7.9	13.7	9.4	6.0	10.5	11.3	8.4
$3,500–$3,999	5.1	4.7	2.4	8.2	9.2	9.9	7.5	11.3	9.4	8.5	8.4	10.1
$4,000–$4,499	7.0	3.1	2.3	11.0	8.9	8.7	15.2	8.5	7.4	9.3	9.1	9.0
$4,500–$4,999	8.5	6.5	3.3	8.1	8.5	11.6	4.1	8.4	7.8	9.7	8.5	12.6
$5,000–$5,999	13.6	14.2	7.1	12.5	18.9	20.9	13.8	14.4	19.3	12.0	20.5	21.4
$6,000–$6,999	10.3	17.2	10.3	8.5	11.3	14.3	13.1	14.4	16.8	6.7	10.2	13.6
$7,000–$7,999	13.3	7.6	10.7	4.5	2.7	6.1	7.1	2.6	8.9	3.4	2.7	5.4
$8,000–$8,999	9.0	8.4	13.3	.5	.8	2.6	1.7	1.8	4.0	0	.4	2.2
$9,000–$9,999	2.4	6.2	12.3	0	0	1.2	0	0	2.1	0	0	1.0
$10,000–$10,999	1.1	3.1	10.1	.5	.3	.6	0	.4	1.0	.8	.2	.5
$11,000–$11,999	.5	.5	7.3	0	0	.2	0	0	.6	0	0	.1
$12,000–$12,999	.4	1.0	5.4	.2	0	.1	0	0	.2	.3	0	0
$13,000–$13,999	.7	.4	3.7	0	0	.1	0	0	.2	0	0	0
$14,000–$14,999	0	0	2.0	0	0	0	0	0	0	0	0	0
$15,000 or more	0	.5	2.4	0	0	0	0	0	0	0	0	0
Median dollar income[2]	5,100	5,650	8,470	3,770	4,030	4,830	4,080	3,950	5,110	3,610	4,040	4,770

Notes: 1. Recipients of Social Security may be receiving retired-worker benefits, dependents' or survivors' benefits, disability benefits, transitionally insured, or special age-72 benefits. Units with a person reporting receipt of both Social Security benefits and railroad retirement are excluded. This is less than 1 percent of beneficiaries aged 55–61, 1 percent aged 62–64, and 1 percent aged 65 and older.

2. Rounded to the nearest $10.

FOOD STAMPS AND PUBLIC ASSISTANCE

Table 6–13. Food Stamp Recipiency of Households with Householder Age 65 Years Old and Over, Mean Annual Face Value of Food Stamps, and Mean Number of Months Receiving Food Stamps, by Household Money Income and Poverty Status of the Primary Family or Individual: 1984

(Numbers in thousands. Households as of March 1985.)

Characteristic		Household money income												Below current poverty level	
										Median income (dollars)		Mean income (dollars)			
	Total	Under $2,500	$2,500 to $4,999	$5,000 to $7,499	$7,500 to $9,999	$10,000 to $12,499	$12,500 to $14,999	$15,000 to $19,999	$20,000 and over	Value	Stand-ard error	Value	Stand-ard error	Number	Poverty rate
Householder 65 Years Old and Over															
Total	1,085	41	560	250	95	42	36	28	33	4,736	96	6,682	251	777	71.6
Region															
Northeast	198	5	102	38	20	7	7	8	11	4,794	239	7,763	712	128	64.6
Midwest	178	14	72	41	22	8	8	6	7	5,180	462	7,185	733	125	70.2
South	629	20	352	150	43	25	14	11	14	4,595	116	6,194	292	478	76.0
West	80	3	34	21	10	1	7	3	1	5,384	581	6,723	564	46	57.8
Race and Spanish Origin of Householder[1]															
White	678	22	374	162	47	23	16	17	19	4,624	114	6,420	302	485	71.5
Black	090	20	100	00	40	10	10	10	10	4,000	267	7,070	167	080	71.8
Spanish origin	95	3	48	25	9	4	4	2	1	4,855	546	6,277	732	67	70.7
Type of Household															
Family households	442	16	47	169	84	39	32	26	28	7,330	221	9,529	467	220	49.9
Married-couple families	229	8	11	107	37	20	13	14	18	7,245	232	9,875	667	114	49.5
Male householder, no wife present	26	2	7	8	6	–	3	–	1	(B)	(B)	(B)	(B)	14	(B)
Female householder, no husband present	186	7	30	54	41	19	15	12	9	7,673	502	9,441	715	93	49.9
Nonfamily households	643	25	513	82	11	2	4	1	5	3,944	81	4,728	227	557	86.5
Male householder	112	1	92	16	1	–	–	–	2	3,989	188	5,233	858	95	84.9
Female householder	531	24	421	66	10	2	4	1	3	3,934	90	4,620	206	461	86.9
Size of Household															
One person (living alone)	617	25	513	74	5	–	–	–	–	3,881	79	4,188	53	537	87.1
Two persons	260	15	32	130	49	9	13	7	5	6,591	203	7,595	504	133	51.2
Three persons	100	–	11	20	28	12	12	5	12	9,207	594	11,974	1,183	38	38.1
Four persons	48	–	2	14	6	7	3	7	8	(B)	(B)	(B)	(B)	27	(B)
Five persons	21	–	–	6	2	4	2	4	3	(B)	(B)	(B)	(B)	13	(B)
Six persons	26	1	–	3	3	8	2	3	5	(B)	(B)	(B)	(B)	16	(B)
Seven persons or more	15	–	3	3	2	1	4	1	1	(B)	(B)	(B)	(B)	13	(B)
Mean size of household	1.55	1.35	1.11	1.88	2.10	3.41	2.21	2.14	1.59	(X)	(X)	(X)	(X)	1.53	(X)
Presence of Children Under 18 Years Old															
Households with children under 18 years old	138	–	18	38	21	24	13	14	11	9,094	898	10,955	895	89	64.5
Households with children under 6 years old	60	–	5	17	9	12	8	2	6	(B)	(B)	(B)	(B)	43	(B)
Households with no children under 18 years old	946	41	542	213	74	18	23	14	22	4,490	93	6,058	245	687	72.6

Table 6–13. (continued)

Characteristic	Total	Under $2,500	$2,500 to $4,999	$5,000 to $7,499	$7,500 to $9,999	$10,000 to $12,499	$12,500 to $14,999	$15,000 to $19,999	$20,000 and over	Median income (dollars) Value	Standard error	Mean income (dollars) Value	Standard error	Below current poverty level Number	Poverty rate
Work Experience in 1984 of Householder															
Total civilian hhldrs	1,085	41	560	250	95	42	36	28	33	4,736	96	6,682	251	777	71.6
Worked	52	4	5	12	11	4	2	3	12	(B)	(B)	(B)	(B)	18	(B)
Worked at full–time jobs	14	2	–	3	4	4	–	1	1	(B)	(B)	(B)	(B)	8	(B)
40 weeks or more	8	2	–	–	2	2	–	1	1	(B)	(B)	(B)	(B)	4	(B)
27 to 39 weeks	–	–	–	–	–	–	–	–	–	(B)	(B)	(B)	(B)	–	(B)
26 weeks or less	6	–	–	3	1	2	–	–	–	(B)	(B)	(B)	(B)	4	(B)
Worked at part–time jobs	38	2	5	9	8	–	2	2	11	(B)	(B)	(B)	(B)	11	(B)
40 weeks or more	22	–	3	6	4	–	–	2	7	(B)	(B)	(B)	(B)	5	(B)
27 to 39 weeks	–	–	–	–	–	–	–	–	–	(B)	(B)	(B)	(B)	–	(B)
26 weeks or less	16	2	2	3	3	–	2	–	4	(B)	(B)	(B)	(B)	5	(B)
Did not work	1,033	38	555	239	84	38	34	24	21	4,655	95	6,325	229	758	73.4
Total Money Earnings in 1984[2]															
With earnings	52	4	5	12	11	4	2	3	12	(B)	(B)	(B)	(B)	18	(B)
Without earnings	1,033	38	555	239	84	38	34	24	21	4,655	95	6,325	229	758	73.4
Tenure															
Owner occupied	508	23	210	128	53	28	21	19	26	5,413	289	7,682	445	330	64.9
Renter occupied, including no cash rent	577	19	350	123	42	14	15	8	7	4,426	112	5,803	255	447	775

Notes: (B) Base less than 75,000

(X) Not applicable

1. Persons of Spanish origin may be of any race.

2. Excludes a relatively small number of households reporting 'no income.'

Source: U.S. Bureau of the Census, *Current Population Reports, Series* P-60, No. 150

Table 6–14. Elderly Recipients of Public Aid and Average Monthly Cash Payments Under Supplemental Security Income and Public Assistance: 1970–1985

(As of December. Public assistance data for all years include Puerto Rico, Guam, and Virgin Islands. SSI: Supplemental security income. SSI data are for federally administered payments only. Excludes vendor payment for medical care, i.e., payments made directly to suppliers of medical care.)

Program	1970	1975	1978	1979	1980	1981	1982	1983	1984	1985
Payments										
Supplemental Security Income (million dollars)	(X)	5,878	6,552	7,075	7,941	8,593	8,981	9,404	10,371	11,060
Aged	(X)	2,605	2,433	2,526	2,734	2,818	2,824	2,814	2,973	3,035
Public assistance (million dollars)	8,443	10,434	12,024	12,402	14,048	(NA)	(NA)	(NA)	(NA)	(NA)
Old-age assistance (million dollars)	1,862	5	5	9	9	9	8	8	8	(NA)
Recipients of payments:										
SSI, total[1] (thousands)	(X)	4,314	4,217	4,150	4,142	4,019	3,858	3,901	4,029	4,138
Aged	(X)	2,307	1,968	1,872	1,808	1,678	1,549	1,515	1,530	1,504
Public Assistance										
Old-age assistance[2] (thousands)	2,061	18	19	19	19	19	19	18	18	18
Average monthly payments (dol.):										
Aged	(X)	91	100	123	128	138	146	158	158	164
Old-age Assistance[2]	75	21	22	42	39	41	36	36	36	(NA)

Notes: NA = Not available   (X) = Not applicable

1. Includes items not shown separately.

2. Average monthly recipients and payments for the year.

Source: U.S. Social Security Administration, *Annual Statistical Supplement* to the *Social Security Bulletin; Social Security Bulletin,* monthly; and *Public Assistance Statistics,* monthly.

Table 6–15. Households with Householder Age 65 and Over by Number of Selected Means-Tested Public Noncash Benefits Received, Types of Means-Tested Cash Public Assistance, and Poverty Status of the Primary Family or Individual: 1984

(Numbers in thousands. Households as of March 1985)

Noncash Benefit	All income levels					Below current poverty level					Above poverty level				
	Total	Not receiving cash public assist-ance	Receiving cash public assistance Total	AFDC or other assist-ance	SSI	Total	Not receiving cash public assist-ance	Receiving cash public assistance Total	AFDC or other assist-ance	SSI	Total	Not receiving cash public assist-ance	Receiving cash public assistance Total	AFDC or other assist-ance	SSI
Households with Householder 65 Years Old and Over															
Total	18,155	16,462	1,694	231	1,531	2,683	1,748	935	116	860	15,473	14,714	759	115	671
Not receiving noncash benefits	14,711	14,627	84	21	64	1,257	1,226	31	1	30	13,453	13,400	53	20	84
Receiving at least one noncash benefit	3,445	1,835	1,610	211	1,466	1,425	522	904	115	829	2,019	1,313	706	95	637
Noncash Benefits Totals															
Food stamps, total	1,085	324	761	128	683	777	195	582	86	532	308	129	179	43	152
School lunch, total	185	78	107	67	57	93	28	65	43	33	93	50	42	24	23
Public housing, total	1,157	825	333	37	306	444	221	224	24	208	713	604	109	14	98
Medicaid, total	2,381	836	1,545	194	1,417	1,075	214	860	104	796	1,306	622	685	90	621
Receiving One Noncash Benefit Only															
Total	2,338	1,627	711	61	659	676	401	275	24	256	1,662	1,226	436	37	403
Food stamps only	231	184	48	10	39	133	99	34	7	29	99	85	14	3	10
School lunch only	48	46	1	–	1	16	15	1	–	1	31	31	–	–	–
Public housing only	718	711	7	3	4	156	154	2	2	–	562	557	5	2	4
Medicaid only	1,341	686	655	48	615	371	133	238	16	226	970	553	417	32	389
Receiving Two Noncash Benefits															
Total	858	189	668	91	618	541	106	435	46	409	317	83	234	45	209
Food stamps and school lunch only	18	16	2	–	2	11	10	1	–	1	7	6	1	–	1
Food stamps and public housing only	44	41	3	1	2	32	30	2	–	2	12	11	1	1	–
Food stamps and Medicaid only	542	64	477	58	451	393	42	351	34	335	149	23	126	25	115
School lunch and public housing only	4	2	3	3	–	3	–	3	3	–	2	2	–	–	–
School lunch and Medicaid only	48	13	35	20	21	14	2	13	8	7	34	11	23	12	14
Public housing and Medicaid only	201	54	148	9	141	89	23	65	2	68	113	31	82	7	78
Receiving Three Noncash Benefits															
Total	242	19	223	52	187	204	15	189	41	162	38	4	34	11	25
Food stamps, school lunch, and public housing only	–	–	–	–	–	–	–	–	–	–	–	–	–	–	–
Food stamps, school lunch, and Medicaid only	59	1	58	37	29	44	1	42	28	21	16	–	16	9	8
Food stamps, public housing, and Medicaid only	182	17	165	14	157	160	13	147	13	141	23	4	18	2	17
School lunch, public housing, and Medicaid only	–	–	–	–	–	–	–	–	–	–	–	–	–	–	–
Receiving All Four Noncash Benefits															
Total	7	–	7	7	2	5	–	5	5	2	3	–	3	3	–

Source: U.S. Bureau of the Census. *Current Population Reports*, P-60, No. 150.

VII

SOCIAL CHARACTERISTICS

ATTITUDES

Figure 7–1. Percent of People Who Think Age 40 is Young, by Age

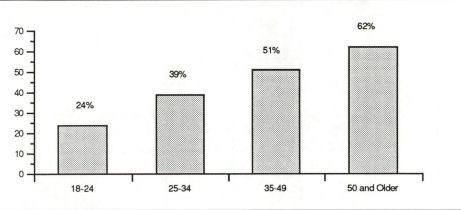

Source: NBC News/*Wall Street Journal*/Poll, April 1986.

Figure 7–2. *Question:* **Taken All Together, How Would You Say Things Are These Days — Would You Say That You Are Very Happy, Pretty Happy, or Not Too Happy?**

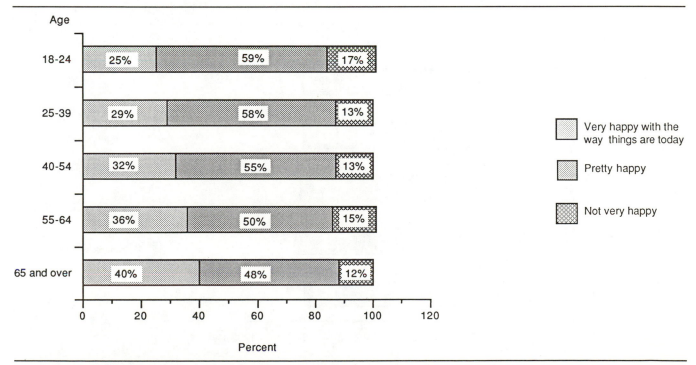

Source: Surveys by the National Opinion Research Center, General Social Surveys, 1982, 1983, and 1984 combined. From *Public Opinion,* February/March 1985. Reprinted with permission of the American Enterprise Institute for Public Policy Research.

Figure 7–3. *Question:* **People Feel Differently About What Years Are the Best Times of a Person's Life. Which of These Do You Think is the Best Time of Life?**

Childhood	Teen-age years	The twenties	The thirties	The forties	The fifties	Retirement years	By age:
22%	29%	42%	9%	4%	1%	3%	18—29 years
22%	21%	28%	31%	13%	4%	5%	30—44 years
17%	16%	24%	22%	20%	13%	8%	45—59 years
14%	14%	19%	20%	16%	11%	31%	60 years and over

Notes: Multiple responses per respondent. Don't know/no answer (not shown) ranged from 4–8%.

Source: Survey by the Roper Organization (Roper Report 84-4), March 17–24, 1984. From *Public Opinion*, February/March 1985. Reprinted with permission of the American Enterprise Institute for Public Policy Research.

Figure 7–4. *Question:* **How Much Discrimination Is There Against Old People in the United States?**

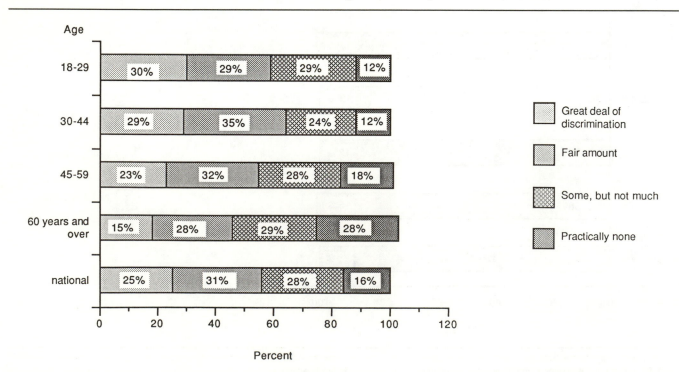

Source: Surveys by the Roper Organization (Roper Report 84-3), February 11–25, 1984. From *Public Opinion*, February/March 1985. Reprinted with permission of the American Enterprise Institute for Public Policy Research.

COMMUNITY SERVICES

Table 7-1. Percent of People Age 65 Years and Over Living in the Community Who Had Used Community Services During the Preceding Year by Age and Sex: United States, January–June 1984

Service	65–74 years			75 years and over		
	Total	Male	Female	Total	Male	Female
			Number			
Sample	3,731	1,625	2,106	2,251	822	1,429
			Number in thousands			
Estimated population	16,227	7,048	9,178	10,063	3,685	6,378
			Percent			
Senior center	14.7	11.5	17.1	15.8	13.8	17.0
Special transportation for the elderly	3.6	1.8	4.9	7.2	3.8	9.1
Senior center meals	7.6	6.1	8.8	9.3	8.9	9.4
Home-delivered meals	1.2	1.1	1.3	3.2	2.4	3.7
Homemaker service	0.8	0.5	1.0	2.7	1.0	3.6
Home health services[1]	2.3	2.3	2.4	5.5	4.8	6.3

Notes: 1. Includes visiting nurses and home health aides.
Source: National Center for Health Statistics *Advancedata,* No. 124, 1986.

Table 7-2. Percent of People Age 65 Years and Over Living in the Community Who Had Used Community Services During the Preceding Year by Living Arrangement and Limitation of Activity: United States, January–June 1984

Service	Living alone			Living with others		
	Total	Moderately to severely limited[1]	Not limited to slightly limited[2]	Total	Moderately to severely limited[1]	Not limited to slightly limited[2]
			Number			
Sample	1,809	429	1,380	4,173	1,064	3,109
			Number in thousands			
Estimated population	8,018	1,919	6,099	18,272	4,677	13,595
			Percent			
Senior center	20.3	18.8	20.8	12.4	7.5	13.1
Senior center meals	11.9	11.6	12.0	6.4	4.4	6.7
Special transportation for the elderly	10.5	15.4	8.4	2.4	2.7	2.2
Home-delivered meals	3.8	10.3	1.7	1.2	2.4	0.7
Homemaker service	3.0	10.4	0.5	0.9	1.7	0.5
Home health services[3]	4.2	13.2	1.4	3.1	8.6	1.2

Notes: 1. One is moderately limited if one is limited in the kind or amount of one's major activity. One is severely limited if one is unable to perform one's major activity.

2. One is slightly limited if one is limited in outside activity only. The "non limited" category includes persons with unknown responses.

3. Includes visiting nurses and home health aides.

Source: National Center for Health Statistics *Advancedata,* No. 124, 1986.

CRIME

Table 7–3. Arrests, Persons Age 65 and Over, 1986

(1986 estimated population 198,392,177)

Offense charged	Total all ages	Total 65 and over	Male Total all ages	Male 65 and over	Female Total all ages	Female 65 and over
TOTAL	10,392,177	92,488	8,586,328	78,010	1,805,849	14,478
Percent distribution[1]	100.0	.9	100.0	.9	100.0	.8
Murder and nonnegligent manslaughter	16,066	233	14,083	208	1,983	25
Forcible rape	31,128	203	30,780	203	348	—
Robbery	124,245	209	114,495	194	9,750	15
Aggravated assault	293,952	2,500	255,176	2,261	38,776	239
Burglary	375,544	542	345,886	485	29,658	57
Larceny-theft	1,182,099	15,078	819,754	8,713	362,345	6,365
Motor vehicle theft	128,514	164	116,348	154	12,166	10
Arson	15,523	88	13,397	75	2,126	13
Violent crime[2]	465,391	3,145	414,534	2,866	50,857	279
Percent distribution[2]	100.0	.7	100.0	.7	100.0	.5
Property crime[3]	1,701,680	15,872	1,295,385	9,427	406,295	6,445
Percent distribution[1]	100.0	.9	100.0	.7	100.0	1.6
Crime Index total[4]	2,167,071	19,017	1,709,919	12,293	457,152	6,724
Percent distribution[1]	100.0	.9	100.0	.7	100.0	1.5
Other assaults	593,902	4,065	503,732	3,498	90,170	567
Forgery and counterfeiting	76,546	202	50,612	152	25,934	50
Fraud	284,790	1,841	161,523	1,190	123,267	651
Embezzlement	10,500	30	6,678	29	3,822	1
Stolen property; buying, receiving, possessing	114,105	335	101,069	290	13,036	45
Vandalism	223,231	615	199,882	525	23,349	90
Weapons; carrying, possessing, etc.	160,204	1,322	148,372	1,259	11,832	63
Prostitution and commercialized vice	96,882	457	33,553	375	63,329	82
Sex offenses (except forcible rape and prostitution)	83,934	1,665	77,278	1,651	6,656	14
Drug abuse violations	691,882	1,542	591,806	1,363	100,076	179
Gambling	25,839	1,035	21,390	968	4,449	67
Offenses against family and children	47,327	260	40,250	230	7,077	30
Driving under the influence	1,458,531	18,115	1,290,900	16,752	167,631	1,363
Liquor laws	490,436	2,177	407,942	1,964	82,494	213
Drunkenness	777,866	15,271	708,317	14,556	69,549	715
Disorderly conduct	564,882	5,818	461,975	5,023	102,907	795
Vagrancy	32,992	422	29,052	387	3,940	35
All other offenses (except traffic)	2,272,589	18,276	1,923,173	15,488	349,416	2,788
Suspicion	7,455	23	6,217	17	1,238	6

Notes: 1. Because of rounding, the percentages may not add to total.
2. Violent crimes are offenses of murder, forcible rape, robbery, and aggravated assault.
3. Property crimes are offenses of burglary, larceny-theft, motor vehicle theft, and arson.
4. Includes arson.
Source: Federal Bureau of Investigation. *Uniform Crime Reports for the United States: 1986,* July 1987.

Table 7–4. Sex, Race, and Ethnic Origin of Murder Victims Age 65 and Over: 1986

Age	Total	Sex			Race				Ethnic Origin		
		Male	Female	Unknown	White	Black	Other	Unknown	Hispanic	Non-Hispanic	Unknown
18 and over[1]	17,204	13,115	4,087	2	9,109	7,655	404	36	2,542	11,571	3,091
65 to 69	386	258	128	–	224	155	6	1	15	280	91
70 to 74	290	175	115	–	208	79	2	1	13	216	61
75 and over	474	233	241	–	339	128	7	–	13	359	102

Notes: 1. Does not include unknown ages.

Source: Federal Bureau of Investigation. *Uniform Crime Reports of the United States: 1986,* July 1987.

EDUCATION

Figure 7–5. Percent of Total and Elderly Population With Less Than 5 Years of School And With 4 Years of High School or More

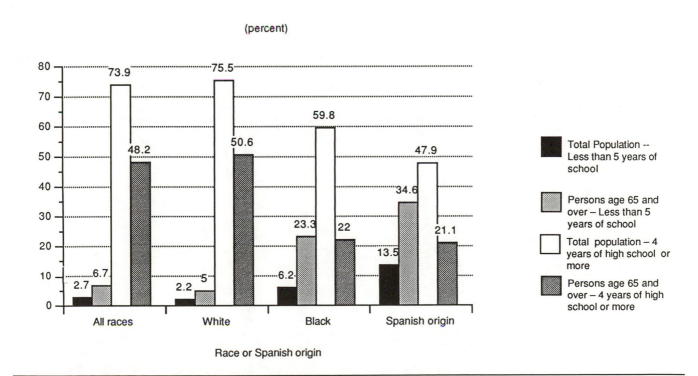

(percent)

Notes: "All races" includes other races not shown separately. Persons of Spanish origin may be of any race.

Source: U.S. Bureau of the Census, *1970 Census of Population,* vols. I and II; *1980 Census of Population,* vol. 1, chapter C; *Current Population Reports,* Series P–20, No. 403; and unpublished data.

Table 7–5. Educational Attainment of the Population 65 Years and Over and 25 Years and Over, by Sex: 1959 to 2000

(Figures are for March of year indicated. Base date of projections is March 1979.)

Sex and year	Median school years completed			Percent high school graduates		
	65 years and over	25 years and over	Ratio, 65 and over to 25 and over	65 years and over	25 years and over	Ratio, 65 and over to 25 and over
BOTH SEXES						
1959	8.3	11.0	0.75	19.4	42.9	0.45
1965	8.5	11.8	0.72	23.5	49.0	0.48
1970	8.7	12.2	0.71	28.3	55.2	0.51
1975	9.0	12.3	0.73	35.2	62.5	0.56
1981	10.3	12.5	0.82	41.8	69.7	0.60
1985	11.3	12.6	0.90	46.2	72.3	0.64
1990	12.1	12.7	0.95	53.3	75.6	0.71
1995	12.2	12.7	0.96	58.4	78.2	0.75
2000	12.4	12.8	0.97	63.7	80.4	0.79
MALE						
1959	8.2	10.7	0.77	18.1	41.3	0.44
1965	8.3	11.7	0.71	21.8	48.0	0.45
1970	8.6	12.2	0.70	25.9	55.0	0.47
1975	8.9	12.4	0.72	33.4	63.1	0.53
1981	10.1	12.6	0.80	40.8	70.3	0.58
1985	11.0	12.7	0.87	45.0	73.2	0.61
1990	12.1	12.8	0.95	52.7	76.7	0.69
1995	12.2	12.9	0.95	57.8	79.4	0.73
2000	12.4	12.9	0.96	62.4	81.4	0.77
FEMALE						
1959	8.4	11.2	0.75	20.4	44.4	0.46
1965	8.6	12.0	0.72	24.7	49.9	0.49
1970	8.8	12.1	0.73	30.1	55.4	0.54
1975	9.3	12.3	0.76	36.5	62.1	0.59
1981	10.4	12.5	0.83	42.5	69.1	0.62
1985	11.5	12.5	0.94	47.0	71.4	0.66
1990	12.1	12.6	0.96	53.7	74.6	0.72
1995	12.2	12.6	0.97	58.8	77.1	0.77
2000	12.4	12.7	0.98	64.6	79.4	0.81

Source: U.S. Bureau of the Census, *Current Population Reports,* Series P-20, Nos. 45, 99, 158, 207, 295, and 356, and unpublished data.

PARENT–CHILD RELATIONS

Figure 7–6. Responsibility of Children to Their Elderly Parents

(Children should feel a great deal of responsibility to make sure their elderly parents . . . . .)

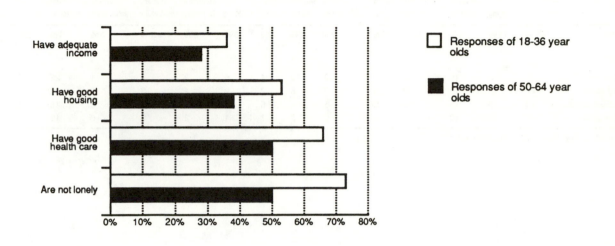

Note: Sample size = 997

Source: Survey by National Research, Incorporated for The American Council of Life Insurance. November 2–18, 1984. From *Public Opinion*, April/May 1985. Reprinted with permission of the American Enterprise Institute for Public Policy Research.

Table 7–6. People Age 65 Years and Over Who Lived Alone and Had 1 Child or More by Frequency of Seeing Children and How Quickly a Child Could Get There: United States, January–June 1984

Frequency of Seeing Children	Total	How Quickly a Child Could Get There		
		Minutes	Hours	Days
		Percent of total		
Total	100.0	71.6	25.1	3.4
At least				
Daily	23.4	22.9	0.0	0.0
Weekly	40.3	36.7	3.5	0.0
Monthly	16.2	9.4	6.7	0.0
Yearly	17.5	2.3	13.0	2.2
Never	2.7	0.0	1.5	1.0

Note: Based on an estimated 5.6 million (1,272 in sample) people with 1 child or more.

Source: National Center for Health Statistics *Advancedata*, No. 116, 1986.

RECREATION

Table 7–7. Favorite Evening Pastimes

(Question: What is your favorite way of spending an evening?)

	Watching television	Reading	Resting, relaxing	Home with family	Dining out	Visiting with friends	Movies, theater	Cards, games	Dancing	Listening to music	House, yard work	Sewing, needlepoint	Other mentions	No opinion	Number of interviews
						April 11-14, 1986									
NATIONAL	33%	14%	14%	13%	10%	8%	6%	4%	3%	3%	3%	3%	19%	2%	1,552
AGE															
Total under 30	28	9	15	14	16	12	10	4	5	3	2	1	22	2	318
30–49 years	27	15	16	18	10	7	5	2	2	4	3	2	22	2	596
Total 50 & older	43	19	13	9	6	5	4	6	2	2	3	5	16	1	630
65 & older	47	19	13	7	3	6	2	7	1	2	2	6	12	1	319

Source: Gallup Report No. 248, May 1986

Table 7–8. Multimedia Audiences By Age—Summary: 1986

(In percent, except as indicated. As of Spring.)

	Total population (1,000)	Television Watchers					Radio Listeners		Newspaper Readers	
					News					
		Prime time	Cable	Pay	Early	Late	Week-day	Week-end	Daily	Sunday
Total, 1986	170,599	82.3	44.5	27.6	50.6	41.6	81.4	66.1	60.5	65.6
18–24 years old	27,990	75.3	44.1	33.1	36.4	30.9	93.8	81.6	52.6	58.7
25–34 years old	40,798	82.5	44.5	30.0	41.1	38.3	88.2	71.4	53.1	64.5
35–44 years old	30,486	83.5	49.1	34.7	41.5	41.6	83.3	64.8	62.6	68.1
45–54 years old	22,494	84.4	48.6	31.7	54.5	47.9	80.9	61.8	67.6	70.0
55–64 years old	22,366	85.4	44.1	23.7	66.3	50.2	73.5	58.6	68.2	70.9
65 years old and over	26,465	83.3	36.8	9.9	74.5	45.1	62.5	52.9	65.4	63.3

Source: Mediamark Research Inc., New York, NY, *Multimedia Audiences,* Spring 1986 (copyright).

Table 7–9. Participation in Activities: 1983

(Represents percent of respondents who said they participated once or more during 12 months prior to interview.)

Activity	All persons	60 years and over
Walking for pleasure	53	42
Swimming	53	16
Visiting zoos, fairs, amusement parks	50	26
Picnics	48	29
Driving for pleasure	48	35
Sightseeing	46	31
Attending sports events	40	16
Fishing	34	17
Bicycling	32	7
Boating	28	9
Canoeing or kayaking	8	1
Sailing	6	2
Motorboating	19	7
Running or jogging	26	2
Attending concerts, plays, etc.	25	12
Camping	24	6
Backpacking	5	(z)
Outdoor team sports	24	2
Tennis	17	1
Day hiking	14	5
Golfing	13	7
Birdwatching, nature study	12	13
Hunting	12	5
Off-road vehicle driving[1]	11	2
Sledding	10	(z)
Waterskiing	9	(z)
Snow skiing	9	1
Horseback riding	9	1
Ice skating	6	(z)
Other activities	4	3
No participation	11	30

Notes: Z Less than .5 percent
    1. Includes motorcycles; excludes snowmobiles.
Source: National Park Service, and U.S. Bureau of the Census, *1982–1983 National Recreation Survey,* 1985.

Table 7-10. Involvement in Outdoor Recreation, by Age Groups

Indicators of involvement summarized over all activities	Age		Total sample
	60 years and over	Less than 60 years	
Average number of activities participated in once or more in prior 12 months	2.9	8.2	7.2
Percentage of respondents indicating they participate in no outdoor recreation activities	30	7	11
Average number of activity days of participation in previous 12 months	12.4	42.9	37.1
Average number of days respondents used various recreation areas in previous 12 months:			
Yards and similar areas	5.4	7.6	7.2
Neighborhood parks, etc.	2.5	5.1	4.6
Community or regional parks, etc.	1.8	4.6	4.0
More distant parks	1.5	3.1	2.8
Average estimated expenditure for outdoor recreation in previous 12 months (dollars)	$391	$350	$355

Source: U.S. Department of the Interior. National Parks Service. *1982–1983 Nationwide Recreation Survey*, 1986.

Table 7-11. Reasons for Enjoying Favorite Outdoor Activities, by Age Groups

(Percentage of respondents who gave selected reasons why they enjoy their favorite activities[1])

Reason	Age		Total sample
	60 years and over	Less than 60 years	
Enjoy nature and outdoors	72	68	68
Get exercise or keep in shape	59	68	66
For peace and quiet	46	47	47
Get away from problems[2]	44	57	56
To be with family or friends	35	55	53
Like people who do activity	30	35	34
Own and enjoy using equipment	23	27	27
Enjoy solitude	21	26	25
Something new or different	18	22	21
Other reasons (not on list)	14	9	10

Notes: 1. Percentages are based on the respondents who cited one or more activities they "particularly enjoyed."
2. "To get away from day-to-day living or problems."

Source: U.S. Department of the Interior. National Park Service. *1982–1983 Nationwide Recreation Survey,* 1986.

Table 7–12. Constraints on Favorite Outdoor Activities, by Age Groups

(Percentage citing constraint[1])

Reasons	Age		Total sample
	60 years and over	Less than 60 years	
Not enough time	30	60	56
Personal health reasons	22	6	8
No one to do activity with	14	18	17
Not enough money	12	21	20
No place to do activity	11	20	19
Inadequate transportation or too far	10	15	14
Crowded activity areas	7	14	13
Personal safety problems in activity areas	4	5	5
Poorly maintained activity areas	3	6	5
Pollution problems in activity areas	2	4	4
Inadequate information on activity areas	1	5	5
Other reasons (not on list)	14	11	11

Notes: 1. Percentage of respondents who gave selected reasons why they do not do their favorite activities "as often as they would like." Percentages are based on those respondents who cited one or more activities they "particularly enjoyed."

Source: U.S. Department of the Interior. National Park Service. *1982–1983 Nationwide Recreation Survey,* 1986.

RELIGION

Figure 7–7. Importance of Religion

(*Question:* How Important Would You Say Religion Is In Your Own Life — Very Important, Fairly Important, Or Not Very Important?)

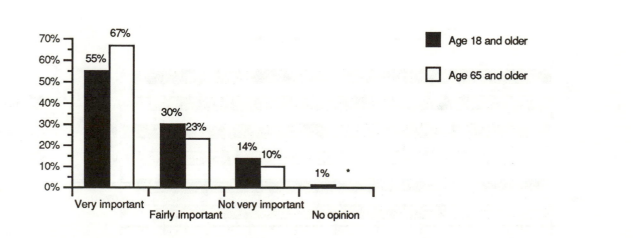

Notes: * Less than 1%.

Surveys conducted during five selected weeks in 1986 (telephone and personal). National data based on 6,633 interviews. Data for age 65 and older based on 1,217 interviews.

Source: "Religion in America." *The Gallup Report,* No. 259, April 1987.

Figure 7–8. Religious Preference: Major Faiths

(*Question:* What is Your Religious Preference—Protestant, Catholic, Jewish, Or An Orthodox Church Such as the Greek or Russian Orthodox Church?)

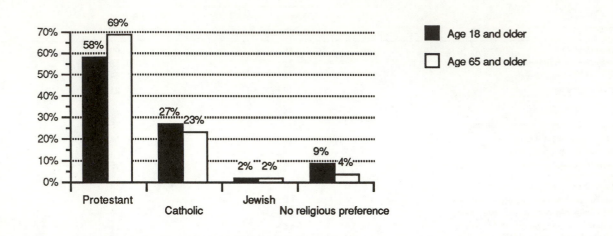

Notes: Data based on four surveys conducted during 1986 (personal and interviews). National data based on 6,221 interviews. Data for age 65 and older based on 1,247 interviews.

Source: "Religion in America." *The Gallup Report,* no. 259, April 1987.

SEXUALITY

Figure 7–9. *Question:* Do You Like Sex?

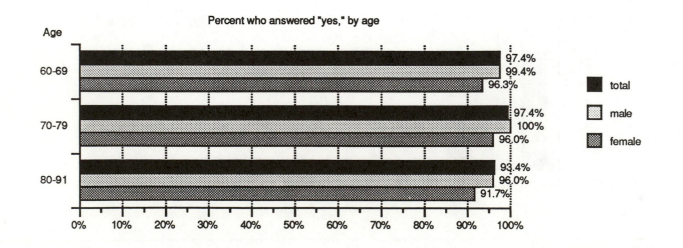

Note: Data based on survey of 800 persons between the ages of 60 and 91 years.

Source: Copyright © 1981 by Bernard Starr, Ph.D. and Marcella Bakur Weiner, Ed.D. From the book *The Starr-Weiner Report on Sex & Sexuality in the Mature Years.* Reprinted with permission of Stein and Day Publishers.

Table 7–13. How Often Would You Like to Have Sexual Relations If You Could Whenever You Wanted To?

(Adjusted frequencies for age groups)

CATEGORY	60–69			70–79			80–91		
	Total	Male	Female	Total	Male	Female	Total	Male	Female
When in the Mood	57 (13.0%)	16 (10.3%)	41 (14.5%)	35 (14.0%)	7 (7.2%)	28 (18.3%)	7 (13.2%)	1 (4.5%)	6 (19.3%)
Three Times a Week or More	127 (29.0)	66 (42.6)	61 (21.6)	59 (23.6)	30 (30.9)	29 (19.0)	7 (13.2)	5 (22.7)	2 (6.5)
Twice a Week	102 (23.3)	38 (24.5)	64 (22.6)	54 (21.6)	22 (22.7)	32 (20.9)	7 (13.2)	4 (18.2)	3 (9.7)
Once a Week	93 (21.3)	25 (16.1)	68 (24.0)	61 (24.4)	25 (25.8)	36 (23.5)	17 (32.1)	7 (31.8)	10 (32.2)
Three Times a Month	1 (0.2)	1 (0.6)	0	4 (1.6)	1 (1.0)	3 (2.0)	0	0	0
Twice a Month	19 (4.3)	5 (3.2)	14 (4.9)	12 (4.8)	6 (6.2)	6 (3.9)	4 (7.5)	3 (13.6)	1 (3.2)
Once a Month	18 (4.1)	2 (1.3)	16 (5.7)	12 (4.8)	2 (2.1)	10 (6.5)	7 (13.2)	2 (9.1)	5 (16.1)
Less than Once a Month	17 (3.9)	1 (0.6)	16 (5.7)	12 (4.8)	4 (4.1)	8 (5.2)	2 (3.8)	0	2 (6.5)
Never	4 (0.9)	1 (0.6)	3 (1.1)	1 (0.4)	0 (0.0)	1 (0.7)	2 (3.8)	0	2 (6.5)
Total Responses	438	155	283	250	97	153	53	22	31

Note: Data based on survey of 800 persons between the ages of 60 and 91 years.

Source: Copyright © 1981 by Bernard Starr, Ph.D. and Marcella Bakur Weiner, Ed.D. From the book *The Starr-Weiner Report on Sex & Sexuality in the Mature Years.* Reprinted with permission of Stein and Day Publishers.

Table 7-14. How Often Do You Have Sexual Relations?

(Adjusted frequencies for age groups)

CATEGORY	60–69			70–79			80–91		
	Total	Male	Female	Total	Male	Female	Total	Male	Female
When in the Mood	26 (6.2%)	9 (5.8%)	17 (6.5%)	15 (6.2%)	7 (7.6%)	8 (5.4%)	2 (4.0%)	1 (5.0%)	1 (3.3%)
Three Times a Week or More	57 (13.7)	27 (17.5)	30 (11.4)	24 (10.0)	10 (10.9)	14 (9.4)	4 (8.0)	2 (10.0)	2 (6.7)
Twice a Week	65 (15.6)	28 (18.2)	37 (14.1)	28 (11.6)	15 (16.3)	13 (8.7)	0	0	0
Once a Week	85 (20.4)	36 (23.4)	49 (18.6)	36 (14.9)	20 (21.7)	16 (10.7)	8 (16.0)	5 (25.0)	3 (10.0)
Three Times a Month	6 (1.4)	3 (1.9)	3 (1.1)	1 (0/4)	0	1 (0.7)	0	0	0
Twice a Month	30 (7.2)	10 (6.5)	20 (7.6)	23 (9.55)	10 (10.9)	13 (8.7)	4 (8.0)	3 (15.0)	1 (3.3)
Once a Month	40 (9.6)	20 (13.0)	20 (7.6)	25 (10.4)	8 (8.7)	17 (11.4)	4 (8.0)	1 (5.0)	3 (10.0)
Less than Once a Month	39 (9.4)	10 (6.5)	29 (11.2)	23 (9.55)	12 (13.0)	11 (7.4)	8 (16.0)	5 (25.0)	3 (10.0)
Not Active	69 (16.5)	11 (7.2)	58 (22.1)	66 (27.4)	10 (10.9)	56 (37.6)	20 (40.0)	3 (15.0)	17 (56.7)
Total Responses	417	154	263	241	92	149	50	20	30

Note: Data based on survey of 800 persons between the ages of 60 and 91 years.

Source: Copyright © 1981 by Bernard Starr, Ph.D. and Marcella Bakur Weiner, Ed.D. From the book *The Starr-Weiner Report on Sex & Sexuality in the Mature Years.* Reprinted with permission of Stein and Day Publishers.

Table 7–15. How Often Do You Reach Orgasm in Your Sexual Experiences?

(Adjusted frequencies for age groups)

CATEGORY	60–69			70–79			80–91		
	Total	Male	Female	Total	Male	Female	Total	Male	Female
Always	169	84	85	105	42	63	14	9	5
	(42.4%)	(57.5%)	(33.7%)	(48.4%)	(49.4%)	(47.7%)	(33.3%)	(45.0%)	(22.7%)
Most of the Time	133	43	90	65	27	38	16	6	10
	(33.4)	(29.5)	(35.7)	(30.0)	(31.8)	(28.8)	(38.1)	(30.0)	(45.5)
Sometimes	91	18	73	42	13	29	11	4	7
	(22.9)	(12.3)	(29.0)	(19.3)	(15.3)	(22.0)	(26.2)	(20.0)	(31.8)
Never	5	1	4	5	3	2	1	1	0
	(1.3)	(0.7)	(1.6)	(2.3)	(3.5)	(1.5)	(2.4)	(5.0)	(0)
Total Responses	398	146	252	217	85	132	42	20	22

Note: Data based on survey of 800 persons between the ages of 60 and 91 years.

Source: Copyright © 1981 by Bernard Starr, Ph.D. and Marcella Bakur Weiner, Ed.D. From the book *The Starr-Weiner Report on Sex & Sexuality in the Mature Years.* Reprinted with permission of Stein and Day Publishers.

VOTING PATTERNS

Table 7–16. Voting–Age Population, and Percent Reporting Registered and Voted: 1972 to 1984

CHARACTERISTIC	VOTING–AGE POPULATION (mil.)							PERCENT REPORTING THEY REGISTERED							PERCENT REPORTING THEY VOTED						
	Presidential election years				Congressional election years			Presidential election years				Congressional election years			Presidential election years				Congressional election years		
	1972	1976	1980	1984	1974	1978	1982	1972	1976	1980	1984	1974	1978	1982	1972	1976	1980	1984	1974	1978	1982
Total	**136.2**	**146.5**	**157.1**	**170.0**	**141.3**	**151.6**	**165.5**	**72.3**	**66.7**	**66.9**	**68.3**	**62.2**	**62.6**	**64.1**	**63.0**	**59.2**	**59.2**	**59.9**	**44.7**	**45.9**	**48.5**
18–20 years old	11.0	12.1	12.3	11.2	11.6	12.2	12.1	58.1	47.1	44.7	47.0	36.4	34.7	35.0	48.3	38.0	35.7	36.7	20.8	20.1	19.8
21–24 years old	13.6	14.8	15.9	16.7	14.1	15.5	16.7	59.5	54.8	52.7	54.3	45.3	45.1	47.8	50.7	45.6	43.1	43.5	26.4	26.2	28.4
25–34 years old	26.9	31.7	35.7	40.3	29.3	33.4	38.8	68.4	62.3	62.0	63.3	54.7	55.5	57.1	59.7	55.4	54.6	54.5	37.0	38.0	40.4
35–44 years old	22.2	22.8	25.6	30.7	22.4	24.2	28.1	74.8	69.8	70.6	70.9	66.7	66.7	67.5	66.3	63.3	64.4	63.5	49.1	50.1	52.2
45–64 years old	42.3	43.3	43.6	44.3	43.0	43.4	44.2	79.7	75.5	75.8	76.6	73.6	74.3	75.6	70.8	68.7	69.3	69.8	56.9	58.5	62.2
65 years and over	20.1	22.0	24.1	26.7	21.0	23.0	25.6	75.6	71.4	74.6	76.9	70.2	72.8	75.2	63.5	62.2	65.1	67.7	51.4	55.9	59.9

Source: U.S. Bureau of the Census, *Current Population Reports,* series P-20, No. 405 and earlier reports.

Table 7–17. Deviation From the National Vote for Republican Presidential and Congressional Candidates by Age Groups

	Presidential					Congressional			
	1968	1972	1976	1980	1984	1970	1974	1978	1982
60–64 years	+5	+2	+6	+1	−8	+9	+7	+5	0
65–89	+1	+5	0	+1	−3	+8	+14	−4	+4
70–74	+1	+12	+15	+5	−9	+10	+4	0	−1
75 and over	+8	+4	+8	+17	+6	+6	+6	+10	−2

Notes: Data indicate, for example, that in 1968 those 60–64 years old were 5 percentage points more Republican than the nation in the presidential vote. Gallup data are used here.

Surveys have been combined from two Gallup polls for each year as follows: *(for 1968)* October 17–22 preelection and November 9–14 postelection; *(for 1972)* October 13–16 preelection and November 10–13 postelection; *(for 1976)* October 22–25 preelection and November 12–15 postelection; *(for 1980)* November 7–10 and November 21–24—both postelection; *(for 1984)* October 26–29 preelection and November 9–12 postelection. Preelection leaners are included.

Surveys have been combined from two Gallup polls for each year as follows: *(for 1970)* October 9–14 and October 22–25; *(for 1974)* October 11–14 and October 18–21; *(for 1978)* October 13–16 and October 27–30; *(for 1982)* October 15–18 preelection and November 5–8 postelection.

Source: Public Opinion, April/May 1985. Reprinted with permission of the American Enterprise Institute for Public Policy Research.

Table 7–18. Percent of Voting Age Population 65 Years and Over by State

State	Percent	State	Percent
Alaska	5%	Montana	16%
Colorado	12	New Hampshire	16
Utah	12	Ohio	16
Hawaii	13	Oklahoma	16
Nevada	13	Vermont	16
Texas	13	Alabama	17
Wyoming	13	Arizona	17
California	14	Connecticut	17
Georgia	14	Minnesota	17
Louisiana	14	Mississippi	17
Maryland	14	New Jersey	17
New Mexico	14	New York	17
South Carolina	14	Kansas	18
Tennessee	14	Maine	18
Virginia	14	Massachusetts	18
West Virginia	14	North Dakota	18
Delaware	15	Oregon	18
District of Columbia	15	Wisconsin	18
North Carolina	15	Iowa	19
Washington State	15	Missouri	19
Idaho	16	Nebraska	19
Illinois	16	Pennsylvania	19
Indiana	16	Rhode Island	19
Kentucky	16	Arkansas	20
Michigan	16	South Dakota	20
		Florida	23

Note: Figures are projections for November 1, 1984, made in March 1984.

Source: Public Opinion, April/May 1985. Reprinted with permission of the American Enterprise Institute for Public Policy Research. Data from Bureau of the Census, Department of Commerce.

TOBACCO AND ALCOHOL

Table 7–19. Drinking by Age and Sex: Quantity, Frequency, and Variability

Age by Sex	N	Percent Abstainers	Percent Moderate 1–60/Month	Percent Heavy 60 + Month	Percent of All Drinkers Who Are Heavy Drinkers
Men					
Total (all ages)	(762)	25	54	21	28
61–70	(91)	38	53	8	13
70+	(72)	41	45	13	22
Women					
Total (all ages)	(1,010)	40	54	5	8
61–70	(102)	61	38	1	3
70+	(103)	61	39	0	0

Source: U.S. Dept. of Health and Human Services, National Clearinghouse for Alcohol Information. "Special Population Issues," *Alcohol and Health* Monograph No. 4, 1982.

Table 7–20. Cigarette Smoking by Persons 20 Years of Age and Over, According to Sex, Race, and Age: United States, 1966, 1976, 1980, and 1983

(Data are based on household interviews of a sample of the civilian noninstitutionalized population)

Sex and age	Current smoker[1]				Former smoker			
	1985	1976	1980[2]	1983	1985	1976	1980[2]	1983
	Percent of persons							
All males								
45–64 years	51.9	41.3	40.8	35.9	24.1	37.1	36.9	40.1
65 years and over	28.5	23.0	17.9	22.0	28.1	44.4	47.4	48.1
All females								
45–64 years	32.0	34.8	30.8	31.0	8.6	15.9	17.1	18.6
65 years and over	9.6	12.8	16.8	13.1	4.5	11.7	14.2	18.7

Notes: 1. A current smoker is a person who has smoked at least 100 cigarettes and who now smokes; includes occasional smokers.

2. Final estimates. Based on data for the last 6 months of 1980.

Source: Division of Health Interview Statistics, National Center for Health Statistics. Data from the National Health Interview Survey. Data computed by the Division of Epidemiology and Health Promotion from data compiled by the Division of Health Interview Statistics.

TRAVEL AND TRANSPORTATION

Figure 7–10. Drivers by Age and Sex, 1985

(Estimated. Numbers in thousands.)

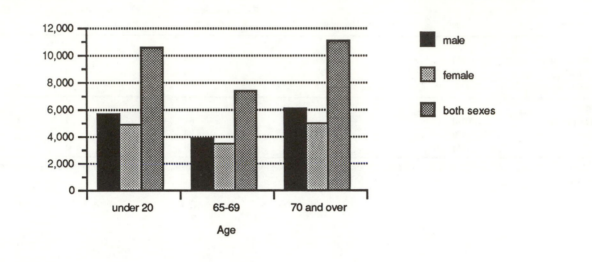

Source: U.S. Department of Transportation, Federal Highway Administration.

Table 7–21. Distribution of Person Trips by People Age 65 and Over and Mode of Transportation: 1983

	Age				Age	
	65 and Over	All			65 and Over	All
Private Vehicle						
Auto, Van-Driver	47.2	44.4	*Other Means*			
Auto, Van-Passenger	30.0	27.0	Walk		10.4	8.5
Pickup	6.5	10.1	Bike		.3	.8
Other Private Vehicle	.2	.5	School Bus		.0	2.6
Subtotal-Private	83.9	82.0	Airplane		.1	.1
			Other		2.7	3.8
Public Transportation			Subtotal-Other		13.5	15.8
Bus, Streetcar	2.3	1.7				
Train	.2	.2	Total		100.0	100.0
Subway, Elevated Rail	.1	.3	All Modes		7.2	100.0
Subtotal-Public	2.6	2.2				

Source: U.S. Department of Transportation, Federal Highway Administration, *Personal Travel in the U.S.,* vol. 1, 1986.

Table 7–22. Average Daily Person Trips, Travel, and Trip Length by Age and Sex: 1983

	Age								
	5–15	16–19	20–29	30–39	40–49	50–59	60–64	65 and Over	All Ages
	Average Daily Trips								
Male	2.3	3.3	3.5	3.3	3.1	2.8	2.7	2.2	2.7
Female	2.3	3.4	3.4	3.6	3.2	2.8	2.1	1.6	2.7
All	2.3	3.3	3.4	3.4	3.1	2.8	2.4	1.8	2.7
	Average Daily Person Miles of Travel								
Male	16.8	22.0	32.4	35.1	38.4	29.9	26.6	14.6	25.5
Female	15.4	20.8	29.6	27.8	31.4	21.1	20.9	10.5	21.1
All	16.1	21.4	30.9	31.3	34.9	25.2	23.7	12.2	23.2
	Average Trip Length (Miles)								
Male	7.5	6.8	9.3	10.8	12.5	10.8	9.9	6.6	9.5
Female	6.6	6.1	8.8	7.7	9.8	7.6	9.8	6.8	7.9
All	7.0	6.4	9.0	9.1	11.1	9.0	9.8	6.7	8.7

Source: U.S. Department of Transportation, Federal Highway Administration, *Personal Travel in the U.S.*, vol. 1, 1986.

Table 7–23. Distribution of Person Trips by Purpose and Age: All Persons, 1983

	Age								
	5–15	16–19	20–29	30–39	40–49	50–59	60–64	65 and Over	All Ages
Earning a Living									
To or From Work	1.4	13.1	26.4	26.3	28.2	26.6	21.7	6.3	20.4
Work Related Business	.4	1.1	2.3	3.3	3.2	4.1	2.1	1.5	2.4
Subtotal	1.8	14.2	28.7	29.6	31.4	30.7	23.8	7.8	22.8
Family and Personal Business									
Shopping	10.3	12.4	16.7	18.5	19.8	22.1	24.0	30.6	18.2
Doctor/Dentist	1.1	.6	.8	1.2	1.3	1.2	1.7	3.6	1.2
Other Family Business	9.8	10.2	15.5	20.5	19.2	15.8	18.4	18.1	16.1
Subtotal	21.2	23.2	33.0	40.2	40.3	39.1	44.1	52.3	35.5
Civic, Educational, and Religious	37.8	24.7	6.9	5.0	4.3	6.1	4.9	7.6	11.8
Social and Recreational									
Vacation	.4	.1	.2	.3	.3	.3	.4	.2	.3
Visiting Friends	12.2	15.7	13.8	9.0	7.6	8.5	10.4	10.4	11.0
Pleasure Driving	.5	.5	.4	.4	.5	.7	.4	1.3	.5
Other Social and Recreational	19.3	19.8	15.7	14.0	14.1	12.9	14.6	17.7	15.8
Subtotal	32.4	36.1	30.1	23.7	22.5	22.4	25.8	29.6	27.6
Other	6.8	1.8	1.3	1.5	1.5	1.7	1.4	2.7	2.3
Total	100.0	100.0	100.0	100.0	100.0	100.0	100.0	100.0	100.0

Source: U.S. Department of Transportation. Federal Highway Administration, *Personal Travel in the U.S.*, vol. 1, 1986.

Table 7–24. Age of Drivers in Fatal Accidents

Age of Driver	1985	1984	1983	1980	% Change, 1980 to 1983	% Change, 1983 to 1984	% Change, 1984 to 1985
14 years & under	212	205	203	240	– 15%	1%	4%
15 to 19 years	7,365	7,604	7,263	10,085	– 28%	5%	– 3%
20 to 24 years	11,269	11,397	10,716	13,537	– 21%	6%	– 1%
25 to 34 years	15,261	15,228	14,470	16,503	– 12%	5%	0%
35 to 44 years	8,971	8,560	8,068	8,366	– 4%	6%	5%
45 to 54 years	5,114	5,081	4,992	5,912	– 16%	2%	1%
55 to 64 years	4,065	4,056	3,862	4,339	– 11%	5%	0%
65 yrs. or older	4,448	4,314	4,026	3,813	6%	7%	3%
Unknown age	1,456	1,513	1,506	1,270	19%	0%	– 4%
Total	58,160	57,958	55,106	64,065	– 14%	5%	0%

Source: U.S. Department of Transportation, National Highway Traffic Safety Administration, *1985 Traffic Fatalities Preliminary Report.* 1986

Figure 7–11. Distribution of Persons Age 65 + by Frequency of Wearing Seat Belts

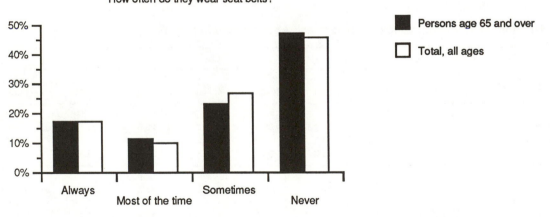

Source: U.S. Department of Transportation, Federal Highway Administration. *Personal Travel in the United States, 1986.*